The concept of international organization

The concept
of international
organization

Edited by
Georges Abi-Saab

unesco

Published in 1981 by the United Nations
Educational, Scientific and Cultural Organization
7 place de Fontenoy, 75700 Paris
Printed by Réunies de Chambéry

ISBN 92-3-101742-X
French edition: 92-3-201742-3

Preface

Since its inception at the end of a 'great and terrible war', Unesco has been involved in efforts to strengthen the structure of peace. International organizations, of which Unesco is one, form part of this structure and reflect the institutionalization of the global system.

As a dynamic system, the world and its institutions are in continuous change, both quantitatively and qualitatively. The number of international organizations, as well as their membership and functions, have increased dramatically over the period of a generation. This development is bound to continue so long as the world becomes more complex and interdependent. Under the circumstances, international organization is indispensable for the proper co-ordination of the system through the co-operation of its members. Viewed in this light, international institutions are the necessary instruments leading towards a better world.

The road to a better world, however, requires careful thought as well as concerted action. In order to improve the performance of international organizations in the operation of the world system, we must increase our understanding of their nature. The study of international organization, therefore, is a prerequisite for any rational development of a new international order.

Unesco's contribution to the study of international organization dates back some years and consists in encouraging research and study in this field. A systematic programme on international organization was first proposed by the General Conference of Unesco in 1970 and later reaffirmed by the General Conference in 1974. At the same time, a number of international meetings of experts held between 1972 and 1976 worked out the details of the programme.

These were incorporated finally within the framework of Unesco's Medium-Term Plan for 1977–82 and appear as part of the objective, 'Promotion of the Study of the Role of International Law and of International

Organizations in the Establishment of a Peaceful World Order'. This objective, along with peace research and peace education, has thus become the expression of Unesco's commitment to the reinforcement of peace in the next few years.

Publication of the present volume is one of the concrete manifestations of that commitment. This book is a collection of articles most, of which appeared as a special issue of the *International Social Science Journal* (Vol. XXXIX, No. 1, 1977). These articles have been revised and supplemented by new ones in order to introduce the reader to the concept of international organization in its fullest dimension.

The chapters are grouped in three parts and thus treat three aspects of the subject-matter: the first combines a historical and typological approach; the second deals with methodological and procedural aspects; and the third presents three world perspectives on international organization. By bringing together the ideas of eleven authorities in this field, Unesco has sought to provide an overview of several facets of international organization from various points of view. Each author brings with him, or her, not only objective knowledge but also subjective interpretations of the subject-matter. Their combined effort constitutes a selection of readings designed particularly for the student of international affairs.

The authors are responsible for the choice and the presentation of the facts contained in this book and for the opinions expressed therein, which are not necessarily those of Unesco and do not commit the Organization. Unesco wishes to thank the contributors to this volume for their studies and the general editor for bringing them together and for writing the introduction. It is hoped that the results will add to our understanding of the weaknesses and strengths, the achievements and shortcomings, the performance and potential of international organization as a means of bringing about a more peaceful world order.

Contents

Introduction
The concept of international organization: a synthesis

Georges Abi-Saab

The term 'international organization' brings to mind two different meanings : one might want to refer to the way in which international society is organized, that is, the institutional framework and structures of that society in general; likewise, one might designate by the term a given international organization, a specific institution or entity.

Although the ultimate goal of a study of international organization, as in any scientific inquiry, is to understand the phenomenon as a whole, i.e. in its broadest sense, it is only by studying international organizations as specific entities or institutions that we can progressively come to an overall view of the institutional framework which moulds international relations in general. Thus, it is in its narrowest sense that the term 'international organization' is used in what follows.

Historical evolution and definition
of the international organization

HISTORICAL EVOLUTION

As with any concept, that of international organization is evolutive in character. Although we can trace attempts at intercommunal institutional

---

GEORGES ABI-SAAB (Egypt) is Professor of International Law and Organization at the Graduate Institute of International Studies, Geneva. His most recent book is *International Crises and the Role of Law: The United Nations Operation in the Congo 1960-1964* (Oxford University Press, 1978). His previous publications include studies on the International Court, the United Nations system, the law of war, and in his main field of interest which is the impact of the Third World on contemporary international law and organization.

co-operation back to ancient times, the contemporary concept of international organization is of comparatively recent origin. In its present form, it is the outcome of a rapid evolution in practice and ideas that began early in the nineteenth century.

The industrial revolution, through its impact on the structures of production, communication and trade, laid the foundations for an international division of labour carried to an unprecedented degree and, consequently, for the interdependence of the different regions of the world. But at the same time, it gave states a potential for mass destruction which exacerbated antagonisms and opened the way to total war.

The emergence of contemporary international organizations was in a large measure a response to this rapid technological and economic evolution, and to the political and social upheavals that accompanied it. Their development is the result of the consolidation of two trends which took hold during the course of the nineteenth century, and which constitute their immediate origins.

The first trend reflects the development of the conference system, which became current practice after the Congress of Vienna (1814-15). Even before the nineteenth century, several European conferences were called in the aftermath of major wars, in order to settle their outcome (e.g. the conferences of Westphalia (1648) and of Utrecht (1713-14)). But the distinctive feature of the Congress of Vienna (and the Concert of Europe which went along with it) was its prospective concern with the maintenance of peace within the new order it had established in Europe and its attempt to achieve this through regular consultations among the great powers, thus granting them a privileged position in the new European system.

And, while this system did not function as planned (because of differences between the great powers) and the conferences were sporadic rather than regular, the technique of diplomacy by conference, or parliamentary diplomacy, beyond the narrow limits of peace settlements, became none the less standard procedure every time a crisis threatened the European order.

Another contribution of the Congress of Vienna was the technique of multilateral treaties. In fact the final act of the Congress was the first instrument to be couched in this form. Multilateral treaties were rapidly used beyond the context of collective peace settlements, and became the instruments of international regulation and international legislation; at a later stage they provided the legal means for the creation of international organizations.

The two Hague Conferences of 1899 and 1907 represented one more step in the direction of today's concept of international organization. The aim of these conferences, which were convened outside the context of any crisis, was to settle in general the fundamental problems of war and peace. And, while they did not manage to impose compulsory arbitration or to prohibit recourse to war, the resulting conventions, still applicable today, codified procedures for the peaceful resolution of disputes, and attempted to humanize war and limit its ravages. In addition, the conferences showed a marked trend towards periodicity and universality of participation, without however fully attaining either.

While this first trend foreshadowed the goals and orientations of international co-operation within the major international organizations still to come, it was the second trend—the emergence of international unions—which provided the institutional framework for this co-operation.

Either through international river commissions or other international unions, an authentic international administration gradually came into being, providing ongoing institutional activity in the context of multilateral treaties for technical co-operation among States, especially in the field of international communications. While remaining responsible to the periodic conferences of the contracting parties—conferences which did not always abide by the unanimity rule in voting—the permanent body, usually called the 'bureau', fulfilled not only the functions of secretariat and preparation from one conference to another, but also sometimes fulfilled executive and control functions within the framework of the convention itself. The secretariat, or bureau, was the transitional factor between the conference technique and that of the organization.

The two trends came together with the foundation of the League of Nations, although the novel concept of international organization which it represented was not immediately perceived. Little distinction was made between 'organs' and 'organization'. The organs of the organization were considered by some authors to be no more than common organs of the Member States, thereby denying the separate identity of the organization; sometimes certain organs of the League were called organizations, etc.

None the less, with hesitant steps forward in the search for practical solutions and in scientific analysis, a clearer and more coherent idea gradually took form, which came into its own in the era of the United Nations.

DEFINITION

What is this idea that started to take shape? Definitions are manifold, both in legal and political literature.

Three elements come out from these definitions: the basis, which is a treaty, serving as a constitution from a legal point of view, and representing a political will to co-operate in certain fields, from a political point of view; the structure, or the institutional aspect, which guarantees some permanence and stability in the functioning of the organization; and the means, which are the functions, powers and spheres of competence, reflecting a certain degree of autonomy of action for the organization in relation to its members. From a legal standpoint, this means that there exists a decision-making process which allows the expression of an autonomous 'will' of the organization, not necessarily identical to the will of each member, and which justifies its separate legal existence, i.e. its legal personality. However, from a political viewpoint, it is not so much the spheres of competence or the legal powers that count, but rather their practical effect, which is to make of the organization a relatively autonomous actor in the international system.

Legal definitions are limited to organizations composed primarily of States, given the requirement of a constitutive treaty ; [1] political definitions, on the other hand, tend to encompass more than just this category and include as well transnational entities which take shape beyond frontiers and governments. Indeed, for the jurist, international organizations are secondary entities, created by States, which are the principal actors of the international system; and yet for some political analysts, the essence of international organizations lies in their non-territorial character, which becomes more and more pronounced the further the organizations get, in membership and functions, from the State system. The autonomy of the organization is measured, not in relation to its members, but in relation to the State or territorial system. [2]

The concept of international organization stemming from these definitions covers a broad range of entities, very different in membership, structure, functions, and real importance, and this is reflected in the numerous classifications put forth in this respect.

Methods of approach

Definitions are generally too concise to encompass the phenomenon in all its facets. They are more a starting-point than an end-product in the search for an overall understanding of international organizations.

Several methods of approach have been used to this effect in the more detailed study of international organizations; they can be schematically classified into three broad categories.

DESCRIPTIVE METHODS

Chronologically the first to have been employed, these are methods that use historical and legal analysis to describe the institutional framework of the organizations and their activities.

Legal analysis

From a legal viewpoint, the structure and functions of the organization are described in terms of its constitutive treaty and its practice. The method consists, then, in the study of the constitutional law of the organization, the content of which obviously depends on the extent of the powers granted to the organization by the member States, and on the distribution of these powers among the different organs of the organization. The same legal problems arise in relation to all organizations, but their resolution varies from one constitutive treaty to another. Some of these common problems are methods of reviewing the legality of the acts of the organization and those of the member States which are regulated by the constitutive treaty; the extent and distribution of powers among the different organs of the organization, and the modalities of their exercise by the organs ; the legal effect of decisions and resolutions adopted by the different organs ; their legislative power ; the amendment of constitutive treaties, etc.

Other legal problems, of an external nature, arise in connection with the legal status of the organization as an entity : its legal personality under the domestic law of member States and under international law and the consequences thereof, such as its privileges and immunities, its treaty-making power, its international responsibility, etc.

A trend towards a more analytical legal approach is taking shape, with a transition from the study of the constitution of one organization to the study of the comparative constitutional law of several organizations, usually in regard to a single problem. But it cannot yet be said that there is a general law applicable to all organizations; thus far we can detect no more than general trends.

Historical analysis

The descriptive historical or political approach studies the historical circumstances and conditions of the creation and growth of the organization, and of the cases and crises with which it has or has not dealt. The international organization is considered an arena of diplomatic history and is treated as such. Sometimes, it is examined in the context of a broader historical investigation (for example, in the study of a crisis, a chapter might focus on the part the organization played in the crisis); but it is just as possible to write the diplomatic history of the organization itself.

Most of the early literature and general works on international organizations, or on a specific international organization, are syntheses of these two methods. They include a brief legal description of the constitutional structure of the organization or organizations with which they deal, and a brief historical presentation of their practice, without going too far in either direction. In other words, they remain on the level of legal, political, and historical description.

ANALYTICAL METHODS

Analytical methods of political science are consciously or unconsciously inspired by systems analysis. They can be situated at two different levels.

Macro-analysis

At the level of macro-analysis, efforts have been made to explain alterations in the structures and functions of the international organization by changes in the international system. This can be viewed in two ways: either the international organization is considered a system and the international system is looked on as its environment; or the organization is considered an element (actor or subsystem) of a broader set, the international system.

The study of this interaction can proceed in a global way, over a very long period, for example from the Congress of Vienna to the present day; and an attempt can be made to show how each of the international systems, deriving respectively from Vienna, from Versailles, and from the Second World War, created its own institutions and left its imprint on their structures and functioning.[3]

But this approach has especially inspired studies that attempt to explain alterations in the universal international organizations of the post-war period, and especially the United Nations, in terms of changes in the international system. These organizations were founded upon the presumption of a post-war international system based on a continuing alliance of the victors. This presumption proved not to be justified by the facts, and the cold war produced a rigidly bi-polar international system, which became more flexible in the mid-1950s thereby allowing for the emergence of a third force, the Third World. The system changed again following the Cuban crisis of 1962, and was distinguished by the pursuit of a greater détente between the superpowers and by their attempt to re-establish their control in the face of the rise of the Third World. The North-South conflict marked this period. The energy crisis of 1973, reflecting the revolt of the

Third World, was one more turning-point in the development of the international system, in which two radically different visions tried to assert themselves. On the one hand, we find the vision of the Third World, seeking a new international economic order which is, in fact, also a new political order, one that is less hierarchical, and more equitable and egalitarian ; and on the other hand, we have the vision of the superpowers, attempting to consolidate their hold and extend their zones of influence by seeking to adjust the present hierarchical system in order to preserve it, even at the cost of a transition from a flexible bi-polarity to a limited multi-polarity (thereby returning to the original presumption of the United Nations system).

It can be shown how each of these alterations in the international system has been reflected in modifications of the membership, the organic structures, and the functioning of international organizations (whether they be universal, regional, or of limited membership), as well as in changes in their respective roles and relative importance in the international system.[4]

Micro-analysis

At the micro-analytical level, it is the international organization itself which is the system to be analysed. The study therefore concentrates on inter-actions within this system, in order to discover their specific qualities and their correlations.

Study of the international organization as a system can proceed in different manners. The international organization can be analysed as an *institutional system*, by describing its formal and informal structures and their way of functioning as elements of a system, in terms of their mutual relations and interactions.[5] The international organization can likewise be studied as a *political system*. David Easton was the first to use this concept to analyse national political systems in terms of (a) resources and means (inputs); (b) products or results (outputs); and (c) the conversion function, which transforms inputs into outputs.[6]

This triptych can also be used in analysis of the international organization as a political system.

Inputs are the interests and demands of the member States, and especially, the influence they use to promote and to give effect to these interests and demands within the organization or through its intermediary. The formal aspect of this influence is the right to vote ; but influence also comprises the means which a State possesses to bring others to vote in a desired way, by persuasion, pressure, etc.[7] In this context we can also situate the phenomenon of groups within international organizations (especially the universal ones)—groups whose goal is to maximize the influence of their members.[8]

The *output* is, formally, always a resolution or decision of the organization. But the importance lies in its content. In the internal political system, the decision is necessarily related to the exercise of one of the governmental functions: to a legislative, executive, or judicial act. On the international level, the functions are not the same and the distinctions between them not so clear. None the less, a distinction can be made between two levels: that of the taking of a position (corresponding to the legislative and judicial acts) and that of action (corresponding to the executive act).

Consequently, the output of the international organization as a political system can be as follows.

Collective action. The organization not only decides what must be done, but will do it itself using its own resources. This implies the use of the collective material resources of the organization, in addition to its legal and political resources. It is the maximum that a State or group of States (whose demands are confirmed by the resolution) can obtain from the organization.

Collective legitimization. Here there is a separation between the decision and its execution : the resolution takes a position in favour of a demand (which can either be on a general or normative level, or bear on a specific and concrete question) which thus becomes the position of the organization, without, however, committing the resources of the organization to carry out the decision. If the interested State or States possess the necessary material resources, they can act directly, reinforced by this collective legitimization of their action (which would have been open to different interpretations without this collective taking of a position in their favour).

Condemnation. It is the negative form of collective legitimization, serving as a moral pressure, in cases where the interested States do not possess the necessary resources to undertake the action covered by the collective legitimization.

The *conversion function* covers the dynamic analysis of the process of transformation of inputs into institutional outputs. This approach has been primarily used to analyse the process of decision-making in international organizations, taking into account not just the formal mechanisms of decision-making described in the constitutions of the different organizations, but also all factors which influence either directly or indirectly the decision-making process, and attempting to show their relative importance within the process.[9]

Another approach to analysing internal political systems is to consider them from the point of view of the functions they fulfil.[10] One attempt to adapt this approach to the study of international organizations seeks to analyse the United Nations system on the basis of the following six functions: (a) articulation and aggregation of interests; (b) communication; (c) socialization and recruitment; (d) conflict management ; (e) redistribution ; and (f) integration.[11]

This analysis of the political system in terms of its functions is not incompatible with its analysis in terms of inputs and outputs. Indeed, the authors who developed that approach refer to the first three functions as 'input functions' and the last three as 'output functions'.

Analysis of the international organization as a system does not mean that there is no interaction or exchange between that system and its environment. Indeed, at least a part of the input comes from the environment, and the output is intended at least in part for the environment, although, by feedback, it can once again bring its influence to bear on the system as an input.

Moreover, by studying the international organization as a system one can see better how this system is integrated within the larger context of the international system and to what extent the organization plays the role of actor or arena therein.

By focusing on the inputs and outputs one unconsciously puts oneself in the position of States, a position that sees the organization essentially as an arena of interaction. But, by concentrating on the decision-making processes, one tends to emphasize the role of the autonomous will of the organization as an actor in the international system. However, these two methods of analysis are complementary and each can accommodate the two possible roles of the international organization.

An international organization becomes an actor to the extent that it has (or develops) the ability to influence its environment, i.e. when the organization's institutional output affects the international system instead of simply reflecting it within the organization. But, even if it is only an arena, this does not mean that the organization will have no effect on the issues it deals with. In the first place, the multilateral context of the organization invariably changes the dimensions of these issues, which may be of bilateral origin. Secondly, this context has an influence on the members' position and the content of their demands in so far as they must be formulated according to the terms of reference laid down by the constitution of the organization. Therefore, even as an arena, the international organization affects the inter-actions taking place within it in the same way that a prism deflects the rays of light that cross it.

INTERPRETATIVE METHODS

The interpretative methods lie halfway between the descriptive and the analytical methods. While relying on a theoretical frame of reference (though less formal and abstract than the analytical methods), they remain closer to the phenomena they interpret, using the theory not only as an explanatory tool but also as a guide for action.

Within this category are two diametrically opposed types of approach relating to two functions of the international organization as a political system, namely, conflict and integration. They are: (a) the functionalist approaches, which are openly integrationist; (b) the conflictual approaches, which encompass but go beyond the Marxist explanation of the phenomenon of international organization.

The functionalist theory

This theory was given its first theoretical formulation by Mitrany.[12] Like the adepts of world federalism, Mitrany proceeds from the postulate that the root of international problems and the real obstacle to international co-operation is the division of the world into sovereign States. These States are exclusive and jealous of their independence, although they no longer constitute the ideal framework for providing human communities living within their borders with all technical, economic and social services they need.

Mitrany criticizes, however, the method proposed by the world federalists, which is a formal and constitutionalist one aiming at the creation of a world federation. Because from the start it tackles the problems of security which are the most politically sensitive and cut straight to the heart of sovereignty, the method's reach and efficiency are very limited.

Mitrany proposes a more flexible and indirect approach instead. He considers that security problems (war and peace) originate in material conditions towards which international co-operation ought to be directed in the first place. Entrusting certain technical, economic and social tasks to the organization at the international level demonstrates that some of the needs can be satisfied better at the international rather than at the national level. The multiplication of such organizations chips away at State functions creating transnational pressure groups of technicians, recruited within the States, in favour of transferring action to the international level. This will end in the individual transferring his allegiance from the national State to the international organization that caters for his needs.

In addition, the growth of this kind of international co-operation has a 'spillover' effect necessarily, overflowing the technical sphere into the political sphere whose scope and importance will dwindle progressively. This can lead to world federalism, but it would be the result of the processes and habits of international co-operation rather than the starting-point.

This theory has been severely criticized, particularly its underlying presumptions, which do not necessarily correspond to reality: that all the causes of war are material and can therefore be eliminated by rational means ; that there is a clear and net dichotomy between the technical and the political spheres; that the commitment to technical co-operation will necessarily spread to the political sphere; and that individuals will transfer their allegiance as State functions move to international organizations. These presumptions ignore the subjective factors and go counter to post-war experiences, whether it be the rise of nationalism and particularism or the primacy of politics. In addition, the theory does not sufficiently take into consideration the dangers presented by the concentration of power in the hands of international bureaucrats and technocrats. However, in spite of these flaws, the functionalist theory provides international organizations with a good strategy of action.

Recent efforts have been made to refine this theory and escape some of the criticism. Rather than take up the theory in the abstract, the *neo-functionalist* studies concentrate on specific experiences, notably regional integration efforts (and, in particular, European integration), in order to prove the postulates of the theory, test their validity and refine them in the light of practical experience.

The conflictual theory

The conflictual theory is not explicitly formulated but is subjacent in the attitude of the socialist countries and in some recent trends in the study of international organizations.

The socialist countries, applying Marxist theory to international organizations, consider them to be one of the arenas for the class struggle that reflects the power relations at the international level. However, the organizations can serve as a useful framework for conflict and accommodation as long as the values and demands of the adversary are not transformed into the values and demands of the organization itself. It is therefore a setting for conflict and accommodation principally between superpowers.

A new version of this theory sees the organization as a superstructure or process that aims at institutionalizing the hegemony of the centre over the periphery in the North-South conflict.

While this viewpoint is in line with Marxist thinking, it is not accepted by the socialist countries because it puts them in the dominating and exploiting 'centre', and therefore they take exception to it.

The methods of approach described above are not mutually exclusive. It is not unusual to find alternation between them in the same study. Since each of them sheds a particular light on the phenomenon of international organization, they can cumulatively increase our understanding of this phenomenon.

Chronologically, studies devoted to international organization have called, first of all, on descriptive methods and later have gone on to methods which are analytical, although imbued with the spirit of functionalism. In addition, within the analytical methods one finds a passage from micro-analysis, i.e. the study of the international organization as such, to macro-analysis, i.e. the study of the organization's place and role in the international system.

The current trend is to call less on abstract theoretical analysis than on interpretative methods; and within the latter, more on conflictual than on integrationist theories, at least in the study of universal organizations. As for the study of regional organizations, it continues to be dominated by neo-functionalism.

Group perspectives

The object of the various methods of approach is to try to grasp the reality of the phenomenon of international organization. But, in turn, this reality is to a large extent shaped by the principal actors in the international system, i.e. the States.

It is thus impossible to obtain a thorough understanding of the concept of international organization without taking into consideration the way in which the main groups of States conceive of international organizations. In fact, this determines their attitude with respect to and within these organizations and consequently greatly determines what these organizations are and do.

THE WESTERN GROUP

Since its inception, the present system of universal international organizations has born the stamp of the Western group. Not only are its historical antecedents to be found in co-operative experiences between mainly European and Western countries, but the system was created largely by these States. These organizations were conceived as a means of setting up a new international order: peaceful, democratic and liberal; in other words, to project on to the international sphere the essential traits of the Western political and social system.

The Western conception of international organizations was from the start teleological and expansionist with respect to the tasks and powers of international organizations. This is a conception that joins the functionalist and integrationist theories and considers the international organization an actor in the international system. The cold war has accentuated rather than changed this perspective. The ascendancy, at that time, of the Western group, and especially the United States, within universal international organizations enabled them to have their positions and their actions endorsed as those of the organizations themselves. This view is also reflected in Western literature on international organizations.[13]

However, with the rise of the Third World within universal international organizations and the consequent loss of control by countries of the West, especially the United States, increasingly finding themselves in the minority, the attitude of the Western group progressively evolved: they tried to impose consensus as the only decision-making process (which means the loss of the organization's autonomy *vis-à-vis* its members and the elimination of its role as an actor to become a simple arena); to stop the expansion of the organization's tasks and powers; to deal with important questions outside universal organizations or at least confine them to the bodies and organizations where they continued to have the upper hand or at least a blocking vote; and even to use the threat of withdrawal or non-participation as a means of pressure.

The radical change in the Western group's approach to universal international organizations denotes a restrictive and conflictual attitude. This attitude, which first appeared in practice, has now begun to filter down into recent Western, and especially American, literature on international organizations.

But this recent reserve with regard to universal international organizations has been accompanied, as a substitute solution, with an increasing emphasis on the promotion of regional and partial organizations and a fascination for the European integrationist experience, which goes beyond functionalism to become openly federalist.

THE SOCIALIST GROUP

The socialist group's perspective of international organizations followed a path opposite to that of the Western group.

Although having had only a limited and unhappy experience of international organizations during the period of the League of Nations, the

U.S.S.R.'s post-war participation in the system of universal international organizations, especially the United Nations, constituted a guarantee against encirclement and consecrated its new status as a world power and later that of a superpower.

But for the socialist States international organizations belong to the superstructure; they can only reflect the power relations and serve as another arena in the class struggle at the international level between progressive and reactionary forces. As long as the socialist States are a minority, risking the domination of their adversaries, within these organizations, it is important that the organizations remain within the strict limits of their initial mandate and powers as laid down by their constitutive treaties. Consequently, the socialist States have from the beginning adopted a restrictive interpretation of the mandates and the role of international organizations, considering them as arenas rather than as actors, and opposing all extension of their powers and activities, notably the move from deliberative activities to operational ones, except for the specific cases provided for in the constitutions. This restrictive attitude was accentuated during the cold-war period in view of the Western ascendancy within universal organizations, and the role they played in certain East-West conflicts, such as the Korean war.

However, with the easing of bi-polarity and with the rise of the Third World and its enthusiasm for the extension of the role of international organizations, the socialist States have accepted some extension in the operational activities of international organizations in the economic sphere. On the other hand, they continue to insist, as far as the maintenance of peace and security is concerned, on the strict respect of the initial texts, especially Chapter VII of the Charter of the United Nations which, in making the operational activities in this field the exclusive prerogative of the Security Council, gives a preponderant role to the five permanent members.

The socialist conception of international organization has evolved from a purely conflictual and restrictive conception to a more flexible attitude that allows for some expansion in the role and activities of universal international organizations, to the extent that they are jointly controlled by the superpowers according to the initial hierarchical scheme of the Charter.[14]

THE THIRD WORLD

Most Third World countries were not yet independent at the end of the Second World War. Few of them participated in the establishment of the contemporary system of universal international organizations. But from the time of their independence these countries have adopted a teleological and evolutive attitude towards these organizations.

As the weakest members of the international community, they have always considered international organizations to be the most propitious vehicle for changing the hierarchical and stratified structures of the international system into a more equal and just system.

Accordingly, they have always considered international organizations as important actors in the international system and have always looked very favourably on the extension of their activities and the growth of their powers.

For different reasons, this attitude coincided with, and at the same time went beyond, the Western group's attitude during the cold war and rigid bipolar period (the period of Western ascendancy over universal international organizations). However, with the rise of the Third World, the expansive attitude of the Western group has progressively become much more restrictive. Confronted with this turn of events, the Third World countries have adopted an increasingly demanding and combative attitude, trying to use international organizations as a battlefield and as a means of radically transforming the international system into what has come to be called a new international economic order, but which in fact goes well beyond the purely economic dimension of the international system.[15]

Therefore, one can say that at present the approaches of the three major groups coincide only in their conflictual vision of international organizations. While the perspectives of the Western and socialist groups come closer together in their rather restrictive attitude concerning the activities and role of international organizations—except where these can still be jointly controlled by them—the Third World, given its majority in universal organizations, perseveres in its expansive attitude towards these activites and this role, and seeks to bring about, through their instrumentality, a radical change in the international system.

The foregoing has been a brief synthesis of the different approaches used to grasp the phenomenon of international organization. The following chapters take up these different aspects individually in greater detail and depth.

This work will have achieved its goal if it serves as an epistemological introduction to the study of international organization.

Notes

1. Cf. the chapter by Michel Virally in this volume.
2. Cf. the chapter by Johan Galtung in this volume.
3. This approach is implicit in the work by Stanley Hoffmann, *Organisations Internationales et Pouvoirs Politiques des États*, Paris, 1954.
4. Oran Young, 'The United Nations and the International System', *International Organization*, Vol. 22, 1968; also Wolfram Hanrieder, 'International Organizations and International Systems', *The Journal of Conflict Resolution*, Vol. 10, 1966; Stanley Hoffmann, 'International Organization and the International System'; *International Organization*, Vol. 24, 1970.
5. Mahdi Elmandjra, *The United Nations System: An Analysis*, London, 1973.
6. David Easton, *The Political System*, Chicago, 1953; *A Framework for Political Analysis*, Englewood Cliffs, N.J., 1965; *A Systems Analysis of Political Life*, New York, 1965.
7. Robert Keohane, 'Political Influence in the General Assembly', *International Conciliation*, No. 557, March 1966.
8. Cf., for example, Samaan Boutros Farajallah, *Le Groupe Afro-asiatique dans le cadre des Nations Unies*', Geneva, 1963.
9. Robert Cox and Harold Jacobson (eds.), *The Anatomy of Influence: Decision-making in International Organization*, London, 1974. The authors use the same dynamic approach in their chapter in this volume, but place it on the level of macro-analysis. In other words, here the inputs are modifications in the international system, and the output is modification in the international organization itself. The 'conversion function' is the process of decision-making, not of the organization, but of the international system as a whole, with a view to institutionalizing new power relations.
10. Gabriel Almond, 'Introduction : A. Functional Approach to Comparative Politics', in Gabriel Almond and James Coleman (eds.), *The Politics of the Developing Areas*, Princeton, N.J., 1960; Gabriel Almond and G. Bingham Powell, Jr., *Comparative Politics : A Developmental Approach*, Boston, 1966.
11. Robert Gregg and Michael Barkun (eds.), *The United Nations System and its Functions : Selected Readings*, Princeton, N.J., 1968.
12. David Mitrany, *A Working Peace System*, London, 1943.
13. Cf. the chapter by Rosalyn Higgins in this volume.
14. Cf. the chapter by Grigorii Morozov in this volume.
15. Cf. the chapter by Mohammed Bedjaoui in this volume.

Part I

Evolution
and definition
of international
organization

I Rise and development of international organization: a synthesis

Pierre Gerbet

The proliferation of highly disparate international organizations is a characteristic of our day; their importance varies considerably, but the very fact that there are so many is evidence of an awareness of increasing interdependence. In 1976 there were more than 300 governmental organizations and 3,000 non-governmental organizations—and these figures are rising yearly.

To understand the nature of a phenomenon which has assumed such importance, we shall do well to inquire into its origins and the circumstances of its development. Several factors affect the establishment of international organizations. First, there is the nature of the existing international system; it may consist of empires or States bent on hegemony—in which case all forms of egalitarian organization are precluded—or of a variety of States seeking some degree of equilibrium and co-operation among themselves. Another factor is the geographical coverage of the international system: it may either be divided up into politico-cultural groups affording the possibility of regional organization only, or it may cover the whole globe, thereby providing a basis for a world organization. Here transport and communication facilities are of great importance, for they admit of interregional links, thereby increasing the interdependence of different countries, even the most far-flung, in so far as economic and technological activities develop and are pursued on a world scale.

In order for these facilities to be used, both leaders and the people—or at least the élite—must feel that they belong to a regional or world com-

PIERRE GERBET is Professor of International Relations at the Institut d'Études Politiques, Paris. His books include: *Les Organisations Internationales* (5 editions, 1972); *Les Palais de la Paix, Société des Nations et Organisation des Nations Unies* (1973, with V. Y. Ghébali and M. R. Mouton) and *Les Missions Permanentes auprès des Organisations Internationales* (1971, with Jean Salmon, Michel Virally and V. Y. Ghébali).

munity governed by legal and moral principles which are compatible or identical. They must believe that they have more to gain than to lose by participating in international organizations, and they must show that they are willing to co-operate.

Lastly, historical circumstances have to be taken into account. In peacetime, the setting up of an international organization is a long process, despite the efforts of idealists and the increase in contacts between neighbouring countries. But wars provide a powerful boost to such action, for they oblige groups of States to engage in certain forms of international co-operation, in order to defend themselves against an outside enemy or to maintain peace after their victory. The cause of international organizations advanced considerably as a result of the three victorious coalitions of 1815, 1918 and 1945 which led to the successive creation of the Concert of Europe, the League of Nations and the United Nations.

Before the nineteenth century

History, prior to the nineteenth century, affords relatively few examples of international organizations.

The early civilizations grew up in isolation from each other, with vast distances between them, and were reluctant to communicate with foreigners, who were often regarded as 'barbarians'. These civilizations were encompassed by large States which dealt with their neighbours exclusively on a footing of relative strength. International organizations were neither necessary nor possible. Any such body was bound to be a fringe organization, set up within circumscribed geographical areas, still beyond the pale of the great empires, when several political units belonging to the same cultural area realized that they had common interests. More often than not, they formed defensive leagues. Thus, the small Chinese States, between the seventh and the fifth century B.C., threatened by the Kingdom of Chu, held assemblies in order to discuss the organization of their military strength. In ancient Greece we find a few forms of international organization, such as the *amphictyonies*—councils of arbitration between cities that used the same sanctuaries—and especially the political confederations, which had councils empowered to take majority decisions, and sometimes an assembly, levying contributions to maintain contingents under a single commander. Leagues of cities, in far more embryonic form, were also established in ancient Italy before the Roman Empire extended its domination.

In medieval Europe, within the politically divided Christian community, certain coalitions were formed outside the great monarchical

States, in fragmented Germany and Italy. The antagonistic leagues of Italian cities sought to maintain their relations on a balanced footing. Between the fourteenth and sixteenth centuries some fifty trading towns in northern Europe belonged to the powerful Hanseatic League, the purpose of which was to protect their trade: it was directed by a general assembly in which a majority vote prevailed and which was alone entitled to declare war. The League of Swiss Cantons came into being in the fourteenth century for the purposes of defence, and led to the creation of a confederation.

Examples of the same kind might perhaps be found in pre-Columbian America and in Africa before the arrival of the Europeans, but as yet little is known about that aspect of the history of these continents.

While these various bodies have certain features in common with international organizations proper as we know them today (an assembly, a council, weighted voting, majority voting, financial contributions), they were not part of a continuous process of development. Most of them disappeared with the expansion of the great empires or the constitution of centralized States, which were equally opposed to the idea of an organization linking them with their neighbours.

The modern age was not favourable to the emergence of international organizations. National States became consolidated under the authority of princely dynasties. The principle of sovereignty became more firmly entrenched with centralization. Rivalries in Europe were accompanied by struggles for maritime and colonial expansion. Some of the great States imposed their hegemony at the expense of others: the hegemony of Spain in the sixteenth and early seventeenth centuries gave way to the continental hegemony of France in Europe under Louis XIV and the colonial and maritime hegemony of Great Britain in the eighteenth century, and then, again, the continental hegemony of France in Europe under Napoleon. To prevent any one of them from achieving over-all hegemony, the dominant powers increasingly practised a policy of power balance expressed by forming coalitions. From the seventeenth century onwards, the principle of the balance of power became the basic principle of European public law. Unfortunately, this equilibrium was unstable, for it could be maintained only by breaking alliances and by waging war.

This was why thinkers advocated 'peace plans' to establish concord among the princes. From the seventeenth century onwards the idea of a 'society of nations' developed—in other words, an organized group of States, belonging not only to Christian Europe, as still conceived at the end of the Middle Ages, but to the world opened up by the great discoveries. Starting from the Renaissance, the idea of a universal human society took shape—a society founded on natural law whose rules, dictated by reason, would be valid for all. Thus, in 1623, the Frenchman, Emeric de Crucé proposed that there should be a world assembly, presided over by the Pope; all the princes were to be represented in it, as well as Turkey, China and Japan. Already, a 'one-world' view was being taken.

Other thinkers confined themselves to the European context: William Penn, for instance, in 1693, and the Abbot of Saint Pierre in 1713. Their main concern was to establish peace, for they thought that, once war was eliminated, trade would develop and prosperity would ensue. Like their predecessors at the end of the Middle Ages, they advocated a permanent assembly composed of representatives of the princes, taking decisions by majority vote, and with a combined army responsible for giving effect to those decisions.

These projects had no effect upon the political situation. No monarch took up the idea or proposed to other monarchs that a European congress be set up. International relations in the eighteenth century were still founded upon the sovereignty of the princes and the maintenance of a balance of power between the five dominant States—Great Britain, France, Austria, Prussia and Russia. Conflicts were numerous. Moreover, the projects of those who produced plans for peace were considered Utopian by other thinkers ; Jean-Jacques Rousseau and Kant after him took the view that a congress of delegates of States would not be viable and that it would break up in the event of disagreement. The former considered that peaceful relations could not be established between peoples until they had got rid of the avaricious and bellicose princes. As for the latter, in 1795 he also expressed the view that, in order to live in peace, States should become republics and then advocated a European federation with a constitution, on the pattern of the United States of America, whose confederation, established in 1778 by the settlers in revolt against Great Britain, had been transformed into a federation in 1787.

Thus, by that time, most of the 'maximalist' conceptions of international organization had already been formulated (majority decisions and even federation). In practice, during the subsequent slow development of international organization, the sovereignty of States was generally respected, and for a long time action was confined to consultation and voluntary co-operation.

The nineteenth-century contribution: the Concert of Europe and administrative unions

It was in the nineteenth century that the first lineaments of international organization as we know it today appeared. The circumstances then were, on the whole, more favourable, but at the same time some obstacles were becoming more difficult to surmount.

After the wars at the time of the French Revolution and Empire, the need for peace was felt more strongly, and it was realized that a balance of power in Europe was essential. The scientific and industrial revolution and the extraordinary development of facilities for transporting men and merchandise and for communicating ideas led to an increase in trade, the establishment of a single economic area, the international division of labour and a sense of universal community. The advance of democratic ideas, the belief that all human beings were of equal value, fostered the notion of egalitarian participation by all States in international organizations responsible for ensuring peace and progress. Admittedly, during most of the nineteenth century international relations concerned only Europe, which was the centre of world political, military and economic power, but also a breeding-ground for discord and strife, the other parts of the world being either isolated or under the control of the European powers. But with the emergence of new powers at the end of the nineteenth century (the United States, Japan), the field of action for international organization gradually extended beyond the confines of Europe.

These conditions making for internationalism were, however, counteracted by the growing strength of nation-States and the development of nationalism. The States, which played the leading part in international relations, kept strengthening their political and administrative structures and their military capacity, especially in the latter half of the century. The development of international law led to a more precise definition of the notion of territorial jurisdiction, sovereignty and independence. The nationalist movement throughout the nineteenth century, culminating in the Europe embodied in the Treaty of Versailles, could have been conducive to the establishment of peace among the peoples. But more often than not national feeling and even chauvinistic nationalism prevailed. The national wars of the latter half of the nineteenth century, in particular those which led to a unified Italy and a unified Germany, set entire peoples against each other and left bitter and ineffaceable memories in their wake. Territorial competition shifted from Europe to the colonies. Rivalries between the major industrial powers went hand in hand with economic tension.

This was the background against which, in the nineteenth century, several parallel and more or less unrelated moves were made towards international organization; not till the twentieth century, and then only gradually, was any conjunction of efforts achieved. Instances of such moves are the Concert of Europe and the great diplomatic conferences, action to promote arbitration and disarmament, and the establishment of permanent international administrative unions to deal with technical questions.

The Concert of Europe was the political system established by the victors over Napoleon in order to preserve the balance of power in Europe. The object was to maintain in peacetime the coalitions formed during the war by institutionalizing diplomatic conferences on the basis of a pledge to take joint action.

In the final phase of the struggle against Napoleon, Great Britain, Prussia and Austria had been in constant consultation with each other. The Austrian, Metternich, had recognized the advantages of this, as had the Englishman, Castlereagh who, not wishing to make specific commitments, preferred the system of consultation. As a result, periodic conferences were instituted at which those in power could exchange views on any questions that arose. This was a new method of diplomacy. Up to that time, international conferences were held solely for the purpose of drawing up peace treaties; governments wishing to communicate with each other merely exchanged notes through their ambassadors. Henceforth statesmen could have direct conversations and more easily exchange their points of view. Conferences, or congresses, were held at various levels: heads of State at the beginning, then prime ministers and ministers of foreign affairs, and very often ambassadors. The number of participants was usually limited to the five great powers (the four that had defeated Napoleon, plus France from 1818). The Kingdom of Sardinia and later the Kingdom of Italy participated from 1856 onwards; likewise Turkey. The minor powers were excluded, except—in the latter half of the century—those that were interested in the solution to a particular question. Of varying composition, these conferences were also of various types. Besides the major diplomatic ones, conferences of a more limited nature were held (concerning the Crete affair in 1896, intervention in China in 1900, Balkan affairs in 1912 and 1913).

This system of conferences did not amount to a genuine form of international organization: there was no constitution, no headquarters, or permanent secretariat. Meetings were not held regularly, and each time the agreement of the participants had to be obtained, after lengthy negotiations concerning the place of meeting and the agenda. The place varied according to either the problem to be dealt with or prestige considerations on the part of the powers involved. It was difficult to convene conferences at short notice, particularly in times of crisis, when there was the greatest need for them. Nevertheless these conferences had become the normal setting for multilateral diplomacy. The idea of a multinational secretariat began to be mooted. After the Congress of Vienna (1815), the host country had the prerogative of chairing the conference, and one of its diplomats was responsible for the secretariat. From the time of the Congress of Berlin in 1873, and in particular at the Hague Conferences in

1899 and 1907, each delegation provided a secretary and the host country the secretary-general.

Endowed as it was with still very empirical conference machinery, did the Concert of Europe, as a political system, constitute an actual organization? Such was certainly the case during the first years. The idea of the collective responsibility of the great powers was in the air—the idea of joint supervision in order to maintain peace and equilibrium in the interest of all. Admittedly, States retained their sovereignty, and did not undertake to abstain from war or to defend each other's territorial integrity. But the great powers formed a directive body, an actual government of Europe, at least when they were in agreement. The primary purpose of the Concert was to maintain the European status quo, which was founded on the principles of legitimacy and equilibrium. It gave its support to the anti-liberal intervention of Austria in the Kingdom of the Two Sicilies (1821) and of France in Spain (1823). However, there was no collective intervention. Castlereagh, unlike the conservative powers, wished to guarantee neither thrones nor frontiers. Already the dilemma of international organizations arose: should they promote stability or change?

Then the nature of the action taken by the Concert of Europe changed with the disappearance of the Holy Alliance. It became an instrument of mutual restraint as regards foreign policy. Under the impetus of the liberal powers (Great Britain and, later, France) and despite the reluctance of the conservative powers (Austria, Prussia and Russia), the concert helped Greece, and subsequently Belgium, to become independent, thereby endorsing the principle of nationhood. But the Concert was powerless before the liberal and national explosion of 1848, and the establishment of a unified Italy and a unified Germany. When the great powers came into conflict with each other, the Concert had ceased to exist. The Congress of Paris in 1856 convened to work out the peace terms at the end of the Crimean War. It fulfilled that task, but Napoleon III could not induce it to realize his dream—the peaceable revision of the 1815 treaties—owing to the opposition of the great powers.

The Concert of Europe regained a certain amount of ground during the last thirty years of the nineteenth century; in particular, the Congress of Berlin in 1878 settled outstanding problems after the Russo-Turkish war according to the principle of 'compensation' (the expansion of Russia was checked, Austria received Bosnia and Herzegovina, and Great Britain was given Cyprus), while formally acknowledging the independence of Montenegro, Serbia and Romania and the autonomy of Bulgaria. Subsequently, the Concert of Europe was to remain a forum for the settlement, by the European powers, of a number of problems external to Europe: collective intervention (in China in particular), joint measures to abolish

slavery and the slave trade, the laying down of rules governing the occu-
pation of colonial territories (Conference of Berlin in 1885 and Conference
of Brussels in 1890).

With the resurgence of the threat of war in Europe at the beginning
of the twentieth century, international conferences were again held (in
Algeciras for the Moroccan crisis in 1906, in London for the Balkan crisis
in 1913), but these were mainly improvised in times of crisis. The balance
of power in Europe was no longer maintained by the Concert of Europe,
but by the two blocs of allied powers taking part in the arms race and
caught up in the automatic mechanisms of mobilization. Moreover, since
the end of the nineteenth century, international conferences had begun to
go beyond the European context. The United States had a seat at the first
Hague Conference, in 1899, acted as arbitrator in the Russo-Japanese
conflict in 1905 and participated in the Algeciras Conference in 1906. The
United States and a number of Latin American countries participated in
the second Hague Conference in 1907.

Alongside the Concert of Europe and the intermittent attempts to
establish a balanced political system, the nineteenth century saw the rise,
in a far more embryonic form, of two trends which, in the following century, were to make an important contribution to efforts towards the international organization of States: mediation or arbitration and disarmament.

Mediation, a technique employed in the field of international relations
since ancient times, was highly empirical in character, since it had no
adequately developed body of international law to rest upon. Arbitration,
widely used from the twelfth to the fifteenth centuries but later dropped
by the great monarchies which preferred mediation so as to preserve their
sovereignty, was central to the plans for the establishment of a European
or world organization put forward from the end of the Middle Ages
onwards with a view to ushering in the reign of peace. The Congress of
Paris (1856) in vain advocated the use of the good offices of a friendly power.
When conflicts arose recourse was had to treaties and compromises, however, between English-speaking countries and in the sphere of inter-
American diplomacy. They bore mainly on questions of frontiers. The
success of the 'Alabama' arbitration in 1872 gave wide currency to the
idea that this technique should be tried out whenever there was a threat
of war. Arbitration thus became the panacea of pacifist movements.

However, it proved impossible to set up a permanent court of arbitration or to make arbitration compulsory. The Hague Conferences of
1899 and 1907 laid down the principle of compulsory arbitration and
established a code for arbitral procedure, but did not succeed in setting
up a genuine international court of justice. It was impossible to get the
great and lesser powers to agree on a system for electing judges or to

establish a list of questions of relatively secondary importance concerning which arbitration might be made compulsory. The permanent tribunal established in 1899 was no more than a list of judges from which any parties willing to accept this procedure could make a choice.

At the same time the idea of disarmament, or at least of demilitarization, started to attract attention. The 1817 Treaty between Great Britain and the United States demilitarized the Great Lakes. The 1856 Congress of Paris neutralized the Åland Islands and the Black Sea, but the neutralization of the latter was to be denounced unilaterally by Russia in 1870 and officially abrogated by the Conference of London in 1871. The need for disarmament became particularly apparent at the end of the nineteenth century on account of the growing cost of modern weapons and their highly lethal character. The Hague Conference, which was convened on the initiative of the Czar in 1899, was the first of many conferences on disarmament in the twentieth century; a second was held there in 1907. These conferences adopted declarations aimed at humanizing war and statements on the desirability of disarmament. They were unable to curb the arms race, but at least they had the merit of bringing the problem to the attention of the international public.

Lastly, in another field, that of economic and technical activities, governments agreed to establish genuine international administrative bodies.

There was, of course, no question of organizing international economic life, since, according to the liberal view, it was supposed to be governed by its own laws. The measures taken by governments were aimed above all at eliminating obstacles (establishment by the German States of the Zollverein or Customs Unions in 1834, adoption of free trade by Great Britain in 1846, by France in 1860, and subsequently by the other European countries). Even with the return to a moderate form of protectionism at the end of the nineteenth century, there was a real world economy whose centre was industrialized Western Europe; the United States developed separately. Waterways common to several countries, together with straits, were to be accessible to everyone. Successive treaties established, for trading purposes, freedom of passage through the Turkish Straits (1829), the Danish Straits (1857), the Suez Canal (Convention of Constantinople, 1888) and the Panama Canal (Treaty of 1901 and 1903). It was decided that the Rhine (1815), the Elbe (1821), the Scheldt and the Meuse (1839), the Danube (1856), the Congo and the Niger (1885) would be open to international trade. Permanent commissions were set up to ensure freedom of navigation of the Rhine (1815) and the Danube (1856).

However, owing to the considerable advance in communication facilities and the intensification of trade, permanent co-operation among States at the technical level was necessary; it was all the more readily accepted because there was less danger in this field than in the political sphere of offending national susceptibilities or going against vital interests. A great many international conferences were held, in the latter half of the nineteenth century, on a wide variety of subjects. The number of agreements increased, and, above all, many international organizations of a technical nature, which had permanent administrative organs, were set up by multilateral conventions. Approximately fifty were founded before 1914; in the communications field, for instance, the International Telegraph Union (1865), the Universal Postal Union (1878), the Railways Union (1890) and the Universal Radiotelegraph Union (1906). The speed of transport made the risk of epidemics greater and necessitated the establishment of the International Sanitary Convention (1853), the International Office (1853) the International Office of Public Health (1904) and the International Health Office (1907). The development of industry led to the establishment of the International Bureau of Weights and Measures (1875), the International Union for the Protection of Industrial Property (1883) and the International Statistics Office (1913). The Union for the Protection of the Rights of Authors over their Literary and Artistic Property (1884) and the International Agriculture Office (1905) were also founded.

The international character of these permanent administrative bodies was more or less pronounced. The majority were under the supervision of one Member State. Others were responsible to an international commission, in this respect resembling the river commissions system, with multinational secretariats. These offices gave rise to many contacts between national administrative bodies and established the habit of co-operation at the technical level, thereby laying the foundations of international civil services.

The development of the administrative unions was merely the expression, at intergovernmental level, of a trend towards internationalism which was evidenced to an even greater extent in private activities. A wide variety of social bodies in different countries developed relations with each other. Private international associations had been set up in connection with every kind of activity: humanitarian, religious, ideological, scientific and technological. There were virtually no frontiers, as far as capitalist firms were concerned. At the beginning of the twentieth century, there was a marked contrast between the intensity of the economic, technical and cultural relations between countries and social groups—relations which were often established and maintained through governmental or non-governmental organizations—and the absence of an international political order. The nation-States remained faithful in most of their political dealings to the traditional machinery of military alliances and diplomatic arrangements. The paradoxical nature of this situation did not escape an enlightened section of the public, particularly in Great Britain, France and the United States, where a movement developed for the peaceable organization of the world. The socialist parties, for their part, considered that the impossibility of organizing peace was due to the bourgeois structure of States, and, while deciding to combat war by means of strike action, placed all their hopes in the union of the international proletariat. In 1914, however, socialists in the belligerent countries obeyed their duty as patriots.

On the eve of the First World War, the level of achievement as regards international organization was uneven, but encouraging for the future, perhaps less on account of the results obtained, which were still very slight, than by virtue of the lessons which could be drawn from these first attempts.

Political consultation and multilateral conferences had become well-established practices. But their ineffectiveness in times of crisis was due, at least in part, to the fact that there were no permanent institutions which could, in periods of tension, provide a forum for discussion, carry out inquiries and formulate impartial recommendations. Progress had been made in respect of arbitration and even international justice, but these were not in themselves sufficient to resolve international conflicts of any importance, which needed to be dealt with more broadly, from a political angle. Co-operation had developed in technical matters, but had exerted no influence on political relations. The administrative unions were concerned with a great variety of fields, but there was no co-ordination between them.

All in all, tangible form had been given to important components of international organization, but discretely, whereas the interdependence of problems called for an over-all approach. Perhaps, if the First World War had not broken out, gradual progress towards establishing a more systematic international organization would have continued to be made and, in time, effective solutions would have been found. But the 1914 conflict speeded up the normal course of events, and the League of Nations was established.

The case of the League of Nations

Even before the inception of the League of Nations, major advances had been made in respect of the techniques of international organizations, thanks to the co-operation of the Allies during the war.

The conduct of military operations necessitated frequent meetings between statesmen and constant contacts between military staff and administrations. Diplomatic channels no longer sufficed. Permanent inter-Allied bodies had to be set up to co-ordinate the war efforts of the Allies. The first of these was the Inter-Allied Commission, established in 1916, as a result of a decision taken by Asquith and Briand; it dealt with all matters of importance, and it comprised prime ministers, the ministers of the relevant departments and the technical experts required for the study of the different problems. The Commission expressed opinions, and its proposals had to be approved by governments, but the fact that it comprised persons in positions of political responsibility made it possible for points on which there was agreement to be brought out. Lloyd George, who had become Prime Minister of Great Britain, greatly enlarged the scope of the system. He proposed that meetings between heads of government be supplemented by the establishment of an inter-Allied permanent staff responsible for working out overall strategy. After the Caporetto disaster, the Allies, constrained by necessity, established a Supreme War Council, which was assisted by a permanent secretariat and exercised authority over a number of specialized inter-Allied organizations. On the military side, it was provided with an Inter-Allied Naval Council, a Military Council, a Transport Council, a Blockade Council, a Propaganda Committee and an Inter-Allied Munitions Council.

At the economic level, an extensive organization had gradually been set up. With a long war in prospect, it was not possible to give free play to the market economy, which would have led to competition between Allies for the purchase of foodstuffs and raw materials, increases in prices and freight charges and the improper use of maritime shipping, already reduced by submarine warfare. On the proposal of the French Minister of Trade, Etienne Clémentel, his representative in London, Jean Monnet, and a British senior official, Arthur Salter, 'Executive Commissions' were set up, first of all for wheat, then for oils and fats, meat and sugar, under the authority of the Inter-Allied Provisions Council. An Allied Maritime Transport Council was established, with an Executive Commission the members of which included Salter, Monnet, an Italian, Attolico, and, subsequently, an American. The basic idea was to pool resources. The members of the Commissions employed an original method to achieve this: being government representatives, but not tied by excessively rigid instructions, they examined the problem from all sides, sought the most effective solutions in a climate of mutual trust and persuaded their governments to accept them. From the spring of 1918 they thus controlled the movements and food cargoes of all Allied and neutral ships, and were able to regulate the flow of provisions so as to leave the necessary shipping free for the transport of American troops.

This imposing collection of Councils and Commissions operated under the authority of the Supreme War Council. As Sir Maurice Hankey, the head of the international secretariat of the Council, pointed out subsequently, it is not too much to say that this organization covered every sphere of inter-Allied activity and constituted a true organ of international government. The Councils at ministerial level could be compared to a ministerial cabinet, and the Commissions working for them to ministerial departments. These Executive Commissions had the authority to deal with all questions in their field; however, if these questions were too weighty for the permanent representatives to decide upon, they were brought before one of the ministerial councils and, if they involved a high-level political matter, they were dealt with by the Inter-Allied Supreme Council. Thus, under the pressure of circumstances, the Allies came to achieve a unified command in both the economic and military fields.

Such an all-embracing organization could have continued to exist in time of peace. In fact, it did so only in part. At the political level, the wartime organization became the nucleus of the Peace Conference. The Council of Ten was simply the Supreme War Council. Moreover, it was under that name that it met to discuss the military clauses of treaties with Germany and Austria on the basis of drafts prepared by its military, naval and air committees. The secretariat of the Supreme Council was transferred from Versailles to Paris and attached to the general secretariat of the Peace Conference, and the latter confirmed the multinational character of the secretariat of international conferences. A leading role in it was played by Sir Maurice Hankey. For reasons of efficiency and prudence, the Council of Ten was reduced to a council of four heads of government (Wilson, Lloyd George, Clemenceau and Orlando), with the occasional participation of Japan. A new directive body on a world scale was thus constituted. The Council of Four ceased to exist after the Treaty of Versailles had been signed, but the Supreme War Council continued to meet to consider the other treaties. In January 1920, however, its permanent sessions ceased, but it subsequently met on several occasions until November, in order to settle problems that arose in giving effect to the treaties; this afforded the League of Nations time to organize itself in Geneva and, by and large, eliminated the need for it to take decisions concerning the application of the treaties, except in regard to questions referred to it. With the exception of the United States, the group of victorious great powers reassembled as the council of the League.

However, the inter-Allied wartime organization of economic matters disappeared far more rapidly, despite the fact that there was a need for it in a period of reconstruction. Clémentel and Monnet would have liked it to continue to distribute raw materials where they were most urgently needed, seeing in it the adumbration of a system to regulate international economic life. All the Commissions had been grouped together at the beginning of 1919 under the authority of a Supreme Economic Council. President Wilson, who had advocated free access to raw materials, was interested. But the scheme was unfavourably received by American economists, who rejected the controls which they had been obliged to accept during hostilities, being against the idea of the general control of raw materials in peacetime. The British, who were initially interested, preferred to go back to the practices of free trade, fearing that the control of raw materials would be used by France as a means of keeping Germany under its thumb. The Supreme Economic Council ceased to exist in April 1919; the Executive Commissions were gradually dismantled, although France would have liked these economic bodies to serve the purposes of the groundwork for peace and the instrument of economic sanctions for the use of the league. However, this wartime experience was not in vain: Jean Monnet and Arthur Salter, who had played the leading parts in it, met again at the League, where, in a similar spirit but in far less favourable conditions, they directed their efforts towards the development of international economic and financial co-operation. Subsequently, Jean Monnet evolved from his experience of the Executive Commissions a doctrine of joint action which he was to put into effect in the European Communities.

The League of Nations was the work of the victorious coalition. It corresponded to a trend in public opinion which had become more pronounced among the Allies and in the neutral countries during the war and which incorporated the already familiar ideas of the limitation of armaments, the development of arbitration and the possible application of sanctions as well as the newer and more daring idea of a 'League of Nations', a permanent organization in the service of peace. However, the creation of the League was, above all, the work of one man, President Wilson. Convinced that the United States should play a part in world affairs, but that its role should be a moral one and be exercised impartially, he had at a very early stage conceived of the idea of an international organization piloted by the United States, an organization which would make it possible to do away with the system of armed equilibrium which generated wars and forced the smaller nations to accept the domination of the larger ones. He looked for an association of nations founded on the right of peoples to self-determination, both small and large States being entitled to the same respect for their independence and territorial integrity, which would be vouched for by reciprocal guarantees. These were the ideas he expressed in the last of his fourteen points on 8 January 1918. Wilson considered that the establishment of this world organization was essential to a peace settlement and that it was in this direction that the first efforts should be made. He compelled his two partners, Lloyd George and Clemenceau, who were far more sceptical, first of all to negotiate the Covenant of the League of Nations, which would be incorporated in the peace treaties. It is conceivable that, had he not made this demand, it would have been impossible, after the treaties had been drafted, to reach agreement concerning a projected international organization. Wilson led the discussions himself, and the Covenant of the League of Nations was adopted on 28 April 1919. The American President's success was to be short-lived, however, as he was unable to gain the support of Congress and the United States remained outside the League, thus greatly weakening it.

In what way did the League of Nations, as an international organization, constitute an advance? First of all, by virtue of its institutional structure. The idea of a small council in which the great powers had a permanent seat was taken over from the Concert of Europe. But they were no longer alone; the smaller powers were represented in the Council as non-permanent members. When their number increased, the Council, in which each member had one vote, ceased to be a directive body. However, the influence of the great powers, each of which had its group of 'followers', remained preponderant. The Council normally met every three months, or more often if necessary.

The Assembly was held each autumn in Geneva, and all Member States participated in it, on an equal footing, with one vote each. This was the most notable innovation in the new organization, constituting a guarantee that international life had been 'democratized'. The Assembly provided all States, big and small, with a forum in which to state their case and appeal to world opinion.

An international secretariat, directly based upon the experience of the inter-Allied bodies which had existed in wartime, was entrusted with the administrative tasks, and played a very important role on account of its permanent character, the qualifications of its members and the fact that they were independent of governments. The international civil service was to develop considerably.

A Permanent Court of International Justice, provided for by the Covenant, began work in 1922, in The Hague. It was composed of fifteen members, appointed by the Council and Assembly of the League and independent of States. It played a useful role, though limited in that it was not concerned with the most important conflicts between States—political ones—but only legal disputes not involving vital interests. In addition, its jurisdiction was not binding.

The League had many shortcomings. The fields of competence of the Assembly and the Council were not clearly defined. Out of respect for each country's national sovereignty, decisions of the Council were taken unanimously, except in the case of procedural questions, and this led to paralysis. In principle, the organization was universal: the countries vanquished in the war were admitted, as were the emancipated colonial territories. From forty-five in 1919, the number of members increased to sixty in 1934. But the Covenant provided for the possibility of withdrawal, after preliminary notice had been given, and the totalitarian countries withdrew from the League. In 1939 there were only forty-four member countries left, and the Soviet Union was about to be expelled on account of its attack on Finland. From the beginning, the absence of the United States had caused an imbalance in the institution.

Finally, the very conception of the organization was defective. France, supported by Italy, was in favour of a strong League, capable of keeping a watch on Germany and ensuring that the peace treaties were observed, and possessing for that purpose a military force as a sure means of maintaining collective security. The British and the Americans, however, along with the Commonwealth and Latin American countries, were against this 'international militarism', being apprehensive that an armed force would limit the sovereignty of States. Having no problem of security in respect of Germany and being preoccupied with moralistic considerations, they did not want a 'coercive' League, but a League based on goodwill, whose members would merely undertake to resort to international mediation in the event of a dispute. Fearing that this right might be vitiated by use of the force placed in its service, they considered that the League, as a reflection of international public opinion, should act by exerting moral pressure on States in order to maintain peace. Hence the inadequacy of the provisions of the Covenant relating to collective security. The use of force was not forbidden, but simply governed by regulations, deferred, made subject to the application of peaceful procedures, which were to prove difficult to define. France and its continental allies did not manage to get the 1924 Protocol adopted, the purpose of which was to ensure collective security by means of the formula 'arbitration, security, disarmament': compulsory arbitration, imposed by the Council, would create security, which, in its turn, would make disarmament possible. But the dominions did not wish to take on specific obligations within the League, which remained unarmed. The Briand-Kellogg Pact of 1928 condemning recourse to war was a legal commitment, but too vague and lacking the guarantees of institutional mechanisms which would have made it truly effective. The General Arbitration Act of the same year described the peaceful procedures which were to be substituted for recourse to war, but these were not mandatory. The word 'war' was not defined, which was to lead countries that had committed an aggression to disguise their actions as 'incidents'. Sanctions were in effect subject to a decision by the Council, which made their application uncertain, and there was no body that could intervene. Lastly, disarmament proved impossible; the numerous commissions and conferences that discussed it came to nothing, and Germany's withdrawal from the League was the signal for the resumption of the arms race.

These structural defects were compounded by the fact that the League did not have a chance to work within a homogeneous international system. Victors and vanquished, conservative countries seeking to maintain the status quo and revisionist countries wanting changes in treaties, imperialist countries without respect for any rule, and peaceful countries all remained in conflict with each other.

In these circumstances, the League's political role proved highly disappointing. Minor disputes were settled during the first few years and conflicts avoided (the Vilnius affair in 1920 between Poland and Lithuania, the Åland Islands affair in 1921 between Finland and Sweden and the Greco-Bulgar affair in 1925). Problems concerning minorities were discreetly solved. But the League was never able to face up to a great power. It did not have the courage to stand up to Italy when Mussolini bombed Corfu, nor did it penalize Japan when it invaded Manchuria in 1931; morally condemned by the Assembly, however, Japan left the League in 1933, then attacked China in 1937. The League was not able to prevent Italy from conquering Ethiopia in 1935–36 or to apply effective sanctions against it, after declaring it to be the aggressor. The failure of sanctions—due to Franco-British complicity in ruling out military sanctions before the event and to the delivery of American oil to Italy—marked a turning-point in the history of the organization. Many countries left the League. The illusion of collective security faded. Turkey requested that the demilitarization of the Straits be ended; Switzerland returned to its position of complete neutrality. Italy left the organization in 1937 and attacked Albania in 1939. The League was helpless against Hitler's Germany, which had withdrawn from it in 1933 and which then proceeded to wreck the Treaty of Versailles and to commit aggression against Austria, Czechoslovakia and Poland. The League, which had admitted the Soviet Union in 1934, was unable to prevent it from dividing up Poland or from attacking Finland; it was finally expelled in December 1939, but by then the Second World War had broken out.

This series of failures is to be accounted for partly by the inadequacy of the League's internal machinery, but above all by lack of firmness on the part of the great democracies. They did not apply that policy of collective security of which they could have been the instrument. Since its principal members adopted an attitude of weakness, the international organization was powerless.

In contrast with its failure at the political level, the League's achievement in other spheres appears highly successful. The International Labour Organisation (ILO), which was set up at the request of trade unions, and the constitution of which, like the Covenant of the League, had been included in the peace treaties, comprised all the members of the League. Its structure was unusual, in that workers' and employers' delegates were present as well as government delegates. Thus, not only were States represented, but also the interested social groups. Directed by the French socialist, Albert Thomas, ILO achieved a great deal in the field of social legislation.

The League itself, on which ILO was practically independent, turned towards economic, financial and humanitarian action. General Smuts, a politician from the Union of South Africa, had advocated a League of Nations which would be not only a means of avoiding wars, but also an organ co-ordinating all international activities during peacetime with a view to hastening the advent of a world civilization. It was his view that this organization would be able to impose its law on States in the event of international disputes only in so far as it was able to make its influence felt on peaceful relations between States. But the League was conceived essentially as a political institution: economic and social co-operation was less important than collective security. Furthermore, most of the administrative unions, which were continuing with their activities, refused to place themselves under the direction of the League, although this was provided for by the Covenant, owing to the opposition of the United States, a non-member of the League, and of certain governments which feared that the Geneva-based organization would become too powerful and be transformed into a super-State.

However, under the pressure of the needs of a world emerging from war, the League acquired specialized organs with a view to developing international co-operation in the fields of health, economy and finance, communications and transport. These 'organizations' and 'commissions' were subject to the supervision of the Council and the Assembly and were attached, as regards their functioning to the administrative sections of the secretariat. The League gave a decisive impetus to the provision of aid for refugees and work to counter epidemics. It contributed to the financial revival of certain nations which had been particularly hard hit by the war: Austria's recovery was a typical case of concerted international action. The League's economic services also sought remedies for the disorders of the world economy and organized international conferences for that purpose. More often than not, however, they came up against the ill-will of States, many of which were opposed to economic action on the part of the organization and also to the growing compartmentalization of the world economy, particularly after the crisis of 1929, with prohibitive customs duties, exchange control and immigration quotas. In fact, a considerable proportion of international trade was controlled by private cartels, and international agreements were concluded between countries producing raw materials (tin, rubber) or foodstuffs (wheat, sugar) so as to stabilize prices by reducing production. Despite all these obstacles, the technical organs of the League continued to carry out useful work, adapting to circumstances, foregoing any attempt to induce large numbers of States to subscribe to general conventions and increasing the number of sectoral and regional studies conducted by independent experts.

The success of the League's technical activities was in marked contrast with its political failure. The committee responsible for examining the question of reform of the League observed that universality was the prime condition for its success. Universality was difficult to achieve at the political level, on account of differences in ideologies; it existed in the economic and social field, since those States that had left the League, together with the United States, participated in its technical activities. This being the case, would it not have been worth while to emphasize these activities, making them distinct from political matters, so as to save the organizaiton? This was what was advocated in the report drawn up by Stanley Bruce, an Australian politician. The Bruce Report recommended that a central committee on economic and social questions be established which would take over from the Council and the Assembly responsibility for directing and supervising technical activities. This committee would consist of government representatives and experts co-opted on a personal basis by virtue of their qualifications. Its decisions would be taken by majority vote. The Bruce Report ran counter to prevailing trends in that, for reasons of expediency, it separated technical activities from political obligations, which was contrary to the spirit of the Covenant. But it anticipated the future by putting forward the idea that economic and social activities should be centralized under the authority of a specialized committee, with the introduction of a majority vote and the presence of independent experts within a directive organ. It recognized that economic and social activities should cease to be regarded as secondary to political objectives and that they should constitute an end in themselves. The Bruce Report, published on 23 August 1939, was lost sight of in the war which broke out a few days later. But it had to a large extent paved the way for the creation of the United Nations Economic and Social Council.

The United Nations system and the regional organizations

The League of Nations was the victim of the Second World War which it had been unable to avert. But, by its very failure, it had demonstrated the need for a more effectively structured and more efficient international organization. Yet there were no plans to revive the League, since the United States was never a member and the Soviet Union had been expelled from it.

The United Nations, like the Concert of Europe and the League of

Nations, was created by the victorious coalition. Once again the United States and its President, Franklin Roosevelt, played a decisive role, in that it was their ideas that carried the day. In contrast with the League, which was rapidly set up at the beginning of the Peace Conference, preparations for the establishment of the United Nations were made throughout the period of the war, principally by the Americans and British in conjunction, subsequently joined by the Soviets and the Chinese. It was this sense of solidarity born of the war which alone made success possible. The broad lines of the Organization were laid down at the Dumbarton Oaks Conference (August–October 1944), while the Bretton Woods Conference (July 1945) laid the foundations for an international monetary system. The smaller powers at war with the Axis had an opportunity to put forward their points of view at the San Francisco Conference (April–June 1945), at which the United Nations Charter was drawn up on the basis of the principles already laid down by the great powers. The United Nations, the headquarters of which were to be in New York, began to function at the beginning of 1946.

We shall not attempt to describe the United Nations system, even in brief, but simply to show how it incorporated the various trends which had gradually emerged in the course of the development of international organizations and how it sought to learn from the unhappy experience of the League of Nations.

The first characteristic of the Organization is undoubtedly its universalism, demonstrated from the outset by the presence of the United States and the Soviet Union—a universalism which, since the cold-war period when admissions were suspended, has become the rule. The number of Member States has increased considerably, largely as a result of the accession to independence of colonized countries: the number of members has risen from 51 at the time of the signing of the Charter to 154 on 1 December 1980. All States wish to be members of the United Nations; none has withdrawn its membership. The United Nations has become a world forum, a unique machinery for the conduct of international relations, particularly for the small countries which might be isolated were it not for the United Nations.

Its second characteristic is that it covers a wide variety of activities: something of this was already to be discerned in the League of Nations, but it has been fully realized by the United Nations. The United Nations deals with all human activities: political, economic, cultural, social and technical. Emphasis has been laid on the need for action in the economic and social spheres in order to guard against tensions which jeopardize peace. The Organization's field of action is therefore considerable and has constantly increased, a leading place being given to assistance for development.

The third characteristic of the Organization is the breadth of its institutional machinery and the flexibility of its procedures. The United Nations system as a whole is an impressive structure. The United Nations proper constitutes its centre, with the General Assembly, the specialized Councils (Security Council, Economic and Social Council, Trusteeship Council), the International Court of Justice and the Secretariat, directed by a Secretary-General who, today, has not only administrative but also political functions. Centred on the United Nations and linked up to the Economic and Social Council are fifteen or so Specialized Agencies, some of which are former administrative unions and others former technical organs of the League of Nations, in a considerably developed form. This vast structure is not rigid, however: the relative importance of the principal organs has not always been the same, and by setting up specialized commisions and subsidiary organs it is possible to deal with new problems and to adapt to needs.

The fourth characteristic of the Organization is its capacity for change. The Covenant of the League was incorporated in the peace treaties, and the League itself appeared to be a means of maintaining the status quo; but the United Nations has not, on the whole, had to concern itself with winding up the Second World War. Its Charter was separate from the peace treaties. Nor has it sought to preserve the status quo—far from it. It has shown itself capable of adapting to changing circumstances and to world trends, and its role did not remain the same during the cold war, the period of peaceful coexistence and that of the ascent of the Third World. Its activities have taken different directions in accordance with the successive majorities which have emerged within it.

The fifth characteristic of the United Nations is its relative failure in the matter of collective security. Yet the great powers took the utmost care to make the United Nations an effective instrument in this field. The principle of the sovereign equality of States and majority rule, which prevailed in the other organs, became singularly inoperative in the Security Council, where the five leading powers possessed a 'right of veto'. The agreement of the great powers was regarded as a prerequisite for taking a decision. It was their task to operate a system of military intervention in the event of aggression. The decisions of the Security Council were to be acted on by all members. In this way, world peace would be maintained through the joint action of the great powers. This was a far cry from the shortcomings of the League. It was, more or less, a return to the realism of the Concert of Europe. But the system did not work, on account of the differences which arose among the great powers. In fact, world peace was preserved by the dangerous balance of terror between the two major nuclear powers, though this did not prevent local wars from multiplying.

Nothing was achieved as regards disarmament. And yet, in spite of these unfavourable conditions, the United Nations has done useful work—endeavouring to keep conflicts from spreading, operating the many mechanisms for negotiation, good offices and mediation, and sending observers and emergency forces to intervene between belligerents and to see that a truce or armistice is observed. However, it cannot really deal with the basic causes of conflicts.

This limited nature of the role of the United Nations in the field of collective security is one of the reasons for the development of the regional organizations. These were set up after the Second World War, mainly for security reasons. Alliances multiplied and were often institutionalized in the form of permanent organizations. Economic organizations arose which employed various methods of co-operation or integration. Thus, major regional groupings gradually appeared in a more or less structured form, bringing together countries in the American hemisphere, the North Atlantic, Western Europe, Eastern Europe and the Soviet Union, the Arab League and, later, Africa. This was a relatively new phenomenon except on the American continent, where the efforts of regional co-operation date from the first third of the nineteenth century. After the Concert of Europe, the normal frame of reference of an international organization had been considered, since the end of the nineteenth century, to be worldwide; regionalism now appeared to be a more effective system, because of the geographical proximity, the community of civilization and ideology and the identity of economic and social structures of neighbouring countries.

In fact, the two systems are complementary to each other. Certain problems can as yet be dealt with only within a particular region, while others can be tackled solely at world level. In comparison with the past, this international organization on two levels probably constitutes the most original feature of our time.

Bibliography

GERBET, Pierre, *Les Organisations Internationales,* 'Que Sais-je ?' Collection No. 792, Paris, 1958.

HANKEY, Lord. *Diplomacy by Conference.* London, 1946.

HOFFMAN, Stanley. *Organisations Internationales et Pouvoirs Politiques des Etats.* Paris, 1954.

JENKS, C. Wilfred. *The World Beyond the Charter in Historical Perspective.* London, 1969.

LUARD, Evan (ed.). *The Evolution of International Organizations.* London, 1966.

MANGONE, Gerard. *A Short History of International Organizations.* New York, 1954.

POTTER, Pitman B. Développement de l'Organisation Internationale (1815–1914). *Recueil des Cours de l'Académie de Droit Internationale de La Haye, 1938-II.*

RUSSELL, Ruth, B. *A History of the United Nations Charter.* Washington, 1958.

SALTER, Arthur. *Allied Shipping Control. An Experiment in International Administration.* Oxford, 1921.

SIOTIS, Jean. *Essai sur le Secrétariat International.* Geneva, 1963.

WALTERS, F. P. *A History of the League of Nations.* Oxford, 1960.

Yearbook of International Organizations, 16th ed., Brussels, 1977.

2 Definition and classification of international organizations: a legal approach

Michel Virally

The observation of international organizations brings to light a number of legal problems connected with their existence and operation: laws applicable to them, legal status and capacity, scope and powers of their organs, legal validity of their transactions, regularity of their decisions, responsibility, etc. One may even speak in this regard of a special branch of public international law, namely the law of international organizations. Undoubtedly, then, law has its place among the disciplines concerned with international organizations and which help to promote a better understanding of them.

However, while they may have consequences on the legal plane, the definition and classification of international organizations are not specifically juridical operations, except in the very specific case of determining those categories that certain legal norms are intended to govern. Thus, for instance, various international conventions, such as the Vienna Convention on the Law of Treaties of 23 May 1969 and the Vienna Convention of 14 March 1975 on the Representation of States in their Relations with International Organizations of a Universal Character, provide a definition (and, potentially, a classification) of international organizations. Such definitions and classifications constitute no more than terminological clarifications, intended to establish the scope of application of the conventions in question. Formulated solely to serve certain practical purposes, they are devoid of any scientific value and are as a rule very concise (the two above-mentioned conventions merely say that the term 'international organization' designates intergovernmental organization).

MICHEL VIRALLI is Professor at the Université de Droit, d'Économie et de Sciences Sociales in Paris. He specializes in legal problems of multilateral technical co-operation and in public international law. He has published *L'ONU d'Hier à Demain* (1961) and *L'Organisation Mondiale* (1972) as well as several articles.

To be sure, the science of law, like the other disciplines that concern themselves with international organizations, needs to possess definitions and classifications enabling it to apprehend its subject more precisely and to clarify the significance and bearing of the concepts that it employs. This is why jurists specializing in the study of international organizations have found it necessary to propose their own. In doing so, some took account solely of the legal aspects of the phenomenon considered, or emphasized these aspects unduly. This may be considered to be the result of a regrettable over-specialization. When the same phenomenon pertains to several disciplines, as in the present case, it does not change with the discipline that describes it, and the definition given of it, as also the accompanying classifications, must consequently aim to possess general value if they are to provide a sound basis for a truly interdisciplinary study. Failing this, all one can obtain is a patchwork of items of knowledge pertaining to a variety of disciplines, making synthesis impossible and destroying the unity of the phenomenon that these disciplines seek to describe.

It is in the light of these considerations that the present chapter has been written. It will naturally be for specialists of other disciplines to say whether the concepts formulated by the jurist do in fact possess the general value that he means to confer upon them, and answer their own general requirements, or whether they are too narrowly juridical.

Definition of the international organization

There is no universally accepted definition of the international organization.[1] However, transcending mere differences in formulation, it would seem that a fairly general consensus has been reached concerning what elements should be embodied in such a definition. Even though certain authors omit one element or another from their formulation, they usually take it up again in subsequent analyses. On the other hand, differences and doubts do exist regarding the relative value to be attached to these various elements and their legal designation.

Taking account of these factors, an organization can be defined as an association of States, established by agreement among its members and possessing a permanent system or set of organs, whose task it is to pursue objectives of common interest by means of co-operation among its members.

This definition highlights five specific characteristics of international organizations: their inter-State basis, their voluntaristic basis, their possession of a permanent system of organs, their autonomy and their co-operative function. The last factor alone is the subject of controversy.

INTER-STATE BASIS

There are, of course, international organizations that bring together social groups other than States—even, in some cases, individuals. By virtue of their different social basis, these constitute social phenomena and entail problems that can be compared only in part and with difficulty with those observed in the case of international organizations composed of States. These differences justify the conduct of separate studies, even though useful parallels can be drawn from certain standpoints (for example, that of management methods and administrative structure).

The jurist is careful to distinguish between those international organizations often—and from the point of view of legal language quite wrongly—called intergovernmental (a better term would be 'inter-State') and all the others, designated in the United Nations Charter (Article 71) as 'non-governmental' organizations (NGOs).

However, there is nothing to stop non-governmental social forces from taking part directly in the operation of international organizations understood in this sense (employers' and workers' unions in the International Labour Organisation (ILO), for example).

VOLUNTARISTIC BASIS

All the international organizations currently existing are built on a voluntaristic basis. Only those States belong to them that have expressed the desire to become members (and, in practice, only those remain that have not expressed the desire to withdraw).

From a legal point of view, this characteristic is evidenced by the fact that every international organization is established on the basis of a treaty. In some exceptional cases, resolutions adopted by an international conference have sufficed for the setting up of an organization (this was the case with the Organization of Petroleum Exporting Countries (OPEC)). In law, this may be deemed an agreement in simplified form, possessing the force of a treaty. It is not, therefore, a true exception.

Certain systems of organs, on the other hand, have been established by a resolution of an existing organ—as, for example, UNCTAD in 1964 and UNIDO in 1965, which were both set up in pursuance of resolutions adopted by the General Assembly of the United Nations.

Although the structure of such systems of organs is in many respects comparable with those of an international organization, they are, both *de facto* and *de jure*, subsidiary organs only, as it were organic outgrowths of the organization that created them. This inferior status gives rise to many consequences, particularly with respect to their autonomy on the operational and financial levels.

These differences emerge clearly in the struggles carried on among certain groups of States to obtain the setting up of an independent organization to replace a subsidiary organ (even when it possesses a complex structure). The transformation of UNIDO into a Specialized Agency provides an interesting illustration of the antithesis between the two categories of organization.

PERMANENT SYSTEM OF ORGANS

This characteristic is too self-evident to require comment. Clearly, there is no international organization that does not possess such a system. So long as this has not been established as a permanent entity, it does not, however great its complexity, constitute an international organization but only an international conference (albeit one that possesses a number of features in common with international organizations, particularly with respect to decision-taking processes or procedures).

AUTONOMY

This results from the existence of a system of organs that is distinct from that of its member States, and depends upon the particular nature of the decision-taking process. Autonomy exists in so far as this process is such as to enable the organization to take decisions which are not identical with the sum of the individual decisions of its members. From the legal point of view, it is then possible to speak of the organization's 'individual will'.

This may be achieved either through member States taking part in the decision-taking (application of the majority system, existence of small bodies in whose work not all the members take part at the same time), or through the setting up of decision-taking bodies at least relatively independent of governments.

Understood in this way, autonomy enables the international organization to operate as an agent distinct from its member States. For legal purposes, this can be reflected in the acquisition by the organization of a legal status of its own.

FUNCTION OF INTER-STATE CO-OPERATION

The international organization's *raison d'être* is undoubtedly the function assigned to it by its charter or constitution (that is, by the founder States), whereby it becomes essentially an instrument for the performance of that function. It is its function that determines, from the legal standpoint, its sphere of competence (and can determine the extent of its powers, in accordance with the theory of implied or implicit powers).

For some authors, in particular those who approach the question from the standpoint of systems analysis, the function of the international organization is always one of integration.[2]

For the jurist, such a conception lacks precision; it is too vague and ambiguous to be acceptable. In his view, a distinction should be made between two functions that are radically different in their purpose and their methods, in the present state of international society: co-operation and integration.

Organizations whose function is co-operation have only to deal with the machinery of States (governments), even though they may maintain certain working relations with NGOs and may sometimes even address themselves directly to citizens or to other non-state social groups. They take the form essentially of 'superstructures', in the most precise sense of the term. Their role is to encourage and promote the harmonization and co-ordination of their member States' policies and lines of conduct, possibly (and today exceptionally) to the extent of setting up joint undertakings. While they may themselves undertake various operations using their own resources, they do so in every case in co-operation with the governments concerned.

Organizations whose function is co-operation consequently leave intact the basic structure of the present-day international community, composed of sovereign States. Far from calling in question the existence and role of these States, they enable them better to perform their social functions in those spheres in which the magnitude of the problems involved transcends their individual powers of action. They constitute an instrument in the hands of their member States rather than being able to operate as autonomous agents.

On the contrary, organizations whose function is integration are responsible for bringing their member States closer together by taking over certain of their functions, to the extent of merging them together in a composite whole, in the sector in which they exercise their activity, that is, in their field of competence. In its ultimate form, this fusion will result in the substitution of the organization, as a legal entity, for its members in dealings with third parties (for example, in the case of trade negotiations). Concomitantly, certain essential functions of States (legislation, statutory regulations) will be exercised by the organs of the organization for and on behalf of the organs of States.

By reason of their specific characteristics, organizations whose function is integration possess certain features in common with States, since they may be said to have a population and a territory, even if only from a strictly functional point of view. This could in no way be said of organizations whose function is co-operation.

The distinction outlined above is widely accepted in legal doctrine. What inferences are to be drawn from it is a more controversial matter.

For some authors,[3] both organizations promoting integration and those promoting co-operation constitute, despite their disparities, no more than subsets of a single category, namely that of international organizations. What is involved is thus, in their view, an initial classification of the latter.

For others, including the present author,[4] the disparities outlined above are too basic for the two sets not to be considered as radically separate entities. The organizations whose function is integration may be called supranational organizations, in contradistinction to international organizations properly so-called. The questions is therefore one of definition.

This is more than a terminological quibble. More exactly, the terms are used for their instrumental force. The point is, in short, to determine whether the two types of organization give rise to the same problems, which would justify their being studied together (albeit having regard to the necessary distinctions), or whether they give rise to problems that are substantially different, and should therefore be studied separately.

The difficulty stems from the fact that we are dealing here on the whole with 'ideal' types, in the Weberian sense of the term. In reality, existing supranational organizations (including the European Communities are not pure types. Sometimes, despite their constitutions, they operate as mere co-ordinating bodies, by conferring on the intergovernmental organs more prominence than is provided for in their decision-taking process and by making the rule of unanimity prevail over the rule of majority within those organs.

Despite these tendencies, the legal problems entailed by the operation and activities of the supranational organizations differ too greatly from those arising in connection with the international organizations for it to be possible to study them together, except in respect of specific features. From the standpoint of the legal sciences, in any case, we therefore consider that the two types of organization should be studied separately (which, in practice, is what all jurists do, irrespective of their theoretical positions). It is for this reason that we have retained the concept of co-operation in our definition of the international organization.

It would doubtless be advisable to consider whether this point of view is likely to be confirmed by that adopted by other disciplines. However, it would also be advisable to exercise critical judgement in the actual effecting of the classifications. It should not be taken for granted that all organizations that call themselves supranational or proclaim their objective to be that of integration necessarily deserve to be placed in this category.

In some cases, the means employed and the aims actually pursued amount to no more than co-operation. It is difficult to determine in practice where begins and the other ends. These uncertainties should not, however, lead to the jettisoning of a distinction which, in theoretical terms, is a sound one.

In search of a principle of classification

The classifications proposed by legal doctrine are highly varied and generally seem to have no other purpose than to facilitate the enumeration of existing organizations. In view of this pragmatic attitude, it may be worth inquiring into the functions of a classification and considering whether the classifications customarily used in legal doctrine perform those functions effectively. If not, upon what principles might a more satisfactory classification (or typology) be founded?

THE FUNCTIONS OF A CLASSIFICATION

These may be of a purely practical nature, as has already been illustrated by the example of international conventions. They may also be of a scientific kind: a good classification is intended first and foremost to bring order into the subject to be studied. For this reason, it contributes in its own right to a more thorough and systematic knowledge of that subject and maps out the direction to be taken by future research. Its importance should not be underestimated. The rise of many sciences began with a rational classification of the phenomena being studied and has continued to depend on such a classification. However, classifications perform this function only if they are themselves based on a thorough knowledge of phenomena, sufficient to enable their most essential constant characteristics to be apprehended.

It is, of course, always preferable to arrive at a single classification, providing a universally valid key. Owing to the complexity of the actual situation, it is not always possible to achieve this, particularly in the case of social phenomena. If a plurality of classifications, corresponding to a plurality of points of view, has to be accepted, every effort should at least be made to ensure that these are mutually consistent, lest the subject be so fragmented as to make any overall view of it impossible and to deprive the proposed classifications of much of their value. Such consistency will only be achieved if all the classifications are founded ultimately on a single principle.

Social phenomena are not only complex. Often they are also hybrid— all the more so in that they are involved in a constant process of evolution that modifies them gradually rather than causing sudden mutations. Accordingly, it is often vain to seek to classify them strictly in a certain number of clear-cut and mutually exclusive categories. A specific phenomenon will very often pertain to several categories at one and the same time, either because it is in the process of evolving from one category to another or because it is, by its very nature, hybrid.

This being so, the work of classification should be directed to the establishment of types that constitute a systematization rather than a mere description of the phenomena observed, and will therefore be of a more markedly theoretical nature. The classification of phenomena in terms of these types (or ideal types) will not of course be as exact as in the case of classifications established by the physical and natural sciences. It will, however, bring out the main features of each phenomenon to be classified, corresponding to those of the type to which it is considered to pertain, even if it possesses certain secondary features which ally it to a different type.

THE USUAL CLASSIFICATIONS AND THEIR SHORTCOMINGS

The classifications most frequently used in legal doctrine are based on the composition of international organizations, the purpose of their activities and, occasionally, their powers. As is evident, these different classifications have no connection with one another. In addition, they are often formulated in a very approximative way.

First, in classifications made on the basis of their composition, a distinction is usually made between organizations which are of universal character or have a universal vocation, and regional organizations.

The first are difficult to define. No international organization is totally universal. Because they are built on a voluntaristic basis, it is always possible for some States to refrain from membership in them. Would it be better to say, 'which have a universal vocation', to emphasize the fact that their universality is only virtual? But does an organization such as the World Bank fit in with this definition, founded as it is on economic principles which make it impossible for those States that reject them ever to become members?

Regional organizations are easier to define in terms of composition. But is there not a third category, which finds no place in this dualistic classification, that of organizations which do not have a universal vocation and are not established on a regional basis: such, for instance, as OECD, OPEC and the various councils and boards responsible for primary commodities?

Second, in classifications made on the basis of the purpose of their activity, a distinction is frequently made between political organizations and technical organizations. Other authors prefer to speak of general organizations and specialized organizations, a distinction which corresponds to the same classification, but with the emphasis placed elsewhere. Considered solely from the point of view of their sphere of competence, there is no decisive reason why one of these classifications should be preferred to the other. Again, other authors go further and distinguish between political, economic, financial, social, cultural, administrative, military, etc., organizations. There is no limit to this purely descriptive list, the interest of which is exceedingly limited. It is in fact rather an enumeration than a real classification.

Finally, in classifications made on the basis of their powers, a distinction can be made *inter alia* between consultative, standard-setting and executive organizations, depending on whether they are or are not empowered to take decisions that are binding on their members, and whether they can or cannot themselves carry out their decisions. From a legal point of view, this is a more promising distinction. However, here again it may be wondered whether it amounts to a genuine classification, and upon what bases it is founded. Considered from the standpoint of the binding force of the decisions taken, for example, the United Nations General Assembly would appear to be a consultative body, because its resolutions have the force merely of recommendations, whereas the Security Council would be deemed to be a standard-setting body, because it can take binding decisions. Clearly, such an antithesis in no way represents the reality of the two bodies' respective functions and is indeed completely misleading.

More generally, the slight legal powers of international organizations limit the interest of such a classification.

STRUCTURAL TYPOLOGIES AND FUNCTIONAL TYPOLOGIES

A classification that is to be more systematic—or scientific—than those just reviewed must be established on the basis of a characteristic of international organizations that is as typical as possible but, at the same time, varies significantly from one organization to another.

At first glance, there would seem to be two principles of classification equally worthy of consideration. International organizations consist of systems of organs; they may therefore be classified according to the types of structure to which these systems conform. They are established for the purpose of pursuing objectives of common interest to their members; the nature and particular characteristics of their functions therefore provide a further principle of classification.

On reflection, it is the latter principle that would seem to prevail.

As has already been pointed out, it is an organization's function that constitutes its true *raison d'être*. And it is in order that it may perform this function that its member States have established it and take part in its operation, bearing the costs and accepting the constraints that inevitably derive therefrom. Moreover, the organization's structure is directly determined by this function or purpose. The structure is designed to enable the organization to fulfil the purpose assigned to it as efficiently as possible having regard to the conditions and limitations that the founding States have deemed it necessary to impose, so that it may be achieved in accordance with their interests, as defined by them. In other words, the organization's structure is itself subordinate to the requirements of its function. Experience also shows that, in many cases, modifications occur in the structure as and when these requirements change, and in accordance with them.

It should be noted, lastly, that there are at present no structural—or constitutional—models sufficiently diversified or stabilized to enable a significant typology to be established. Existing international organizations almost all conform to a single model operating at three levels: at the highest level, the plenary intergovernmental organ, at the lowest level the administrative secretariat, and at the intermediary level the plenary intergovernmental organ (in organizations composed of only a small number of States) or limited intergovernmental organ (in the case of world-wide organizations). This general pattern is complicated by a number of adjuncts that are highly varied (and often of variable duration) according to the nature of the functions assigned to the organization in question, the circumstances with which it has to cope, the direction given to its activities, without its being possible to reduce this multiplicity of institutional developments to a few well-defined and significant types. This state of affairs is probably to be explained by the relatively recent character of the phenomenon of international organizations, which have generally come into being to meet particular circumstances and needs without pre-established plan, and by the extraordinary diversity of the functions assigned to them.

The different types of international organization

As a principle of classification, the function of international organizations can, it would seem, be considered principally from three points of view. The first question concerns the extent of the co-operation that it is the organization's mission to bring about: is it open to the international community as a whole, or reserved for certain of its members only?

Second, what is the range covered by this co-operation? Can it extend to all the sectors in which a need for it may be felt, or is it confined to a clearly delimited field of action? Lastly, what are the means used to effect such co-operation, and what type of relations does it institute between the organization and its members (and between the members themselves in their relations with one another)? On these three levels, highly significant differences and even antitheses, having important repercussions, may be identified between the various existing international organizations. It is therefore possible on these bases to establish a typology that, in many respects, is allied to the traditional classifications, while endowing it with the precision which these lacked.

WORLD-WIDE ORGANIZATIONS AND ORGANIZATIONS OF LIMITED MEMBERSHIP

An alternative distinction might be between universal or world-wide organizations and organizations whose membership is restricted. This is, however, a question of terminology, and of no great significance.

World-wide organizations aim to bring about the unification of the international community by grouping within themselves all the States that make up that community or at least that play a prominent part in it, and by seeking to solve the problems that arise at a planetary level or that are liable to affect the international community as a whole.

By contrast, organizations of limited membership seek to promote co-operation among a particular group of States only, restrictively defined on the basis of specific interests which they all share and which distinguish them from the rest of the international community.

In a sense, it may be said that the organizations of a universal character are founded on the principle of inclusion (even if the admission of new member States is subject to the agreement of existing members and if some States or groups of States may be temporarily kept out). On the other hand, the organizations of limited membership are founded on the principle of exclusion, since all States which do not belong to the group on the basis of which such organizations are established are constitutionally excluded from membership.

Because vicinity and geographical proximity often engender a community of interests, many organizations of limited membership have a geo-political basis; they include regional, subregional and inter-regional (e.g. continental) organizations, frequently merged under the generic (and approximative) label of 'regional organizations'. Despite their particular basis, they do not differ substantially from other organizations of limited membership, and therefore constitute no more than a subset within this set, which is considerably broader. The defence of economic interests, for instance, often leads to the constitution of organized groups bringing together States that are geographically remote from one another, for which the term 'regional organization' would be highly inappropriate (OECD, OPEC, COMECON, etc.). Even when some of their members (or even the majority) are situated in the same region, it is not this relationship, but certain well-defined interests, shared with States that do not belong to the region, that constitute the *ratio foederis*.

Organizations of limited membership may be more or less open or closed to the outside world. Their chief purpose may be to protect their members against influences alien to their particular group and to oppose any external intervention. It may be to strengthen the influence of the group and its members in world affairs and to prepare them for more active participation in a process of co-operation extended to include other groups and even to cover the whole world. These two objectives are not, moreover, mutually exclusive. In any case, the organization of limited membership reflects, and cultivates, a particularism, and thus performs a function diametrically opposite to that of the world-wide organization, even if the latter decentralizes its activities and even if a fruitful collaboration becomes established between the two by reason of their complementarity. They represent two contrasting (albeit in practice not necessarily conflicting) models for the structuring of the international community and, consequently, two fundamentally different types of organization.

The distinction between these two types of international organization is probably the one that has the most far-reaching effect. It concerns not only the number of members and the rules relating to their admission; it also entails a whole series of consequences in regard to the establishment of the system of organs, its relations with member States, the purpose of its work, and the whole of its activities.

GENERAL ORGANIZATIONS AND SECTORAL ORGANIZATIONS

Some organizations are established to allow organized co-operation between their members in all fields in which such co-operation may appear useful, without any limitation, or excluding only certain clearly defined sectors (for example, matters of national defence, in the case of the Council of Europe). By reason of this undifferentiated function, they may be called general organizations, whether they be set up on a world-wide basis, like the United Nations or, before it, the League of Nations, or on a regional basis, like the Council of Europe, the Organization of American States, the Organization of African Unity, or the Arab League.

Other organizations have assigned to them a function limited to a single sector of activity, or at least to a set of strictly defined sectors, and may accordingly be called sectoral. These fields of action may be more or less narrow, ranging from the formulation of international measures, co-operation in meteorological questions or in the operation of postal services, to the promotion of international trade or the organization of military defence.

The distinction between general and specialized functions is traditional in domestic law, and the consequences deriving from the principle of specialization have often been studied by jurists; such analyses can to a certain extent be transposed into international law. However, this is probably only a somewhat minor advantage of the distinction, which has far wider implications and of which certain aspects have been brought to light by functionalist theory. It may be noted, in particular, that when the field of co-operation has not been delimited at the outset, the deter-mination of its real extent is apt to give rise to tensions within the or-ganization if the existing balances between its members change, or if circumstances reveal new needs in co-operation that are not felt equally by all. Moreover, the expansion or contraction of the field of co-operation will almost inevitably have direct and important repercussions on the structure of the system of organs and on its operation, and these changes will not necessarily be accepted without resistance by all the members.

Lastly, the coalitions and conflicts of interest that occur in certain areas of activity are liable to have repercussions, with highly varied conse-quences, in other areas or, on the contrary, to clash in these same areas with very different coalitions and conflicts.

In other words, organizations whose fields of competence are of a general nature will not only be led to penetrate into politically sensitive areas; their activities as a whole will take on a more or less pronounced political hue on account of the behaviour of their members. As a result, their manner of operation and the nature of the problems with which they will have to contend will, in the ordinary course of things, differ greatly from those observed in sectoral organizations, whose dominant concerns are of a technical nature.

The classification of certain organizations in one or other of these two types may sometimes give rise to hesitation. This applies, for example, to organizations whose functions extend to an area of decisive political importance, the more so if their sphere of competence is defined in a particularly broad way, as is the case with defence organizations such as NATO or the Warsaw Pact Organization.[5]

Lastly, the different sectors of specialized activity open to inter-national organizations present highly variable opportunities and degrees of political sensitivity, which may result in considerable differences in their operation. A sub-classification would therefore probably be justified. It remains to be established, however, since there are at present no adequate comparative studies on the basis of which it might reliably be formulated.

STANDARD-SETTING ORGANIZATIONS AND OPERATIONAL ORGANIZATIONS

In regard to methods of co-ordination, it is possible to distinguish between two types of organization, according to whether they confine themselves to bringing into harmony and orienting the attitudes and actions of their members, or themselves engage in operational activities. The former may be called standard-setting organizations and the latter operational organizations. The significance and merits of the distinction are at once apparent, stemming as they do from the nature of the relations between the organization and its members, on the one hand, and from the nature of the means employed by the organization, on the other (the one being to a large extent contingent upon the other). The means themselves are not without direct effects on the structure, operation and working methods of the system of organs and, naturally, on the competence and mutual relations of the organs that compose it.

The *standard-setting organizations* are principally concerned with orienting their members' attitudes to avoid their becoming conflictual (or, if they have already done so, to end this situation), and with assisting the attainment of common objectives through the co-ordination of efforts.

Several methods can be used for this purpose. Some of them entail no decision-taking on the part of the organization, except in regard to matters of procedure. Its action may in fact be limited to taking the necessary measures for consultations (which may or may not lead to collective conclusions, but do at least make possible an exchange of information), negotiations (aimed at the conclusion of agreements, which may take the legal form of a treaty or less-binding forms), or public debate. Organizations are characterized by marked differences in style, according to the relative importance they accord to these various processes. Such differences might well provide the basis for a more sophisticated typology—which, however, the scope of this chapter does not allow us to develop.

The orientation of member States' attitudes can also be effected through decisions taken by the organization itself; such decisions may either contain directives to be observed by the States, or they may institute various measures designed to bring pressure to bear on the latter to comply with previous commitments or with the organization's own directives. These measures may, for instance, take the form of a supervision of implementation.

These decisions (which are the outcome of public debate or of private consultations) may themselves be more or less compulsory, according to whether they constitute merely an invitation (or recommendation) or are legally binding on those to whom they are addressed. This is a distinction whose crucial nature from the legal point of view needs no stressing, but which also points up two contrasting models of relations between the organization and its members. In practice, however, the situations in which international organizations are empowered to take binding decisions are rare and usually restricted to technical spheres (with the notable exception of the Security Council, which has made very moderate use of this power).

The co-operation that results from such decisions may be limited to a harmonization of the policies and attitudes of member States through the definition of general rules with which each is expected to comply. It may amount to a positive co-operation, designed to ensure the focusing of individual lines of action on the achievement of specific objectives (international strategy for development). It may even lead to joint operations, for the conduct of which member States provide resources the utilization of which is co-ordinated by decisions of the Organization (joint measures decided by the Security Council, co-ordination of relief work in the event of disasters, etc.).[6]

The *operational organizations* go one step further, in that they themselves take action, using their own resources or resources made available to them by their members, but of which they determine the utilization (and therefore have the operational management). It is true that, in most cases, the resources used by international organizations derive from their member States, but the situation differs considerably, according to whether these resources have been definitively transferred to the organization (as in the case of financial contributions) or are simply supplied to it on an ad hoc basic (as in the case of military contingents or logistical support).

The activities engaged in by some international organizations are almost entirely operational; this applies, in particular, to the financial institutions and especially to the international banks (which may, moreover, possess resources of their own, as does the International Bank for Reconstruction and Development (IBRD). The activities of others combine both standard-setting and operational elements. This is the case with the United Nations (whose activity remains primarily of a normative kind) and with most of the Specialized Agencies (with the exception of the financial institutions). These organizations thus pertain simultaneously to both types, but the relative importance assumed by the operational activities has in fact been reflected in a fairly profound modification of their functions and, frequently, in noteworthy changes in structure and style that have had considerable repercussions upon their actual working.

Notes

1. Many authors, moreover, confine themselves to listing those elements the combination of which seems to them to be implied in the notion of international organization, often in connection with a classification, without seeking to formulate a real definition. See, for instance, S. Bastid, *Droit International Public—Le Droit des Organisations Internationales*, p. 1-3, Paris, Les Cours de Droit, 1969-70 ; Bowett, *The Law of International Institutions*, 2nd ed., p. 9-11, London, Stevens, 1970 ; El Erian, 'The Legal Organization of International Society', in: M. So-RENSON (ed.), *Manual of Public International Law*, New York, St Martin's Press, 1968 ; P. Pescatore, *Cours d'Institutions Internationales*, p. 140-3, Luxembourg, Centre Universitaire de l'Etat, 1970 ; Reuter, 'Principes de Droit International Public', *Collected Courses of the Hague Academy of International Law*, Vol. 103, p. 516 (1961/II) ; H. G. Schemers, *International Institutional Law*, Vol. 1, p. 4-25, Leiden, Sijtoff, 1972 ; G. I. Tunkin, 'The Legal Nature of the United Nations', *Collected Courses of the Hague Academy of International Law*, Vol. III, p. 3–68 (1966/III).

   See also the definition proposed by El Erian, in his first report on relations between States and international organizations, in *Yearbook of the International Law Commission, 1963*, Vol. 2, p. 173–7, and his third report, *Yearbook of the International Law Commission, 1968*, Vol. 2, p. 203, and the discussions to which it gave rise within the commission, *Yearbook of the International Law Commission, 1968*, Vol. I, p. 182–253.

2. See, for example, the explanations given by E. B. Haas, 'International Integration: the European and the Universal Process', *International Organization*, Vol. 15, No. 4, Autumn 1961.

3. M. S. Korowicz, *Organisations Internationales et Souveraineté des Etats Membres*, p. 283-6, Paris, Pedone, and the authors quoted by Peter Hay in *Federalism and Supranational Organization*, p. 76, University of Illinois Press, 1966.

4. M. Virally, 'De la Classification des Organisations Internationales,' *Miscellanea W. J. Ganshof Van Der Meersch*, Vol. I, p. 365-82, Brussels, Et. Bruylant, 1972.

5. Not all authors agree that NATO, and particularly the Warsaw Pact Organization, are international organizations. In view of their organic developments, however, these two institutions correspond in our view exactly to the definition given above. But, in point of fact, only NATO has sought to transcend the purely military sphere and to concern itself with the settlement of international disputes and even with economic and scientific co-operation, albeit without great success.

6. In this connection, a clear distinction should be drawn between joint measures carried out solely by Member States, using their

own resources—as, for example, breaking off of diplomatic relations (Spanish case) or refusal of recognition and boycott (Rhodesia)—and measures carried out by organs of the organization (emergency forces, military-control missions) the elements of which, although furnished by the Member States (military contingents, officers serving as observers), are placed for operational purposes under the sole authority of the organization.

3 Non-territorial actors: the invisible continent

Towards a typology of international organizations

Johan Galtung

Since the time of the Great Discoveries, increasingly accurate maps have been made available to create an image of the world in terms of territory. From this elementary-school indoctrination generations have been trained to see the world in terms of territorial actors, in conflict and co-operation. What is left out of that image is the forgotten continent, an invisible continent of non-territorial actors, the international organizations. Of course, everybody talks about them today, but still mainly as an adjunct to the territorial system, with insufficient emphasis, perhaps, on the system of non-territorial actors as also being a system in its own right, *sui generis*, with its own logic, contradictions and structure.

Actors in the territorial system are organized on the basis of contiguity of territorial 'units'; actors in the non-territorial system on the basis of similarity or interaction. This works like Chinese boxes: inside a territorial actor, e.g. a country, there are associations and organizations (parties, trade unions, farms, factories, firms) and inside a non-territorial actor there may be States—for States may also form associations or organizations. The basic point is always clear, however: membership of a territorial actor is based on location in geographical space; membership of a non-territorial actor on location in some socio-functional space, defined

JOHAN GALTUNG is a Professor at the Institut Universitaire d'Études du Développement (Geneva) and project co-ordinator for the United Nations University. He is a former Professor of Conflict and Peace Research of the University of Oslo and Director General of the Inter-University Centre of Post-Graduate Studies (Dubrovnik, Yugoslavia), and has had numerous assignments for organizations within the United Nations system. He was written many books and articles on a wide variety of social science subjects and contemporary problems, particularly on peace and development. A five-volume collection of his *Essays in Peace Research* has been prepared, three of which have already been published (1975, 1976, 1978).

by similarity and interaction. In the first case vicinity is the guiding principle, in the second case affinity.

In order to come to grips, analytically, with the non-territorial system, the first and basic task is to develop some typologies of international organizations.

Instead of using the traditional classification into intergovernmental, non-governmental, etc., non-territorial actors can be classified, on a scale of increasing non-territoriality, according to the nature of units belonging to the 'international organization': (a) members are national governments and the organization is intergovernmental (IGO); (b) members are national organizations or associations other than governments, and the organization is inter-non-governmental (INGO); (c) members are individuals, and the organization is a transnational (non-governmental) association (TRANGO).

We prefer not to use the term 'international' for any one of these, since the term 'international', in our view, does not necessarily imply any organization or actor at all. The international system is simply the system of nations (actually, the system of States, or countries), in co-operation and conflict—nothing more, nothing less. For that reason we interpret IGO to mean 'intergovernmental' (and not 'inter-national', governmental), INGO to mean inter-non-governmental (and not international non-governmental), and we add to this well-known distinction the trans-national (or, really, trans-non-governmental) organization, the TRANGO, which relates directly to individuals wherever they are found. In the TRANGO there are no 'national chapters' or similar arrangements filtering the direct relation between individuals.

There is also the vitally important special case of the INGO: the business inter-non-governmental organization (BINGO). It links together non-governmental business organizations in various countries and is better known today as the 'multinational corporation'. However, this may be an unfortunate term for at least three reasons. First, 'multi' connotes involvement of more than two nations, but often there are only two, and in that case the term 'cross-national' may be more accurate. Further, the term 'multinational' conceals how asymmetric these corporations are, since they are usually dominated by one country. And, finally, 'corporation' may not be broad enough, for there are other ways of organizing international business than in corporations. (Incidentally, one of these ways would be governmental, as an IGO, which, in that case—when it is for business—would be termed a BIGO.)

The significance of this typology is seen in two important phenomena located at the interface between the territorial and the non-territorial systems. These two systems are by no means unrelated, particularly since the territorial one preceded the other by thousands of years and consequently must have set its stamp on the latecomer.

The relation between the two systems can be usefully discussed under the headings of 'isomorphy' and 'homology'. The propositions are simple:

Proposition 1. The non-territorial actors tend to be isomorphic with the territorial system.

Proposition 2. The non-territorial actors tend to induce homology among territorial actors.

Proposition 3. The propositions above are most valid for intergovernmental organizations (usually), less for inter-non-governmental organizations, and (almost) invalid for transnational organizations. They are also highly valid for transnational corporations.

Characteristic of the two lowest types of non-territorial actors, the IGOs and the INGOs, is that the world territorial structure of nation-States is still entirely visible. If governments are members this is obvious, but it also applies to the typical 'international organization' which is an association of associations (e.g. an association of national associations of dentists, longshoremen, stamp-collectors etc.). An association or organization at the national level becomes a 'national chapter' or a 'mother, sister, or daughter company', depending on the position in the hierarchy, at the level of the non-territorial actor.

Furthermore not only the components of the territorial system are reflected in the non-territorial actor; the relations between them can usually also be rediscovered. For this reason the stronger term 'isomorphy' is used. Relations of power (both resource and structural power) and interaction frequency are often mirrored faithfully. The most powerful chapter comes from the most powerful country—in terms of location of headquarters, recruitment of staff, general perspective on world affairs: frequencies of interaction in the territorial system are mirrored in frequencies of interaction in the organization, and so on. In other words: the territorial system is reproduced within certain non-territorial actors which, for that reason, are not truly non-territorial.

This way of thinking carries us quite far analytically. Non-territorial actors with national components—governmental or non-governmental— can be seen as governed primarily by the principle of isomorphy. This is the baseline, as implemented in the United Nations, when the major victors of the Second World War appointed themselves to permanent Security Council seats, with veto power. Isomorphy is called 'realism' in the plain language of power; and it means that to those who have power in the territorial system, power shall also be given in the non-territorial system. It may further be partially true that the more an inter-governmental organization departs from this isomorphy, the less attention will be paid to it, because its decisions will be seen as not reflecting the 'real world'—meaning the territorial system with its bilateral relations—to which decisions will then be referred.

But this is only a partial truth. A non-territorial actor 100 per cent isomorphic with the territorial system is in a sense only a replication of that system, except that it makes multilateral interaction possible. Small deviations from strict isomorphy will take place when countries are represented by persons, making these organizations a medium in which the smaller powers can more easily express themselves, can be listened to, and perhaps can make some impact on the territorial system. It is not merely a forum in which they can be more easily controlled.

Then, again, there is the opposite view: that this is precisely the forum in which the territorial system is kept alive and even reinforced. For instance, Taiwan had for a long time a power excess because of its position in the United Nations Security Council. One could argue, however, that this was not an excess of isomorphy, but a lack of it, the United Nations being out of date, and serving to freeze the past. One might also extend that argument to other cases and imagine the United Nations brought up to date, in an effort to mirror the territorial system. The argument would then be that any distinction between veto and non-veto is too sharp, too absolute relative to the power distinctions in an increasingly subtle and complicated territorial system.

Of course, in time the internal workings of a non-territorial actor will acquire complex facets never contemplated by its social architects, the lawyers. There will be informal structures in addition to the formal ones. Yet power differentials may actually be magnified rather than reduced in an intergovernmental organization.

In the INGO, all of this becomes much less important, except for the BINGO, of course. Non-governmental members may feel less obliged to act in the name of the national interest, and more free to find the pattern of action and interaction that fits the values of the organization. Thus, one would assume in general that INGOs have national elements—by definition—but that the relations between them are different, for instance much more egalitarian. The world has come to accept the idea of a big-power veto in the United Nations, whether this reflects adequately or even exaggerates territorial power—but it would hardly accept it in an international philatelic association. Needless to say, however, all shades and gradations can be imagined here.

When it comes to transnational organizations, isomorphy breaks down completely: there are neither the national components, nor the relations of the territorial system. Transnational ties uniting individuals across territorial borders might even be stronger than common citizenship. The classical example here is, of course, nation membership as opposed to

State citizenship. The nation, defined as a group of human beings having in common some characteristics, referred to as ethnical, is the most important of all transnational organizations. (Here the unfortunate consequences of the double meaning of 'nation' becomes particularly obvious!) Time and again it proves to be more important than territorially defined State citizenship, but the two are often confused because the nation-State is taken as a norm.

Recent examples would be international scientific unions where the dissolution of national organization has gone quite far. Of course, people in the same discipline from the same country may know each other better, and their interaction is usually facilitated by speaking the same language, but the search for significant colleagues, for meaningful persons with whom to work, to converse, to exchange ideas will not be restricted by such considerations. Few and only particularly repressive countries would imagine organizing their citizens so as to act as a bloc in a transnational organization.

Then there are, of course, the transnational political parties and pressure-groups, such as the World New Left and the Viet Nam solidarity movement. The fact that there may also be co-operation at subnational and national levels does not detract from the transnational character of such world movements, for national identities are usually successfully washed out. Good cases in point are the world hippie movement—or any movement for new life-styles in defiance of the various versions of vertical success-oriented, power-oriented societal orders.

For these reasons we see the transnational organizations as the real non-territorial actors of the future. Only they can be really global actors, since only they (like States) are based on individuals as their components, and are global in their scope.

Isomorphy therefore poses two problems: are the territorial components (the countries) present in the 'non-territorial' actor? Are the territorial relations mirrored? Table 1 provides the answer.

TABLE 1. Three types of non-territorial actors

Territorial components	Territorial relations	Non-territoriality
Present	Present	Low (IGOs, most BINGOs)
Present	Absent	Medium (INGOs)
Absent	Absent	High (TRANGOs)

Let us now turn to the problem of homology, in other words, focus on the non-territorial organizations as giant mechanisms for making all States as similar to each other as possible. Just as a State tries to find its appropriate place (often called its 'natural' position) in a non-territorial organization, so a non-territorial organization is a vehicle facilitating the search for an opposite number within any State. Whether members are governments, non-governmental associations, organizations, or simply individuals, any non-territorial actor will look for like-minded or like-positioned elements in all States around the world. For that is their task: to organize all of their kind, wherever they may be found. And if they do not exist, they can be created, for instance by inviting to international conferences observers who then return to their country with the message imprinted on their minds: 'We must also have something like this.' This means moreover that non-territorial actors become giant mechanisms through which the stronger States that started these organizations can imprint a message on weaker States: you must have this profession and that profession, this hobby and sports association and that ideological movement, you must produce this and that—in order to be full-fledged members of the world. Active membership in IGOs, INGOs, etc., is taken as an indicator of how deeply embedded the country is in the world system—without questioning who started all these organizations, on what social basis, for what purpose, in what image. The same reasoning also applies to regions: the weaker regions will tend to imitate the stronger ones and import the IGO/INGO machinery they have.

Thus, international conferences become giant markets where iso-morphy and homology can be monitored; the former in inter-State, the latter in intra-State relations. They become giant reproduction mechanisms. Power relations in the non-territorial (NT) organization will be compared with power relations in the territorial (T) system, to see to what extent T is reflected in NT. And individuals from any country will compare notes to find to what extent a particular NT is reflected in their part of T—whether it is present at all, and whether their government pays as much attention to it in terms of subsidy and deference as other governments are reported to pay to sister chapters, and so on.

This entire presentation may now gain in depth if we tie it to a simple four-country model of the world with two centre and two periphery countries (see Fig. 1).

In this diagram we have put a dot on top of each circle for the governments, the nuclei of the centres. Obviously, the IGOs connect these dots in various ways. The INGOs do not necessarily connect only the centre of countries—they may also tie periphery elements together. But the chances are they do not: the chances are that the masses are tied to their territorial units because they do not have the resources, that the whole concept of non-territoriality is fundamentally an élite concept. Even such grandiose concepts as 'Europe', even the nation-state is very much of an élite concept because of the way in which such means for developing consciousness as literacy, reading beyond primary school, knowledge of foreign languages are badly distributed, not to mention all the other inequalities and inequities, limited access to transportation and communication, and so forth. Hence, even though we do not have good data on national participation in the type of associations and organizations that are also multinationally organized, we can safely say that those individuals who participate internationally, in conferences and in secretariats, etc., generally belong to the centre of their countries.

Thus, if non-territorial actors (and this includes the transnational ones) essentially link governments and other élite groups together, then there are, in principle, and referring to Figure 1, four types of international organizations: (a) connecting centre countries (horizontal lines, top); (b) connecting centre and periphery countries in the same bloc (vertical lines); (c) connecting periphery countries (horizontal lines, bottom) in same bloc and in different blocs; (d) universal organizations (the whole rectangle).

The first three may be referred to as 'regional' organizations as long as we keep in mind the distinction between horizontal and vertical regions, and are not really non-territorial actors. In the real world, however, a particular organization is often too complex to permit classification in any single one of these types of classes.

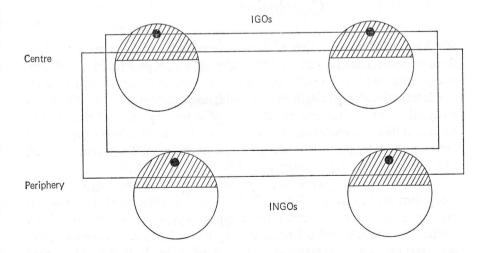

FIG. 1. Non-territoriality as an élitist concept.

Thus, the secretariat of an organization may often be different from the rest of the organization and be transnational even when the rest is intergovernmental or intragovernmental. Much of the history of the large intergovernmental organizations is made up of how the secretariat has tried to transnationalize the national delegates (meeting in conferences/assemblies, in councils or in executive boards), teaching them 'to think in terms of the world as a whole' (the 'world' usually meaning the organization, meaning the secretariat)—and of how the national delegates try to internationalize the secretariat by such methods as secondment, short tenure, return to governmental posts rather than a career in another transnational secretariat, and so on.

The net conclusion of all this is that the two systems, T and NT, are not independent of each other—nor is there any reason why one should expect them to be. The NTs of today are instruments in the hands of the territorial units which know how to use them, and that, as mentioned, is not only the major powers. But this is less true for the transnational organizations, since they are not organized in national chapters, and since the loyalty is to the world level and the individual level, not to the intermediate nation-State level. Their members become less concerned with 'organizing something similar at home' after they have been exposed to patterns in other nations through the medium of transnational conferences. For them an institution found or founded in one country is already a world institution—not something to be used by that country alone and copied elsewhere.

Conclusion

We have tried to conceive of international organizations as a modern form of non-territorial actors. They have their own peculiarities and they are conditioned by the still more important territorial system. In short, the international organizations are ambiguous phenomena, which can be analysed from several and partly contradictory angles, and classified in several different typologies, using as raw material the basic distinction between the intergovernmental, inter-non-governmental and transnational non-governmental organizations (IGOs, INGOs, TRANGOs).

A first typology takes as its point of departure the degree of isomorphism an international organization has with the territorial system, making a distinction between three types depending on whether both territorial elements and relations are reproduced inside the international organization, only the elements, or none of them. It is postulated that the IGOs are more of the first type (together with the BINGOs), the

INGOs more of the second type and the TRANGOs (with individuals as members) more of the third type.

A second typology takes as its point of departure the obvious circumstance, today, that most international organizations connect élites, governmental or non-governmental, profit or non-profit, around the world. The question is what kind of countries are brought together, and a first distinction would be between horizontal organizations (centre–centre, or periphery–periphery) and vertical organizations (centre–periphery). A second distinction would be between universal (open to all of the same kind) and regional (restricted to a geographical region) organizations.

In addition to this, all kinds of distinctions could be made depending on the purpose of the organization—but we have been more interested in characteristics that relate to structure and process so as to see better which role these organizations play in the total world system, which in turn is a combination of the territorial and the non-territorial systems. For this purpose it may be useful to make a distinction between the 'least non-territorial' and the 'most non-territorial' within the present typology, positing against each other a first-order IGO that reflects faithfully the territorial system and essentially brings together centre countries, and an nth order TRANGO bringing together individuals from all over the world. Do they have enough in common to be referred to as international organizations? By definition, yes. But in terms of non-territoriality the former is so little removed from the territorial level as to make little difference, and the latter so much removed from the territorial level that the disparity is probably also insignificant.

This might indicate that it is the in-between types that are the carriers of the most dynamic and interesting aspects of the processes of change in the non-territorial—and thereby the world—system. One may even talk about processes of penetration into the deeper recesses of the non-territorial continent, creating higher levels, less isomorphic, less centristic and more universal organizations, all the time trying to liberate the non-territorial system from constraints placed upon it not by the territorial system as such, but by the particular territorial system that was shaped by Western expansionism during the last five centuries. And that places the international organizations in today's political context in the struggle for a new international economic, political, military, cultural and social order.

Part II

Methodological
approaches
to international
organization

4 The decision-making approach to the study of international organization

Robert W. Cox
and Harold K. Jacobson

The analysis of decision-making is one way of studying power relations. Decisions, of course, do not reveal power directly. What they may show directly is influence, or the way in which power is translated into action. The relative power of contending forces is an inference that can be drawn from a careful observation of the workings of influence.

In drawing this inference, one must include 'non-decisions' within the concept of decisions. When an individual or group or government refrains from taking some initiative or action, this is usually because they have made a calculation showing it likely to be fruitless or possibly damaging to the attainment of their goals because it would encounter opposition too powerful to overcome.[1] Thus, likely opposing power has been taken into account and one possible action eliminated before it ever became part of a record of visible actions. Each decision-maker, individual or collective, carries in his consciousness a picture of prevailing power relations, and these images of the way power is structured are initial determinants of

ROBERT COX, former Director of the International Institute for Labour Studies in Geneva, is now Professor of International Organization at Columbia University, New York. He is author and editor of *International Organisation: World Politics* (1967) and, with H. K. Jacobson, of *Anatomy of Influence: Decision-making in International Organization* (1973). With J. Harrod he is currently engaged in an internationally comparative study of production relations and political and social power.

HAROLD K. JACOBSON is Professor and Chairman of Political Science in the Center for Political Studies of the Institute for Social Research at the University of Michigan, Ann Arbor, Mich. He is the author of *The USSR and the UN's Economic and Social Activities* (1963) and co-author of *Diplomats, Scientists and Politicians: The United States and the Nuclear Test Ban Negotiations* (1966) and of *The Anatomy of Influence: Decision Making in International Organization* (1973). He has contributed articles to various journals and has been a member of the editorial boards of *The Journal of Conflict Resolution* and *International Organization*. His current research involves political aspects of a new international economic order.

the decision process. The 'pre-influence' stage of decision-making is a mental picture of power relations.

The decision process can thus be seen as both a test of the power relations assumed at the start of the action (the mental picture), and a means towards changing these power relations.[2] Decisions can change power relations either by changing the resources available to the actors or by changing the procedures through which they interact so as to give some actors a more advantageous position than others. The study of decision-making is, accordingly, a study of the dynamics of power relations. It begins with an analysis of the structure of existing power relations: and it seeks to understand how the decision process may tend to sustain or to change that structure.

Quite obviously, power relations and decision-making take place within a variety of contexts, more or less broad in scope, more or less consequential. Towards the simple and less consequential end of the scale would be a local friendly society; towards the complex and more consequential, economic policy in a major modern State. The more confined the context studied, the more precision can be given to the concept of a decision. Making an *ex gratia* payment to someone would clearly be a specific decision in the friendly society. National economic policy by contrast involves a multitude of actions all of which might be called decisions, taken by distinct but frequently overlapping sets of people, with different degrees of importance and effectiveness. In such a complex and extensive context, the concept of decision tends to lose the specificity associated with the more simple context. General categories are required to differentiate the kinds of actions which cumulatively constitute a policy—symbolic declarations, strategic programming, tactical allocations, and so forth. The larger the context, the more the specificity of decisions tends to become swallowed up into the decision process as a whole.

This consideration applies to inquiry into power relations at the global level as well as at local or national levels. The choice of a context that is relatively limited in scope and precisely defined implies, on the part of the investigator, an assumption of stability in those other factors in world politics into which the specific decision context fits. It is, of course, possible to allow for changes in the environment of such a limited decision context, but these environmental changes have to be treated as given, as beyond the scope of inquiry. In times of relative stability, a narrower focus with the greater precision of detail it allows, seems like the best way to gain understanding about the inner workings of specific institutions. But in times of more profound and persuasive change, a broader angle of vision is desirable, one that sacrifices detail the better to grasp the shifting outline of the whole into which the separate institutions fit and in relation to which they make sense. This whole is the world system of power relations.

The narrow context

The authors of this chapter completed in 1972 a study of decision-making in international organization which they began in the late 1960s and carried out with the collaboration of several others.[3] It was a comparative study of how decisions were made in eight specialized international institutions of universal or quasi-universal scope: the International Telecommunication Union (ITU), the International Labour Organization (ILO), the United Nations Educational, Scientific and Cultural Organization (Unesco), the World Health Organization (WHO), the International Atomic Energy Agency (IAEA), the International Monetary Fund (IMF), the General Agreement on Tariffs and Trade (GATT), and the United Nations Conference on Trade and Development (UNCTAD). By contrast with the world system of power relations, these specialized organizations provided a set of relatively limited and specific decision contexts. The study covered a period of history, 1945–70, that was one of relative stability in the basic framework of world power relations, although some important changes did modify this framework.

The United States and the U.S.S.R. remained the dominant powers in the world system during the period, and while the U.S.S.R. moved toward parity with the United States in some respects, both declined in their power relative to other States. The main modifications were the increased power and potential for autonomy of Western Europe, and the increased articulation of Third World concerns. The eight organizations studied reflected the structure of world power and adapted to the two major modifications in the framework of world power relations.

As a consequence of this relative stability in the environment our analysis could and did devote primary attention to the interaction among individuals who participated directly in the political processes of the eight international organizations. Building on the tradition of studies of decision-making within local communities and national states,[4] our study sought to explain how influence was acquired and exercised in international organization by analysing how decisions were made. We sought to determine if there were persistent patterns and structures of influence.

We developed a common analytical framework so that our analyses of decision-making in the eight agencies would be comparable. To determine whether or not patterns and structures of influence differed depending on the issue that was being decided, we utilized a taxonomy of decisions involving seven categories: representational, symbolic, boundary, programmatic, rule-creating, rule-supervisory and operational.

Representational decisions affect membership in the organization and representation on internal bodies. They include decisions concerning the admission and exclusion of members, validation of credentials, determination of representation on executive organs and committees, and the manner in which the secretariat is composed, especially at the higher level.

Symbolic decisions are primarily tests of how opinions are aligned; no practical consequences in the form of actions flow directly from these decisions. The intention in symbolic issues is to test the acceptability of goals or ideologies intensely espoused by one group of actors or the legitimacy of long-accepted norms of dominant élites. In some cases these goals or ideologies may relate to broad issues of international politics, in others, to matters specific to the organization's field . . . .

Boundary decisions concern the organization's external relations with other international and regional structures on the matter of (1) their respective scopes, (2) co-operation among organizations, and (3) initiatives taken in one organization to provoke activity in another. . . .

Programmatic decisions concern the strategic allocation of the organization's resources among different types of activity. . . .

Rule-creating decisions define rules or norms bearing upon matters within the substantive scope of the organization. The outcome of the decisions may in some cases be formal instruments such as conventions, agreements, or resolutions. . . . Rules may also be created in less formal ways; for example, speeches by the executive head or others that may never explicitly be the subject of votes may nonetheless articulate widely shared norms or goals with which the organization may come to be identified in the minds of many of its constituents. Such actions may in significant cases be considered as rule-creating decisions.

Rule-supervisory decisions concern the application of approved rules by those subject to them. These decisions may involve various procedures ranging from highly structured to extremely subtle ones. . . .

Operational decisions relate to the provision of services by the organization or the use of its resources in accordance with approved rules, policies, or programmes . . . . Operational decisions may lead cumulatively to programmatic decisions.[5]

Decision-making within each of the categories showed certain distinctive patterns common to most of the agencies studied. Differences among the agencies seemed to arise more from differences in the importance to each of the various categories of decision—differences, that is, in the emphasis on certain categories of decisions and also in the practical consequences in terms of real resources affected that flow from decisions. For instance, symbolic decisions were quite important in ILO and UNCTAD (a category of decisions that by definition does not have significant practical consequences), but relatively unimportant to GATT and IMF. On the other hand, though all of these agencies engaged in rule-creating, the practical consequences of their rules were greater in the cases of IMF and GATT than in those of ILO or UNCTAD, and this affected the way in which decisions were made.

The individuals who were directly involved in decision-making within international organizations (the actors in decision-making) were classified into the following categories: (a) representatives of national governments; (b) representatives of national and international private associations; (c) the executive heads of the organizations; (d) high officials and other members of the bureaucracy of each organization; (e) individuals who serve in their own capacity formally or informally as advisers; (f) representatives of other international organizations; (g) employees of the mass media.

Individuals in the first four categories were active in decision-making in all of the organizations throughout the period studied. Those in the fifth and sixth categories were active in some of the organizations some of the time, but those in the final category played virtually no role, reflecting the minimal attention that public opinion gave to these eight agencies prior to the 1970s.

Different categories of actors tended to be influential in different types of decision. For example, representatives of national governments were influential in symbolic, representational and rule-making decisions. Executive heads were particularly influential in boundary and programmatic decisions. Members of international bureaucracies were more influential in operational decisions than in programmatic ones.

Various measures were used to gauge the influence of different individuals and categories of individuals. One technique that was utilized was simply examining the formal structure of authority: those who held positions of authority in an agency were assumed to be influential. Another technique of analysis was to ask knowledgeable individuals to list the individuals with the greatest general influence in a particular organization. Attempts were also made to construct behavioural indices of influence for individuals in some organizations on the basis of scores achieved for success in initiating and obstructing proposals. Finally, case studies of the interactions involved in particular decisions were used to assess influence in several instances. Each of the techniques had limitations, but by relying on several measures, we were able to obtain a broad and, we felt, reasonably reliable understanding of the relative influence of individuals who directly participated in decision-making in the eight organizations.

We were, of course, more interested in learning what general characteristics make for influence than in identifying which particular individuals appeared to be most influential. Accordingly, we sought to determine how certain general attributes relating respectively to position and personality contributed to the influence of different individuals. Our concept of position included role in the formal structure of authority and in the case of representatives the power of the unit that they represented. In this connection we assessed the changing stratification of the power of the States in the global system. Personal attributes included such factors as charisma, experience, expert knowledge, doggedness and negotiating skill.

Our interest went beyond the static measurement, the comparison, and the analysis of influence of individual actors. We also sought to determine how influence was aggregated behind particular policy orientations. Organizational ideologies were investigated as means of legitimating particular goals and strategies for their attainment. Persistent groupings of actors (whether formal as in the case of caucusing groups, or informal as in recurrent voting patterns) were looked into.

Finally, we sought explanations outside of the internal interaction processes within agencies by considering the environment that set the constraints or framework for the politics of each agency. This environment was conceived as having two aspects. One was the general environment of world politics affecting all intergovernmental organizations. The other was an environment specific to each agency in terms of the conditions most directly relevant to its specific tasks. Each of these environments could be conceived in terms of a stratification of capabilities of States, distinctive patterns of organization or ideology, and configurations of alignments and cleavages of interests among States. This mode of analysis was admittedly 'State-centric' in the sense that it assumed States to be the basic entities co-ordinating the expression of interests through international agencies, but it did, of course, take into account non-State factors in the environment and non-State actors participating in decision-making.

In summary, we sought explanations for how influence was gained and utilized within international organization on two levels: (a) that of the individual actors, those who participated directly in the making of decisions, and (b) that of the environment. The emphasis was on internal processes within agencies. The environment was taken as the given point of departure that set the framework for action and might be expected to explain a large part of the outcome. What could not be explained by the environment was to be understood as the result of the internal decision-making processes.

The principal general findings were first that these eight universal international organizations fell into two broad categories: those in which what we termed 'representative subsystems' dominated decision-making and those in which the 'participant subsystems' dominated decision-making. The 'representative subsystems' are composed of the individuals in the different countries whose interactions (taking place mainly in the countries) determine the policy pursued by that country's representatives through the agency in question. The 'participant subsystem' comprises the interactions (taking place mainly at the headquarters of the agency) among these representatives, the high officials of the agency, and any others directly involved in the internal processes of the agency. The first category (representative subsystem dominated) included GATT, IMF, ITU and IAEA, and the second, ILO, UNCTAD, WHO and Unesco. The policies that were pursued by the organizations in the first category were determined and closely controlled by their most powerful member States. The representatives of the most powerful States constituted an oligarchical élite within these organizations. However these individuals generally enjoyed little autonomy; rather they were required to adhere to detailed instructions formulated by their representative subsystems. Representatives of the most powerful member States were also influential in the organizations within the second category, but beyond setting broad limits the governments of the most powerful member States allowed these organizations considerable autonomy. Within these limits policies were determined by those who participated directly in making decisions within the organizations. These organizations consequently offered considerable scope for executive heads, for members of international bureaucracies and for representatives of less powerful member States. An essential difference between the two categories of organizations was that the activities of GATT, IMF, ITU and IAEA had important consequences for the governments of their most powerful member States while the activities of ILO, UNCTAD, WHO and Unesco were less consequential to them.

Other principal general findings were that these universal international organizations broadly, though in varying degrees, became increasingly involved in activities directed towards the Third World, while individuals reflecting the values associated with rich, industrial, non-socialist societies retained dominant influence. In this sense the organizations became agencies of a type of collective colonialism. At the same time, the governments of these Western societies whose nationals dominated the patterns and structures of influence in the eight organizations were increasingly coming to use separate, limited-membership organizations to deal with the matters of greatest mutual concern to themselves—the Group of 10 paralleling the IMF, for example, and the Development Assistance Committee of OECD paralleling UNCTAD. The study of decision-making in this set of relatively limited contexts thus led to a question that went beyond the study's own framework: how do the decisions of different international organizations relate to each other and to decisions taken in other settings of the broader context of world power relations?

The broad context

Since the above-mentioned study was concluded, further developments have occurred that seem to indicate a period of more profound and accelerating change in world power relations: these include the breakdown of the Bretton Woods system of fixed exchange rates, the dramatic increase in the price of petroleum and the consequential changes in the monetary position of States, the United States' withdrawal from Indochina, the crumbling of the outer ring surrounding the white-minority bastion in southern Africa, continuing momentum of the non-aligned countries in advocating a new international economic order, the more active participation of the People's Republic of China in world affairs. These developments cut across the conventional distinctions between the political and the economic, between State and society. Political and economic, public and private have to be linked together within the structuring notion of the world system. Whereas the focus of interest in the earlier study was on the interactions of individuals in the internal processes of existing inter-governmental agencies, now the decision process is to be conceived in broader terms as the generating of new and modified forms of international organization. What goes on within particular agencies can only be a small part of the total process that is to be seized by the analyst. Such an enlargement of the scope of inquiry calls for some redefinition of the concepts appropriate to it.

The thesis presented here is that for the late 1970s. A somewhat different approach to the study of decision-making in international organization is required than the approach we adopted in the late 1960s. This statement is not to be read as a disavowal of precious work, but as awareness that changes in the world require a further advance from the position reached then.

An approach commensurate with the preoccupations of the present must begin with the world system of power relations. International institutions have to be seen as functioning within that larger system. The starting-point would be a structural picture of power relations which are always the starting-point of the decision process. The approach would then focus on the points of conflict within the system that seem to suggest a potential for structural transformation. Then attention would concentrate on the role of international organization, particularly as to (a) whether international organization tended to stabilize or to transform the existing power relations, and (b) what factors determine the development of international organization. What follows is a sketch of a possible approach along these lines.

Power

The first problem in designing an appropriate model is to define the nature of power. To say in purely abstract terms that power is the capacity to influence the action of others and to achieve autonomy of one's own actions does not advance us very far. It is necessary to enter the historical plane so as to consider the sphere in which the kind of power relevant to this inquiry is exercised. Traditionally, this has been thought to be the sphere of the State and of inter-State relations. Those who regard State power as providing the only hard facts in the study of world polities have as their model the States of the European balance-of-power system that emerged in the seventeenth century and extended by the nineteenth to include North America, Russia, and Japan; they can hardly in the same breath include the 'soft States', of which Gunnar Myrdal wrote, that came into existence in the second half of the twentieth century.[6] The 'state-centric' approach implicitly, though rarely explicitly, refers to a privileged minority among the number of entities now juridically regarded as States.

Criticism of the 'state-centric' approach has led to definition of a 'transnational' approach that would take fuller account of non-State factors in relations among peoples, notably economic relations and movements of people and ideas.[7] Such non-State factors assume increasing importance among other reasons because of the nuclear stand-off among those States possessing weapons of mass destruction and the generally decreasing utility of military force in inter-state relations (as distinct from its impact on domestic politics). If 'State-centric' relations can be thought of as a first level of power relations, corresponding to the *political-security* sphere, then it will be useful to distinguish two further levels both in the 'transnational' category. One corresponds to the distinction between high and low politics, or roughly between political-security and economic-welfare politics.

In the *economic-welfare* sphere—the second level of power relations—we remain within the sphere of the State, in that area where the State plays a role of shaping and channelling the development of society or of responding to the pressures of society. At this second level, financial policy in modern capitalist States has come to play the determining role, and acts as the link between domestic economic-welfare policies of individual States and their international economic relationships.[8]

The third level of power relations arises conceptually outside the sphere of the State, in the realm of society. This is the level of social power or of the dominant and subordinate relationships of classes and social groups. Social power can be expressed in terms both of production and of consumption.

In production relations some groups control others, and increasingly with the internationalizing of production, these control relationships operate between social groups in different countries. There is, accordingly, an international structure of production relations. A control structure of the world economy is implicit in the notion of interdependence now so widely accepted. It is more explicitly present in theories of dependency.[9] The dependency concept is concerned with social power in transnational relations.

It is a moot question whether this control structure is properly thought of as State or non-State in nature. The answer is that it is difficult and decreasingly relevant to try to disentangle how much is State and how much non-State. What, for instance, is the significance of this distinction in considering an industrial co-operation agreement between a European or American-based multinational and a socialist State enterprise? States can muster resources to encourage, strengthen or modify the behaviour of non-State actors. Social groups or non-State interests can influence state policy in these matters. We have to think of social power and the control structure of the world economy as composed of both.

If production is the determining aspect of social power, consumption is its counterpart. We frequently speak loosely of rich countries and poor countries when what we mean is that some countries contain more of the powerful social groups, those able to command the largest share of the world product, while other countries contain more of the powerless, those least able to command a share of the world product. We know that there are rich people in poor countries and poor people in rich countries, but the fact that accounts are made up on a country basis lends a territorial bias to the way we have come to measure social power, for instance by comparing GNP *per capita*.

To summarize, a working definition of world power relations has to bridge the conventional distinction between State and society. An appropriate conceptualization of the world system would take account of (a) the structure of international production relations, from the standpoint of control over production, (b) the consequences of political-security policies of States on their economic-welfare policies and (c) the consequences of economic-welfare policies on international production relations. Thus production relations can be a common yard-stick, to which the other levels of power can be reduced. This approach views the world system primarily in terms of social power.

A model of the world system

World power relations have generally been thought of in terms of the dichotomies of East/West and North/South, corresponding first, to the cold war beginning in the late 1940s, and second, to the debate over international economic relations arising during the 1960s. By taking production relations as the starting-point, it is possible to define a single world system, encompassing but going beyond these two simple dichotomies. The internationalizing of production is the underlying historical process that has linked these segments of the world together and determined their relationships within the whole system.

Very briefly, the internationalizing of production is bringing about a global division of labour in which technological development is concentrated in a *core* area, while physical production of goods is moving increasingly into *peripheral* areas, the two being linked by control mechanisms located in the core area. The multinational corporations are now perceived as technology and control mechanisms of this kind. Between core and periphery are *semi-peripheral* areas struggling not to lose the ability to attain core status.[10]

This world system is to be defined in terms of functional positions in production relations. These functional positions can also be seen as fitting over a territorial map, so that specific functional positions correspond to certain countries. This does not, of course, mean that the activities characteristic of specific functional positions necessarily occupy most of the people in these countries. It does mean that they are the dominant activities, to which other local activities are subordinate, and that they determine the relationship of the country within the world system. In this sense, we can move from speaking of functional positions to speaking about countries. The concepts 'core' and 'periphery' are at the same time functional and geographic. These categories are in the nature of ideal types, which can be thought of as expressing a latent potential rather than a definitive classification of countries.

The structure and the direction of movement of the present world system, from the standpoint of international production relations, can be seen in terms of five categories.

First are the richest countries, moving towards an essentially post-industrial pattern of society. Here are concentrated the research and development capabilities of innovation in production, and the control centres of multinational corporations. The United States is the core of the core, and some countries of Western Europe and Japan might also be assimilated to this status. At most 10–15 per cent of world population live in countries on the threshold of post-industrialism.

Second is a category of advanced industrial countries. The Council for Mutual Economic Assistance (COMECON) group of countries would now be the largest component of this category, but industrialized capitalist countries would be candidates for it in so far as they fail to make the post-industrial category.[11] The status of this second category of countries in the world system is semi-peripheral. Their typical State policies are mercantilist. Their governments seek to reconcile a need for greater links with international production (as a means of acquiring more advanced technology) with a jealous regard to preserve their own autonomy of development so they do not become dependent upon the first generation of post-industrial societies, and are eventually able to make their own transition independently to this status. This category would account for perhaps 15–20 per cent of world population.

Third are the countries of dependent capitalism, those that accept industrialization under the management control of post-industrial centres.[12] These include less-developed countries with a fairly large élite domestic market for consumer durables and now more particularly the export platforms manufacturing for the rich-country markets of the world—countries like Brazil, Iran, the Republic of Korea, Mexico, Singapore, Spain and others. Potentially, they could include another 20 per cent of world population.

These first three categories, which together account for about half of world population, include the most closely integrated or interdependent elements in international production relations. The remaining half of world population live in countries less fully integrated into international production. This population can be divided into two further categories.

Fourth, about 25 per cent of world population live in poor countries that have at present only very limited development prospects within the perspective of existing international production relations, i.e. under the present world structure of social power. The world system makes only very limited use of their labour power or their markets. They do not seem essential to the system. Yet they are there, and any disturbances arising from their condition of frustrated development might be disruptive to the system. Once the niceties of diplomatic dialogue are stripped away, the problems of these countries tend to be regarded by those more integrated into international production as problems of global poor relief and potentially of global riot control.

Fifth, one-quarter of the world population lives in the People's Republic of China, a country that cannot be fitted into the preceding categories. China by conventional statistical measures is poor, but the extent to which its population has been mobilized differentiates it from the undeveloped poor of the fourth category. China is seeking its own autonomous development, rejecting dependent capitalism. In the longer term, it is conceivable that China could connect with the world system in semi-peripheral status, comparable to the way in which the U.S.S.R. expanded its links with the world economy from the late 1960s. It is equally conceivable that China will serve as a contrast model rallying those disaffected by the way the system of international production works and promoting its dialectical contradiction.

The potential sources of conflict within the present world system are grave indeed. Post-industrial societies face the problem of securing a meaningful participation in production, in incomes, in decision-making for that large part of their populations not engaged in the core economic activities. Alienation menaces the heart of the system. The mercantilism characteristic of semi-peripheral countries' defensive postures in the system could spark international conflict. Dependent capitalism is generating increasing income disparities within countries of this category. The capital/labour mix characteristic of transferred technology tends to reduce employment in agriculture, while increasing it only modestly in industry, thus leading to a dramatic rise in the destitute marginal population. Growing incomes disparities and growing marginality encourage repression. When the alienated at the core begin to understand and sympathize with the reactions of the destitute in the peripheries, the crisis of the system can be said to have arrived.

Ideologies
of international organization

Power can never be defined exclusively in physical or material terms. The material aspect of power has its counterpart in ideas. Those who at any time seek to change power relations have to struggle not only against entrenched material interests but also against the legitimacy that accrues to the status quo. Existing power relations define in large measure what problems are worthy of attention, in terms of eliminating what is deemed to be dysfunctional to the existing order. The problematic for science and technology is framed within the parameters of existing power relations. These orientations to behaviour and to applied science we call ideology. Ideology sustains the existing structure of power by mobilizing opinion in favour of it and by directing practical efforts towards solving the problems that arise in the workings of existing power relations.[13]

Ideologies have played an important role in the history of international organization. If we consider only its recent history since the Second World

War, functionalism was an esoteric doctrine of marked influence in shaping the structure and policies of international institutions emerging in the 1940s. [14] Functionalism in essence sought to base international organization upon interests inherent in society rather than making them dependent upon the goodwill of States. In retrospect, functionalism can be seen as the projection upon the world as a whole of the pluralist concept of society which is a prominent aspect of the Western European and North American political tradition.

Functionalism's appeal was mainly to a small number of senior international officials and active promoters of international institutions. Its influence could be seen to wane during the 1960s, to be outclassed by a new dominant ideology of international organization: developmentalism. Developmentalism can be defined as the promotion of economic growth in poor countries by methods consistent with the expansion of a liberal world economy.[15] In practice, this meant creating conditions propitious to the flow of private direct investment or, in other words, encouraging dependent capitalism.

In the 1970s, developmentalism was succeeded by two newer ideologies, transnationalism and globalism. Transnationalism did not depart radically from developmentalism, but shifted the emphasis from developing growth-oriented public services and public policy to the supposed engines of growth themselves, the multinational corporations.[16] Globalism added something new: the ecological perspective. Globalism introduced the notion that there were limits to the total population the world could sustain, to the amount of man-made pollution the ecosystem could cope with. The policy inferences from globalism were restraint in the growth of population and industrial production, and a need for global monitoring and ultimately for global management of the ecosystem.[17]

The fundamental question to ask about ideologies is: do they sustain the status quo of power relations, or do they tend to undermine and revise them? All of the foregoing were status quo supporting ideologies. They all took existing social power relations and the existing structures of the world economy as the given framework. Functionalism would have exalted economic interests and diminished the ability of States to intervene and control these interests. Developmentalism and transnationalism offered programmes for growth within existing structures.

Globalism alone stood on the threshold of a contradiction. It seemed to be saying that the thoughtless growth policies of the past had brought the world into great danger, which could only be averted if the poor of the world were to have fewer children and abandon hopes for rapid industrialization. But latent within the notion of limiting growth is the issue of sharing. Growth-oriented ideologies rely on dividing increments as a means of solving problems and reducing tensions. With no growth, the more intractable problem of redistribution is posed. Globalism, which began as a concern among the affluent minority, becomes readily transformed into an attack on privileges they acquired through the appropriation of a disproportionate share of the world's resources. The demand for a new international economic order formulates this challenge from the Third World as a new revisionist ideology of international organization.

Hegemony and international organization: the environment

The material and ideological aspects of power are united in the concept of hegemony. The hegemony of a particular social group reflects that group's dominance over the material components of power, but it is a dominance expressed through a consensus (i.e. in ideological form) in which the dominant group takes account of the interests of subordinate groups so as to yield them some satisfactions without at the same time endangering their own position of dominance.[18] The interests of subordinate groups are merged in some measure into a programme that can be plausibly represented as of universal interest. This will usually be a programme of expansion under existing power relations in which, though benefits will be unequally distributed, there will be something for all participating groups.

International organization here is regarded as a process that takes place in world power relations—a process in which hegemony becomes institutionalized. When a particular formal intergovernmental institution is established, it crystallizes the hegemonic consensus of a particular time in relation to a particular global task or set of global tasks. Hence hegemony comprises the environmental variables relevant to decision-making in international organization. Hegemony thus replaces the three variables which we used to characterize the general environment in our previous study: the stratification of States in terms of their power, the distribution of States and non-independent territories according to their political and economic characteristics, and the pattern of conflicts and alignments. Hegemony is a historical moving force; it is readjusted as the material and ideological components of world power relations change over time. The specific institutions spawned by hegemony at one point in time face a problem of adjustment to the altered hegemony at a later point in time. Institutions are visible. Hegemony is invisible, a latent force that can only be seized intellectually. Yet hegemony is the secret of the vitality of institutions. Some institutions successfully adapt to a changing hegemony, others fail to. The effectiveness of international institutions is to be gauged by their fit to prevailing hegemony.

The issue of change in institutions is thus secondary to the question of change in hegemony. A change in hegemony can come about through the emergence of a counter-hegemonic force. Bearing in mind the dual nature of power—the conjunction of material and ideological elements—the counter-hegemonic force will result from a combination of (a) an increase in the material resources available to a subordinate group and (b) a coherent and persistent articulation of the subordinate group's demands that challenges the legitimacy of the prevailing consensus.

The first response of the hegemonic group once it becomes aware that the counter-hegemonic force has to be contended with is to try to co-opt it, giving its leading elements a fuller place in the system without really changing the system. Co-optation re-establishes the old hegemonic legitimacy. This is the most likely result in a 'moderate' international system.[19] It results in some gradual change *in* the world system but no radical change *of* the system as a whole.

The alternative of a violent revolutionary change of the international system is hardly conceivable other than through a nuclear war the consequences of which are predictable only as making survival for humanity, and thus of any international system, problematic. Intermediate between co-optation and violent revolution, a negotiated restructuring of power relations may be conceived—one could designate this possibility by the term that evokes the 1976 demand by the Opposition for a restructuring of the Italian political system to reflect a perceived change in the balance of social forces—the demand for a *compromesso storico*. Effective counter-hegemonic challenges may thus lead either to co-optation or to a historic compromise.

At the present juncture, the demand for a new international economic order expresses a counter-hegemonic force in the form of a consensus among a large number of Third World countries. To maintain this consensus is the first condition for an effective challenge. This is difficult because in the existing world economy the interests of Third World countries are to some degree competitive. Moreover, it is a consensus among governments with very different policies—from those seeking growth through attracting foreign investment to those favouring greater self-reliance, from those seeking to mobilize domestic populations and widen popular participation to those using coercion to obstruct any such developments. Nevertheless, the consensus has been maintained and encouraged by such manifestations of a shift in world power as the rise in petroleum prices, the withdrawal of the United States from Indochina and the setbacks to white-minority government in southern Africa.

The more radical elements behind the Third World consensus seek a historic compromise, that would give the Third World countries a greater share of control over real resources. The powerful within the existing hegemony respond by attempting to co-opt some elements of the Third World consensus, to offer them some satisfaction within the existing order without prejudicing their own control, a tactic that might prove attractive to those Third World country regimes fearful of arousing popular pressures.[20]

The question of the reform or reconstruction of international institutions has to be approached in the perspective of inter-institutional relations. Study of any particular institution, for instance IMF or ILO to mention but two within which issues of institutional reform have been raised, quickly leads outside the initial object of study to the broader problematic of hegemony.

Currently, a division of labour is apparent among the variety of institutions participating in the process of institutionalizing a new hegemony. OPEC and the International Atomic Energy Agency group countries have specific interests. They are directly concerned with the use of real resources. Negotiations between representatives of these two groups and others take place through the institutionalized North–South dialogue meeting in Paris, the Conference on International Economic Co-operation. The non-aligned countries meet to maintain the Third World consensus and define its content (e.g. the conference held in Lima in August 1975), and try to maintain a common platform for those countries that have leverage through their resources (especially petroleum) and those poor countries that lack such leverage. The secretariats of the United Nations Conference on Trade and Development and the United Nations Industrial Development Organization provide intellectual support for the countries of the South in the form of data and ideas. The General Assembly of the United Nations, which has no control over real resources, confers legitimacy upon the aims of a new international economic order and thereby acts as a spur to the North–South dialogue which does deal with real resources. When the General Assembly does produce widely agreed conclusions, it is registering through formal proceedings the results of an intricate informal process of negotiations amongst groups of countries, groups defined by mutual and persisting interests.

When one comes to consider some specific institutional issue like the reform of voting rights in IMF, it now has to be seen as conditioned by all these other activities. The decision process through which a new hegemony becomes institutionalized encompasses existing international institutions and what could be called quasi-institutions (various ad hoc forums for negotiation). The process extends, of course, well beyond the central meeting places to include the networks of public officials and private interest groups that shape international policy from within countries. In short, the decision process of international organization is inter-institutional and it also transcends existing institutions, since it must include the explanation for the creation of new or reformed institutions.

Proximate factors in decision-making: individuals and groups

Certain individuals and groups merit special attention since they may play a crucial role in how the institutionalization of world power relations is being shaped, and thus how hegemony is being adjusted. For convenience, these can be called the proximate factors in the decision process. They replace the actors in our previous study.

A first category is that of *foreign-policy directors of powerful States*. These are the individuals whose role requires an accurate assessment of existing hegemony as a basis for action at all times. The pre-eminence of functionalist thinking has perhaps given a bias against paying much attention to personalities like De Gaulle and Kissinger in earlier studies of international organization. Most of these studies have included the middle-level officials of foreign offices and functional ministries who take part in decision-making within international institutions.[21] In times of relative stability, this may suffice. What it implies is that the frameworks for action by these middle-level bureaucrats are fixed. In times of change in the structure of world power relations, it is important to consider how the heads of government and foreign secretaries envisage the role and potential for international institutions. Their intervention can change the limits of action of the middle-level officials. The first category of proximate factors includes only the highest level of national foreign-policy-makers, those with authority to fix the framework of policy for lower-level officials.

A second category includes *special-interest groups whose activities transcend national boundaries*. These include both private or non-governmental interest groups and segments of governmental bureaucracies that serve particular specialized interests. Private- and public-interest group activities that cross national boundaries have been distinguished as transnational and transgovernmental relations respectively. Keohane and Nye have pointed out that intergovernmental institutions are privileged forums for transgovernmental relations.[22] Transnational relations of the non-governmental kind take place through a variety of international interest groups (e.g. the International Chamber of Commerce) or religious, charitable or scientific associations, 'invisible colleges' and clubs (e.g. the Club of Rome).

The level of consciousness characteristic of this second category is likely to differ from that of the first. The first category thinks in terms of hegemony, of the over-all structure of world power. The consciousness of the second category is of the economic-corporative type, concerned with the solidarity of interests of particular groups. The various economic-corporative interests are assigned their place within any particular hegemony. But the construction of hegemony is analytically separate from the pursuit of economic-corporative interests. In general, the action of special-interest groups tends to maintain a *status quo* in hegemony to the extent that satisfaction for particular interests is built into hegemony.

A third category can be called the *empathetic neutral*. The first identified components of this category were executive heads of international institutions. Executive heads have been represented as able to play a critical role in the development of their institutions.[23]

The ground for looking to executive heads for leadership in international organization is similar to the ground on which Karl Mannheim placed the role of the intellectual in a world of conflicting socio-economic interests and ideologies—both can be relatively free from the constraints of particular interests and better than others able to comprehend the conflicting viewpoints of competing interests.[24] The executive head can perform this role not by virtue of his office alone, but to the extent that he has been able to approximate the ideal type of relative detachment.

Thinking of the ideal type rather than one of the offices that may be most conducive to its attainment, this category might be extended to include certain notable individuals who are not executive heads of international institutions but may be placed by events in situations of ad hoc players of similar roles. Indeed, one need not even be restricted to individuals, since the foreign policies of some small countries may play such a role.

Since we are concerned with organization as a process rather than as a set of formal institutions, it is best to define this category in the broadest possible manner as the empathetic neutral. The particular question of interest here is whether a period of profound change in world power relations is more or less propitious for effective initiative by empathetic neutrals than are times of relative stability.

Empathetic neutrals can be thought of as links between economic-corporative and the hegemonic levels of action. Their role in times of change in world power relations would be to help adjust hegemony—to achieve either co-optation or a historic compromise with counter-hegemonic forces by reformulating the hegemonic consensus and programme so as to embrace successfully all the relevant elements. It is a mediating role between the complex of economic-corporative interests and foreign-policy-makers of the most powerful States.

The fourth and final category is what can loosely be called *public opinion.* International institutions are bureaucracies built upon national bureaucracies. The normal political processes of international institutions are intrabureaucratic processes. The non-governmental interests which impinge upon these institutions are expressed through interest-group bureaucracies. Rarely is there any occasion for accountability to any more broadly based opinion. Even those international institutions that ostensibly serve the interests of broad segments of populations, e.g. ILO in relation to industrial labour, or FAO in relation to farmers, have in practice had little or no direct audience with mass constituencies.

In contemplating present and future change, however, it seems useful to inquire to what extent the mobilization of mass-based concern with certain world issues is capable of affecting the reformulation of hegemony and providing a political base for certain forms of international action. It is not inconceivable that the development of forces at work in the world economy could provide conditions propitious for mass-based concern in controlling international production. Popular participation in the process of international organization has clearly not arrived, but it may be wise to retain an open mind as to its future possibility.[25]

In so far as public opinion may be in the picture, the question must be asked: whose public opinion? This may well be a means of mobilizing new political resources behind rich-country positions, since it is in the richer countries that public opinion can most easily become a political force. The poor of the world, as a whole, remain very largely inarticulate. In so far as public opinion becomes a factor in the decision process of international organization, it could under present conditions be to their disadvantage.

This prospect would be altered to the extent that social mobilization extends into the Third World and is expressed through a greater identification of people and governments and a fuller public consciousness in these countries of how international issues impinge upon their own welfare. In the short run, the proponents of a new international economic order have to patch together through diplomatic activity a rather heterogeneous coalition of radical mobilizing and repressive authoritarian regimes. In the long run, they may have to build a more durable popular base of support for their programme among the people of the Third World as a whole, as well as among the populations of the richer countries. At some point along this road, active stimulus to social mobilization will come into conflict with the diplomatic task of maintaining support for the programme from those regimes in the coalition that view mobilization as a threat to established élites. In so far as the balance tips towards a more articulate popular support for Third World goals, the prospects of a historic compromise—a re-negotiated hegemony with all the institutional consequences that flow from it—are enhanced. In so far as the balance tips in favour of the non-mobilizing authoritarian regimes, the likelihood that these will be co-opted into the existing hegemony is high.

In summary, the decision-making approach to international organization analyses how these key proximate factors interact with the prevailing hegemony—the environment—and it seeks to understand the extent to which these interactions support the status quo or promote change in the structure of existing power relations.

Notes

1. The concept of 'non-decision' has been used by Peter Bachrach and Morton S. Baratz in *Power and Poverty, Theory and Practice*, New York and London, Oxford University Press, 1970.

2. 'Power relations' is used here to include both (a) the structure of power, i.e. the relative capability of individuals, social groups, States, etc., and (b) the processes of power or patterns of inter-action in which power is used. Decisions can thus change power relations either by changing relative access to resources, or by altering the procedures of interaction to the advantage of one party or another.

3. Robert W. Cox and Harold K. Jacobson, *The Anatomy of Influence : Decision Making in International Organization*, New Haven, Conn., Yale University Press, 1973. Others contributing to the volume are Gerard and Victoria Curzon, Joseph S. Nye, Lawrence Scheinman, James P. Sewell and Susan Strange. Earlier studies of decision-making include : Chadwick F. Alger, 'Interaction in a Committee of the United Nations General Assembly', in J. David Singer (ed.), *Quantitative International Politics*, p. 51-81, New York, The Free Press, 1968 ; Hayward R. Alker, Jr. and Bruce M. Russett, *World Politics in the General Assembly*, New Haven, Conn., Yale University Press, 1965 ; John Hadwen and Johan Kaufmann, *How United Nations Decisions are Made*, 2nd ed., Leiden, A. W. Sitjoff, 1962 ; Arend Lijphart, 'The Analysis of Bloc Voting in the General Assembly : A Critique and a Proposal', *The American Political Science Review*, Vol. LVII, No. 4, December 1963, p. 902-17 ; Johan Kaufmann, *Conference Diplomacy: an Introductory Analysis*, Leiden, A. W. Sitjoff, 1968 ; Robert O. Keohane, 'Political Influence in the General Assembly', *International Conciliation*, Vol. 557, March 1966, p. 5-64.

4. See especially Robert A. Dahl, *Who Governs? Democracy and Power in an American City*, New Haven, Conn., Yale University

Press, 1963, and Richard C. Snyder, H. W. Bruck and Burton Sapin (eds.), *Foreign Policy Decision Making: an Approach to the Study of International Politics*, New York, The Free Press, 1962.

5. *Anatomy of Influence*, op. cit., p. 9–11.

6. A point of view which in the United States in commonly associated with Hans Morgenthau, *Politics Among Nations*, New York, Alfred Knopf, 1948. This is also the perspective of many European scholars of international relations, /e.g. Ludwig Dehio, *The Precarious Balance: The Politics of Power in Europe, 1494-1945 (Gleichgewicht oder Hegemonie)*, New York, Knopf, 1962. (Original German edition, 1948.) In *The Challenge of World Poverty*, Harmondsworth, Penguin, 1970, Myrdal writes: 'The term "soft State" is understood to comprise all the various types of social indiscipline which manifest themselves by: deficiencies in legislation and in particular law observance and enforcement, a wide-spread disobedience by public officials on various levels to rules and directives handed down to them, and often their collusion with powerful persons and groups of persons whose conduct they should regulate. Within the concept of the soft State belongs also corruption . . .' (p. 211).

7. Robert O. Keohane and Joseph S. Nye (eds.), *Transnational Relations and World Politics*, Cambridge, Mass., Harvard University Press, 1972.

8. The new primacy of finance ministries in the modern capitalist State arises from the way domestic economic welfare policies are conditioned by external economic conditions. Finance ministries are the link between external and internal economies. This has been noted in French scholarship, e.g. Erhard Friedberg, 'L'Internationalisation de l'Economie et Modalités d'Intervention de l'Etat : la "Politique industrielle" ', *Planification et Société*, p. 94–108, Grenoble, Presses Universitaires de Grenoble, 1974, and Christian Palloix, *L'Internationalisation du Capital*, Paris, Maspero, 1975, especially, p. 81–3.

9. This is not the place to give a full bibliography on dependency theory. Suffice it to say that in so far as the study of international organization is to be placed within the larger framework of the world system of power relations, and power is to be understood primarily in terms of what we have called social power, dependency theorists have been particularly prolific in suggesting structural models of the world system. Some of those works which have influenced the authors' thinking in drawing up the present outline are referred to in the notes below.

10. The core/periphery model outlined here may be found also in Immanuel Wallerstein, *The Modern World System : Capitalist Agriculture and the Origins of the European World-Economy in the Sixteenth Century*, New York, Academic Press, 1974, and his article 'The Rise and Future Demise of the World Capitalist System: Concepts for Comparative Analysis',

Comparative Studies in Society and History, Vol. 16, No. 4, September 1974, p. 387–415. Wallerstein's thesis that capitalism became a world system in the sixteenth century would be contested by historians, e.g. the Marxist Perry Anderson, *Lineages of the Absolutist State*, London, NLB Atlantic Highlands Humanities Press, 1974, who saw this period as the consolidation of centralized feudal States on which mercantile capitalism had only limited impact, and Geoffrey Barraclough, *Introduction to Contemporary History*, Harmondsworth, Penguin, 1967, who sees the emergence of something that might be called a 'world system' as an aspect of contemporary history, which begins only on the threshold of the twentieth century. The argument over when the model becomes applicable poes not diminish the usefulness of the model for analysis of contemporary world powers relations. The application of the core/periphery conceptualization to international production relations fits well with the work of Christian Palloix, op. cit. ; Stephen Hymer, 'The Multinational Corporation and the Law of Uneven Development', in Jagdish N. Bhagwati (ed.), *Economics and World Order : From the 1970's to the 1990's*, London, Macmillan, 1972 ; and Keith Griffin, 'The International Transmission of In-equality', *World Development*, Vol. 2, No. 3, March 1974, p. 3–15, among others.

11. The semi-peripheral status of the Soviet Union is suggested in Wallerstein, 'The Rise and Future Demise of the World Capitalist System . . .', op. cit. A somewhat fuller rationale might be given by reference to the innovations in Soviet economic policy observable from the late 1960s when technology was perceived by Soviet economic management as a bottleneck to further growth. Continuing extensive use of capital and labour seemed to be reaching limits that could only be passed through a more technologically intensive use of capital. To acquire such technology, industrial co-operation agreements with European- and United States-based multinationals were encouraged. In order to acquire the foreign exchange to purchase technology, Soviet exports were encouraged; and some industrial co-operation agreements included provision that the Western partner firm should be paid in goods produced by the new technology which it would then undertake to market. Soviet trade and industrial links with the world economy thus increased markedly during the mid-1970s. Of course, the managers of the Soviet economy do not want such increased intercourse or 'interdependency' to reduce their ultimate control over the Soviet economy. These developments in policy and economic relations conform to the semi-peripheral type in the model outlined.

12. Fernando Henrique Cardoso has put aside the notion of 'development of underdevelopment' of André Gunder Frank, and substitutes for it the notion of 'dependent capitalist development' that occurs in the sectors of the Third World integrated

into the expanding economy of international production. See Cardoso, 'Imperialism and Dependency in Latin America', in Frank Bonilla and Robert Girling (eds.), *Structures of Dependency*, Nairobi, Calif., Nairobi Bookstore, 1973.

13. Karl Mannheim, *Ideology and Utopia*, New York, Harcourt Brace, 1936. (Original German edition, 1929.)

14. On functionalism as an approach to international organization, the classic text is David Mitrany, *A Working Peace System*, London, Chatham House, 1943. Important commentaries and developments in functionalist thinking are in Inis L. Claude Jr., *Swords into Plowshares*, Chapter 17, New York, Random House, 1964, and Ernst B. Haas, *Beyond the Nation State*, Stanford, Calif., Stanford University Press, 1964. Cox and Jacobson, op. cit., p. 403-6, contains a critical discussion of functionalism and developmentalism as ideologies of international organization.

15. The report entitled *Partners in Development* prepared for the World Bank by a commission under the chairmanship of Lester B. Pearson is an exemplary statement of developmentalist ideology. See also Robert W. Cox, 'The Pearson and Jackson Reports in the Context of Development Ideologies', *The Year Book of World Affairs, 1972*, p. 187–202, London, Stevens, 1972.

16. There is now an abundant literature which could be bracketed under the heading of transnationalism, which sees the multinational as the engine of global development breaking through the restrictions of an obsolescent nation-State. Most of this literature, to be sure, is American. See, for example, George W. Ball, 'Cosmocorp: The Importance of Being Stateless', *Atlantic Community Quarterly*, Vol. 6, No. 2, Summer 1968, p. 163–70; and his 'Multinational Corporations and Nation States', *Atlantic Community Quarterly*, Vol. 5, No. 2, Summer 1967, p. 247-53 ; Frank Tannenbaum, 'Survival of the Fittest', *Columbia Journal of World Business*, Vol. 3, No. 2, March-April 1968, p. 13-20 ; Harry Johnson, 'The Multi-National Corporation as an Agency of Economic Development : Some Exploratory Observations', in Barbara Ward et al., *The Widening Gap : Development in the 1970's*, p. 242-52, New York, Columbia University Press, 1971; Howard Perlmutter, 'The Tortuous Evolution of the Multinational Corporation', *Columbia Journal of World Business*, Vol. 4, No. 1, January-February 1969, p. 9-18. Most of this enthusiasm for the multinationals dates from the late 1960s. It was soon countered by a barrage of criticism forecasting negative consequences from the expansion of multinationals, a literature that has grown in vigour during the 1970s, and which is both American and non-American in origin.

17. The most widely known statement of the globalist position is probably the report prepared for the Club of Rome by D. H. Meadows et al., *The Limits to Growth*, New York, Universe

Books, 1972. This was based largely on a model developed by Jay W. Forrester, *World Dynamics*, Cambridge, Mass., Wright-Allen Press, 1971. Other exponents of globalism include Harold Sprout and Margaret Sprout, *Toward a Politics of the Planet Earth*, New York, Van Nostrand Reinhold, 1971, and Lester R. Brown, *World Without Borders*, New York, Random House, 1972. The implications for international organization of the globalist position have been drawn in Philippe de Seynes, 'Prospects for a Future Whole World', *International Organization*, Vol. 26, No. 1, Winter 1972, p. 1-17, and by Maurice F. Strong, 'One Year After Stockholm : An Ecological Approach to Management', *Foreign Affairs*, Vol. 51, No. 4, July 1973, p. 690-707.

18. The concept of hegemony in the form used here is derived from Antonio Gramsci, *Quaderni del Carcere*, Turin, Einaudi, 1975.

19. For the concept of a 'moderate' international system, see Stanley Hoffmann, 'International Organization and the International System', *International Organization*, Vol. 24, No. 3, Summer 1970, p. 389-413.

20. This seems to have been the message contained in the circular telegram sent by the United States representative to the United Nations, Daniel P. Moynihan, to United States Secretary of State Henry Kissinger and to all American embassies which was 'leaked' to the *New York Times* (28 January 1976). The telegram referred to 'a basic foreign policy goal of the United States, that of breaking up massive blocs of nations, mostly new nations, which for so long have been arrayed against us in international forums. . . . The nonaligned or the Group of 77, or whatever, are groups made up of extraordinarily disparate nations, with greatly disparate interests. Their recent bloc-like unity was artificial and was bound to break up . . .'. Roger D. Hansen, 'The Political Economy of North–South Relations: How Much Change?', *International Organization*, Vol. 29, No. 4, Autumn 1975, discusses the likelihood of 'the embourgeoisement of OPEC', i.e. of co-optation.

21. See, for instance, Arnold Beichman, *The 'Other' State Department : The United States Mission to the United Nations—Its Role in the Making of Foreign Policy*, New York, Basic Books, 1967, and the extensive study sponsored by the Carnegie Endowment, *Les Missions auprès des Organisations Internationales*, Brussels, Bruylent, 1971–76, 4 vols.

22. See especially Robert O. Keohane and Joseph S. Nye, 'Transgovernmental Relations and International Organizations', *World Politics*, Vol. 27, No. 1, October 1974, p. 39–62.

23. Of the literature on the role of executive heads, note Haas, op. cit. ; Robert W. Cox, 'The Executive Head : An Essay on Leadership in International Organization', *International Organization*, Vol. 23, No. 2, Spring 1969, p. 205–30; and a review article by Mark W. Zacher, 'The Secretary-General : Some

Comments on Recent Research', *International Organization*, Vol. 23, No. 4, Autumn 1969, p. 932–50.

24. Mannheim, op. cit., especially p. 154 et seq., in which he discusses the intelligentsia as 'a relatively classless stratum', which implies that at least some members of this stratum would be capable of 'dynamic mediation [*dynamische Vermittlung*] of conflicting point of view' (p. 161).

25. There has been a great dearth of attention to the relationship of public opinion to international organization, perhaps in large measure because it is but a latent phenomenon in most cases. Williann A. Scott's and Stephen B. Withey's early study, *The United States and the United Nations : The Public View, 1945-1955*, New York, Manhattan Publishing Company, 1958, remains one of the most detailed and conceptually elegant analyses. Not surprisingly, the European Communities have been most attentive to public opinion. A programme of EEC-wide opinion polls has been conducted under the direction of Jacques-René Rabier, Former Director-General for Press and Information in the European Communities. See Commission des Communautés Européennes, *Les Européens et l'Unification de l'Europe*, Brussels, General Directorate for Press and Information of the European Communities, 1972. The United Nations Institute for Training and Research (UNITAR) sponsored a study of press reaction to United Nations activities. See Alexander Szalai, *The United Nations and the News Media*, New York, United Nations Institute for Training and Research, 1972. In an imaginative piece of futurology, three Canadian professors of international law envisage a future world organization polarized between, on the one hand, an élite technocratic, computer-bound intrabureaucratic structure and, on the other hand, a world people's assembly of 'inter-populism' directly representing a coalition of anti-bureaucratic, minority and poor people's groups in rich countries with anti-capitalist, anti-imperialist groups in poor countries. See R. St J. Macdonald, G. Morris, D. Johnson, 'International Law and Society in the Year 2000', *Canadian Bar Review*, Vol. LI, No. 2, May 1973, p. 316–32.

5 Quantitative approaches to the study of international organizations

Mircea Malitza

The origin of quantitative approaches to the study of international relations

The theory of international relations went through the phase of international law early in the century, that of diplomatic history in the inter-war period, behaviourism in the 1950s, when it assimilated a great number of results from psychology and sociology, and is now in the fourth phase, that of 'the rise of analytic and quantitative research concepts, models and methods'.[1]

If we accept schematization, which must be completed with the parallel school of dialectical and historical materialism and the powerful trend of economism, we find that the fourth phase is now in full swing, and that the threshold at which we now stand has several distinctive features: (a) it shows a clear preference for deduction and a renunciation of 'the fallacy of puristic induction', thus exerting strong impulses towards logic formalization and general concepts; (b) it is exerting, along with other social science disciplines, the strongest pressure on modern mathematics, playing the same role of stimulation as did mechanics in the nineteenth century and physics in the first half of the twentieth; (c) experimentation with mathematical models in isolation from the other social science disciplines is inefficient and costly, and consumes much time and energy; (d) it does not eliminate or replace the traditional disciplines such as law,

MIRCEA MALITZA, a former Romanian Minister of Education, is now a Professor at the University of Bucharest, in charge of the Laboratory of Mathematical Theory of Systems. He has undertaken missions to the United Nations, Unesco, UNCTAD and disarmament conferences, and has published widely, including an article on mathematical approaches to the study of international relations and international organizations.

history and sociology; (e) it has an immediate and attractive outlet for action, due to the inoperative nature of existing methods and the urgency of global problems. It is essential for any discipline to achieve consensus on its methodologies, without prejudice to the viewpoints and paradigms of the schools of thought which use them. Just as technology requires a common matrix and industrial co-operation implies unanimously accepted units of measurement, scientific research stands in need of methods with sufficient guarantees, which researchers in various countries can use in their effort to clarify problems and find solutions.

The idea of using mathematics in the study of international relations is a current phenomenon within a more comprehensive trend. The biologist, the aesthetician, the political scientist, the sociologist and even the musicologist, currently applying mathematics in his discipline can quote names of precursors who tried, over the centuries, to do the same thing. Yet it is not so much the gradual maturation of such individual attempts but the general use of mathematics in every discipline of the sciences of society and man, which has yielded results.[2] But prior to this, one thing was absolutely necessary: the evolution of mathematics itself. The reluctance of many authors to apply mathematics in the social sciences is not groundless; but this applies to classical mathematics, tailored specifically to the requirements of the physical and mechanical sciences. Such mathematics are built on the concept of quantity, whereas the new mathematics of structures is based on extending the measurements to such phenomena as centralization, hierarchy, order, organization, affinities, values or decisions. Two of the most significant extensions of measurement have taken place during the past three decades: Shanon's definition of the unit of information and the elaboration of the concept of 'utility', the key which opened to mathematics the closed gate of values. That is why researchers in international relations, as well as biologists, sociologists or aestheticians are no longer prevented by philosophical barriers from using a mathematical methodology. To the traditional objection pointing to the qualitative difference between social phenomena and the physical world, mathematicians are now serenely replying that the new mathematics, too, are qualitatively different from the one applied to physical and mechanical phenomena.

The massive use of computers increased the application of mathematical methods. The computer enhanced confidence in operating with numerous variables. This is all the more important since international phenomena have always been characterized by a high degree of complexity.[3]

While these circumstances are valid for all disciplines of the social sciences, there are at least two specific elements encouraging students of international relations to resort to mathematical tools. Besides being complex, the problems under scrutiny are also urgent and grave. The rapidity and scale of the changes occurring in the world, the arms drive, the anticipated dramatic consequences of confrontations, the difficulty of managing and extinguishing local conflicts, and the alarm signals coming from ecologists are so many sources of pressure on the theory and practice of international relations. Doubts have emerged as to the ability of intuitive reasoning to cope with such problems. Is it advisable to entrust their solution exclusively to common sense, inspiration and pragmatic methods, which have so often failed? And even if the mathematical instrument is not a panacea, what is wrong with applying it to the study of international affairs?

This argument, which has become increasingly accepted in recent years, is reinforced by the ever larger number of global problems on the international agenda. In addition to peace, security and co-operation—the list of universal problems which require joint efforts of the international community has increased considerably. The United Nations has been holding a succession of world congresses on such issues as food, population, energy, resources, the oceans, outer space, development, science tehnology, urbanization and the environment, and soon the priorities will include such themes as the brain, the cell, genetics, the computer, communications and others, the impact of which on human societies will become overriding.

The applicability
of mathematical approaches

The description of and research on international phenomena cannot be properly conducted without the massive use of statistics, and various data. Today no political reasoning can overlook the basic data concerning States and societies, and no situation can be presented without a quantitative description.[4] But the accuracy of the existing data is not satisfactory, nor are their comparability and relevance. Although a valuable statistical survey of the conflicts of the last hundred and fifty years has been undertaken, many characteristic elements of current international life are not considered: the number of bilateral agreements, of meetings at various levels and of negotiations in various fields, the number of disputes settled non-jurisdictionally, the phenomena of co-operation, etc. Everybody agrees that the data are useful in themselves, but mathematics does not stop there. It can provide models of basic processes of international life, helping us better to understand decision-making, conflicts, negotiations, agreements and their observance, the stability of international institutions, innovations, forecasting. At this point opinions differ. Some authors emphasize the contribution of the mathematical instrument to the knowledge and explanation of international phenomena, stopping at the frontier of action and operations. The discretion and modesty with which mathematicians formulate the impact of their methodology on international relations, giving rise to no unfounded hopes, should be noted.

On the other hand, mathematical models lead to an enlargement of the 'conceptual repertory', the building of 'intellectual capital', with 'rich dividends in other investigations'. Thus, the main pay-off is conceptual rather than pragmatic.[5] Similarly, or in the case for instance of the various models of the arms drive,[6] one cannot expect a mathematical model to tell how to end this drive, but the insight the mathematical model gives will greatly help negotiators and decision-makers to grasp certain aspects which may escape the non-mathematical reasoning.

The clarifying and maieutic role of mathematics does not exhaust its potential contributions. We must expect its operational role to be enhanced, with obvious advantages for decision-making and action. One example is supplied by negotiations. It is difficult to find a more complex phenomenon. Because of the imponderables and random elements it involves, negotiation has long been considered as an art. Suppose, however, that each side, before meeting at the negotiation table, sums up its position in a list of its strategies and of the moves it expects from the other side. This is a logical model. The sides could act differently, each of them starting a separate political game in which the partner's role was conventionally given to someone specially trained for the purpose. This is a simulation—the diplomatic equivalent of military manoeuvres and exercises.[7] Lastly, the various strategies and their outcomes could be represented in matrix form, as in the theory of non-zero-sum games, which are, for the time being, the best way of representing a negotiation process. This is a mathematical model.

An explored field: voting at the United Nations

To understand better what the quantitative approach to the study of international organizations actually is we shall examine research into nominal voting at the United Nations. Mathematicians will lend a helping hand wherever a numerical approach is possible. International organizations with a finite membership, which periodically take open votes on a set of basic issues, provide an ideal field for quantitative studies. What are the voting patterns and how do countries line up in such cases? Alker and Russett took four sessions of the United Nations General Assembly and studied the nominal votes in all the commissions, using factor analysis to delimit various groups of voters (Alker and Russett, 1965). Other studies deal in the same way with only Plenary Session voting, but over longer periods of eighteen sessions (Newcombe, Ross and Newcombe, 1970). The type of conclusion drawn by such studies is the identification of a pattern, in this case a tendency towards bipolarization and the failure—at the time—of the attempts by other regions to form stable independent groupings.

The next step was an attempt to account for the vote and confrontations in the General Assembly not by means of caucusing group variables, but by 'environmental variables' describing basic political, economic and social factors of each country (e.g. GNP, defence expenditures, college enrolment) or interactions (regional involvement, trade, etc.). This effort began with an attempt to define 'predictors', i.e. variables significantly predictive of a country's behaviour in voting matters. This led to exploring the relationship of voting patterns with national attribute data also through correlational techniques. Using no fewer than seventy-seven national attributes, Vincent (1971) pointed out the particular relevance of economic growth, even in a period marked by political problems and affiliations. While factor analysis as applied to groupings treated countries as variables and nominal votes as observations, the explanatory and predictive type studies examine the correlations between the countries' attributes and their behaviour as shown by voting.

Other studies have shown that, in order to hold an elective position in the United Nations system, legislative indicators (personnel resources for the organization, committee involvement, etc.) are more significant than environmental interactions or attributes. This shows that the character of the General Assembly is that of a quasi-legislative system (Volgy and Quistgaard, 1974).

Let us pause to examine some of the methods often resorted to in this type of study: multiple correlation, regression analysis, factor analysis. One can measure the amplitude of variations of the true values of a chosen variable from those expected: the average squared misestimate is called variance. If we wish to improve the estimation we take a new variable into account. If the correlation is perfect (1.00) we say that 100 per cent of the variance is explained, which seldom happens. To improve the estimate we add more variables: this is multiple correlation analysis. Another way to proceed is to weigh the relative importance of an independent variable, by asking what change in the dependent variable is produced by a change in a unit of the first one. This is the purpose of multiple regression analysis. In explaining a phenomenon, we may use a great number of variables, among which some are 'more equal than others'. In order to select the essential ones, we use factor analysis, which allows us to measure the intercorrelations among groups and to identify those which are highly correlated with some factors, thus 'loading' them.

These statistical methods are commonly applied to the social and political sciences and especially to the study of national legislative bodies. Although they are full of pitfalls and require many significance tests, they already constitute a battery of well-established procedures.

Studies on voting have been conducted to answer some of the following questions: Who votes with whom, how are the voters grouped and on which subjects, what are the most important problems, whose vote is the most effective? What are the results of the votes? They have also been concerned with delegates' interactions, attitudes and beliefs, the development of the system of international organizations, and with such judicial processes as ratifications and elections. Pondering on this impressive literature we may ask: What purpose has it served and how has it improved the quality of political science studies? What light has it shed on the development of international organizations or the behaviour of States within such organizations?

The goal of any quantitative method is to lend more accuracy to qualitative statements, observations or findings, precisely in order to improve the accuracy and refinement of the methods of political science investigation. Here, for instance, is a proposition, the truth of which can be ascertained even without quantitative studies: 'groups with a high degree of cohesion tend towards a minority position, while groups with a lower degree of cohesion tend to vote with the majority' (Hovet 1960).

Mathematics is called upon primarily to confirm an intuition, to justify and explain it. But it goes beyond this. We know that one problem was more important than another at a particular session, but qualitative observation cannot tell us how much more important it was, nor what weight it had. This must be determined by quantitative means. Looking at the unrotated factor scores on the East–West and North–South conflicts in a series of United Nations General Assemblies (Alker, 1969), one visualizes a new North–South conflict cutting across the old East–West issues, as perceived earlier by certain political writers (Bloomfield, 1960). This can tell us whether the weight of an issue was maintained or not at subsequent sessions, whether it will imperceptibly increase or decrease over time.

At this point, the great ambition of quantitative studies is to uncover non-intuitive truths. According to certain contemporary authors, many mechanisms of the political process are not intuitive, and their manifestations must be detected by means of special analyses of a mathematical (quantitative or structural) type. In the case under discussion a simple analysis cannot reveal whether the number of voting groups in the General

Assembly will increase over time or not. The 'diversification' hypothesis put forward in some works was invalidated by a quantitative study (Russett, 1967).

But quantitative studies cannot be legitimized solely by such refinement of methods and by cognitive and explanatory contributions. Their actual accreditation in political studies may ultimately come about only as a result of their operational and predictive performance. To date, we must admit that, operationally speaking, few quantitative studies on international organizations have served as arguments in decision-making or in the planning of measures or actions.

In the field of forecasting, despite some insufficiently processed signals, such studies failed to foresee the mutations that occurred in the international bodies, notably in 1974, owing to the emergence of a structural reform trend in connection with the new international economic order. The emergence of this overriding issue has changed the pattern of voting in the political field as well, bringing about a different polarization from the one noted in previous studies, hastening the decolonization process and altering positions on some crises long maintained on the agenda of the General Assembly (the Middle East, southern Africa).

Future directions

Is this an essential limitation of quantitative studies, or does it merely arise from difficulties attending any fresh venture? Personally, I think the latter assumption holds true. Furthermore, starting from the example of vote analysis and of those tendencies that the method failed to identify, single out and turn to account, we can learn a good deal about the orientation and management of research and the paths which ought to be explored in order to make quantitative studies on international organizations more relevant.

It will be seen that most quantitative studies focused on situations and issues that readily provided researchers with numerical data. The most attractive among these was the list of nominal votes (roll-call) which could be obtained from international organizations. The roll-call continues to be a major source, the more so as it is now published with the United Nations resolutions, following the introduction of automatic voting systems in the Plenary Session and the Committees of the General Assembly. This circumstance has lured researchers away from the quantitative study of attitudes, cohesion and stand-taking, e.g. in the economic field. There are few roll-call votes in the Second Committee, the top of the list being held by the Plenary Session, the First Committee (political) and the

Third Committee (social). We may say that, had a quantitative investigation—based on means used in the political field—been made of the work of the Second Committee (economic) and of the four conferences on trade unit development such as UNCTAD I (Geneva, 1964), UNCTAD II (New Delhi, 1968), UNCTAD III (Santiago, 1972) and UNCTAD IV (Nairobi, 1976), it would have been easier to detect the process of clarification, polarization, and the emergence of a new cohesion among the developing nations, as well as the increased urgency of the problems posed by relations between the countries producing raw materials and those exporting manufactured goods. We could then understand that the new international economic order, far from being a sudden intrusion on the scene, related by many authors solely to certain contingencies (raw materials, energy, oil), is in fact the logical conclusion of a process that has long been taking place in the international organizations, where it could not only be observed, but also dealt with numerically.

Of late we notice a certain movement away from easy sources of facts and data, and the organization of basic information into systematic bodies, into data banks. We may mention, for instance, Chadwick F. Alger's inventory of existing data on intergovernmental organizations (IGOs) and non-governmental organizations (NGOs). The inventory includes over fifty data sets, which marks an improvement in the study sources available so far (Azar and Ben-Dack, 1975).

Aggregate data for countries are available from United Nations sources as well from several works (Banks and Textor, 1963; Deutsch, 1960; Russett et al., 1964; Taylor, 1972). 'In the aftermath of the behavioural decade, the unsatisfied hunger now beginning is for data, for hard materials to be handled, ordered and analyzed' (McClelland, 1972). But as Burton (1974) remarks, many of the existing bodies of data are gathered for purposes other than the study of the international system and a special effort must be directed towards the acquisition of relevant and unbiased data, as required by a new global approach, and in the light of an updated theoretical outlook.

Improving the methods

In Alger's (1970) survey of literature on international organization, using quantitative methods (published in fourteen major periodicals during the decade 1960-69), forty-three out of sixty-six studies used simple statistical analysis (percentages, averages, ranks, indices), fifteen used varied statistics, and only eight used factor analysis, multiple correlation and regression. This shows that, so far, the use of quantitative methods in the field of international organizations has been dominated by simple data-processing procedures, without recourse to the more refined methodology worked out in other branches of modern political science. Game theory, coalition theory, cluster analysis, stochastic processes and learning theory, the theory of decision-making in conditions of uncertainty, and others are missing. These methods have been refined in recent years through the advances made by the use of mathematical tools in the biological and social sciences, and even in the study of international relations. They represent a clear-cut transition from measuring to modelling.

There is a regrettable but common confusion between the mathematical approach and the quantitative approach, considering the latter as but one modality of the former. Mathematics as a science of structure finds its true vocation in the study of relations, invariance and regularities that may result from data analysis. We now possess models which use quantities, such as logical and topological ones, and others which use graphs or the concepts of mathematical linguistics.

Full recourse has not yet been had to the measurement of interaction by entropy, which can reveal a deeper cohesion than that shown by statistical similitudes and correlations. The type of research considered here can only benefit by the sustained effort to systematize the social indicators.

The systems approach has now given rise to a genuine transfer of mathematical methods from one domain to another, based on the isomorphism of laws in different fields, whose corollary is the possibility of using a model for realities other than those for which it was originally designed.

Connection with other international phenomena

The drive for data and method improvement reflects a fresh approach which is also evident in the linking of phenomena operative in international organizations with other political phenomena. Up to now, most quantitative (and, generally, mathematical) studies have dealt with the interactions of States and the major problems in international affairs for the purpose of analysing conflicts; with the armaments race and arms control; with periods of crisis, equilibrium conditions, and the causes of equilibrium disruption.

Many researchers have emphasized that mathematics has served more frequently to investigate conflict than co-operation, this predilection being in part accounted for by the interest taken in military applications of conflict study. But knowledge of the mechanisms of peace and, primarily, of co-operation, also needs mathematical research. Two examples can be given which are more extensively studied outside international organizations, although they also find a vast field of application within such bodies. They are negotiations and coalitions. These two areas have been subjected to more evolved mathematical tools, upon which they have been exerting a challenging influence destined to improve and refine them. The specific nature of international organizations is more and more insistently being stressed today, as a locus for permanent negotiations and as a means of reconciliation. Coalition theory has been applied more often to inter-party alliances and to military alliances (Holsti et al., 1973) than to group formation within international organizations, where the external criterion of expression by voting has overshadowed the internal mechanism of coalition formation. It is to be expected that the progress made in these areas and the mathematical instruments designed for dealing with them will be more extensively used in the years ahead in studies on international organizations.

Emergence of global problems

Although quantitative studies have also dealt with organizations other than the United Nations, such studies are few. They are concerned with the analysis of the elaboration of legislation and conventions in the International Labour Organisation (Dahl, 1968), and the functioning of the International Court of Justice (Coplin, 1968), as well as with relations with non-governmental organizations at the United Nations Conference on the Human Environment held at Stockholm in 1972 (Thomson, 1974) and the debates on the law of the sea (Friedheim and Kadane, 1970). The conflicts examined by the United Nations and ways to improve the collective security system have been dealt with in several quantitative studies (Haas, 1968, 1970).

An element of novelty which in recent years has increased the number of phenomena that can be submitted to quantitative treatment within international organizations is introduced by the series of world conferences on such urgent and vital world problems as natural resources, energy, development, population, food, the environment, the oceans and, prospectively, science and technology. There is no dossier of a global-type problem which does not include quantitative relations, figures, data and forecasts, expressed in terms of short-range and long-range trends. In this case, mathematics is present in the statistical analysis of various series of data, in the attempts at modelling and assessing situations and the principal conflicting tendencies. The methods are borrowed from classical statistics, but also from econometrics, a field where the more advanced methods are used on a larger scale than in behaviouristic research.

In all these conferences stress has been laid on the need for systems analysis, on the interdependence and interaction of factors, on the need to work out general views—tasks with which mere intuition and the classical approach can no longer cope. It is to be expected that this trend will be maintained and even developed over the next five years.

The use of quantitative methods in international organizations

During the 1960s, international bodies, even those with study centres and the means to finance research, were not much interested in quantitative studies. Now the situation has changed to some extent. First, all the international organizations have set up computation centres and data archives, and have undertaken data processing for their own use. They are sponsoring quantitative research projects and are enhancing co-operation in this direction with non-governmental scientific bodies.

International intergovernmental organizations have increased their contacts with academic research centres using data collected from their own activities, and they have begun to bring up subjects of practical interest and to support such researches. This helps to remove a paradoxical shortcoming: it was difficult to account for the absence of an R&D component from the programmes of large organizations, which in fact have policies for enhancing the role of science in the operation of other institutions and in solving problems. International organizations, especially non-governmental ones, which concerned themselves with certain reforms motivated by questions of a budgetary and administrative nature, are now inclined to undertake more detailed studies in order to revise their structures and adapt them to realities. There is now a whole methodology for analysing the operation of productive or administrative institutions with a view to enhancing their efficiency. Unfortunately, such methods have not been fully employed in matters concerning the reorganization of United Nations economic activities, for instance those of the United Nations Development Programme, although an assessment of structures has included many quantitative aspects. Operational research today can use an advanced apparatus, refined and tested in improving the efficiency of management. In the case of international organizations there is no doubt some difficulty in identifying input and output situations. The basic questions, however, are the same as those in any other information-processing system. The traditional ones are: for input—What? From where? How much? When? For transformation—How? Who? How long? When? For output—What? Whither? How much? When? Perhaps never before have international organizations been confronted, as they are now, with the need to carry out a radical improvement in their structures and procedures, in order to become more efficient and increase their contribution to the solving of fundamental social problems.

The quantitative study of the processes occurring in the day-to-day running of operations, the need for forecasting and for an adjustment to new situations, all justify the establishment, within the Secretariat of each international institution, of a strong computation centre with programmes and models and the most complete data archives. If the introduction of a data-processing and computation component has proved profitable to relatively small enterprises or institutions, the greater its benefits in giant institutions employing tens of thousands of people grappling with increasingly complex tasks and accused daily of red tape and inefficiency. Even if good results are achieved (e.g. averting conflicts, developing a more responsible international consciousness, or tackling essential problems) international organizations still have to make a convincing contribution, in keeping with the predominantly numerical style of our times.

Conclusions

We have so far examined four factors: data, methods, connections with other international policy researches, and the use of quantitative methods by international bodies, to infer from the shortcomings of the past ten or twelve years the prospects for greater relevance and consistency in the field under consideration. At this point of the discussion let us also present an argument to the contrary.

In works by many authors of international studies, the idea has been established that quantitative studies are necessarily technical and non-political in character. Since they are independent of any consideration of values, these methods could be assimilated to the positivist school of thought. Yet our times are characterized by a decline of tendential methods and the rise of normative ones, the latter being value-loaded. According to some authors, the behaviourist revolution is exhausted, and along with it the monotonous succession of technical refinements, devised for analysing all too common phenomena, where results are often tautological, is also beginning to fall into disuse. The intensification of political debate in the world is allegedly reducing the significance of quantitative studies, which are better suited to stable and calmer periods.

Is all this true? Indeed, the arena of international organizations, characterized by a rapid rate of change, is dominated by the demand for a new international economic order, for building a more equitable system of relations, capable of ensuring progress for all in a climate of justice and dignity, for solving such basic global problems as security and disarmament, development and the environment, and for dealing with basic questions in the economic and social field.

This *problématique* is not inimical to quantitative methods; on the contrary, it presupposes the fullest mobilization of such methods. Let us consider, for instance, the question of human needs underlying a new international economic order. Can one devise a better distribution of resources according to human needs without measuring the minimum thresholds in regard to food, water, space and the quality of the environment? There is no issue more stimulating to the progress of mathematics than that of the quality of life, which calls for new mathematical indicators, methods, and even concepts. While everybody agrees that economic problems require quantitative methods, the non-economic factors involved in discussing the new economic order can equally be subjected to mathematical treatment. If we consider the non-economic factors cited in this connection (Laszlo, 1975), the mathematical implications are almost immediate: natural factors (geographic and climatic conditions, territory, natural resources), population factors (distribution of population, migration, growth), ideological-political factors (societal structures, principles of organization). The new international economic order essentially aims to re-design a system, an ambition with obvious computational implications that go beyond the sphere of descriptive and verbal approaches.

A dominant feature of present-day culture is manifest in international organizations: the propensity to action. Repeatedly, the community of engineers, technicians and researchers employed in producing material goods or concerned with innovation has noticed the distance separating it from the community of political researchers, a distance sometimes tantamount to the transition from calculation to words. That is why, without overestimating the contribution of methods still in their early stages, we have every reason to anticipate their increased importance especially if the variety of possible applications is taken into account. What Karl Deutsch called the 'fourth wave' ('the rise of analytic and quantitative research concepts, models, and methods, a movement towards the comparative study of quantitative data and the better use of some of the potentialities of electronic computation') is not yet exhausted. Like any new method or field of inquiry quantitative methods are making headway amid rather general scepticism and under the not-very-encouraging scrutiny of the traditional methodology. Many people will recall Goethe's words regarding the difficulties of communication between various branches of research: 'Mathematicians are a kind of Frenchman, you talk to them, they turn it into their own tongue, and what come out is altogether different.' Precisely in order to facilitate communication, contacts between researchers and diplomats, between theoreticians and practitioners should be more lively. In particular, it would be very useful to all those working in multi-lateral diplomacy to have readable introductions to the methods of statistical data processing and mathematical model building (fields in which gifted scholars like A. Rapoport have demonstrated the possibility of communicating with the general public), and a larger number of elementary textbooks on quantitative methods, such as have been produced for researchers in biology, sociology, linguistics, archaeology and history. Why should the day be so far off when diplomats attending conferences will carry in their attaché-cases, along with documents, a minicomputer to use in calculating simple correlations, comparing several indicators or options, and drawing up the scheme of a political decision? After all, decision-making is opting, and opting is comparing. A comparison is a mathematical relation, just as addition and multiplication are operations. The greatest contribution towards extending measurement to non-physical phenomena has been the measuring of information, by cybernetics, and that of utility in economics and games. If the mathematics of yesterday was not in a position to deal in its own language with certain kinds of phenomena of particular complexity and dynamism, it does not follow that that of today, and especially the mathematics of tomorrow, cannot do this.

Discovering the mathematical mechanisms of our logical reasoning can only prompt us to improve the latter through the former; to the surprise of many, they will then discover, like Molière's character, that they have been speaking mathematically without knowing it.

Notes

1. Harvey Starr, 'The Quantitative International Relations Scholar as Surfer', *Journal of Conflict Resolution*, Vol. 18, No. 2, June 1974.
2. For the use of mathematical methods in contemporary sociology and political sciences, see Johan Galtung, *Theory and Methods of Social Research*, London, Allen & Unwin, 1967, 534 p.; Raymond Boudon, *L'Analyse Mathématique des Faits Sociaux*, Paris, Plon, 1967, 462 p.; F. Chazel, R. Boudon and P. Lazars-

feld (eds.), *L'Analyse des Processus Sociaux*, Paris, Mouton, 1970, 413 p.; *Sotiologhia i Matematika*, Novosibirsk, 1970, 270 p.; Thomas J. Fararo, *Mathematical Sociology*, John Wiley 1973; Karl W. Deutsch, 'Quantitative Approaches to Political Analysis : Some Past Trends and Future Prospects', in H. R. Alker, K. W. Deutsch and J. H. Stoetzel (eds.), *Mathematical Approaches to Politics*, p. 1-62, Elsevier, 1973; Hayward Alker, Jr., *Mathematics and Politics*, Macmillan, 1965, 152 p.; Jacques Attali, *Analyse Economique de la Vie Politique*, Paris, Presses Universitaires de France, 1972, 219 p.

3. Davis Bobrow and Judah Schwartz, *Computers and the Policy Making Community: Applications to International Relations*, Englewood Cliffs, N.J., 1968.

4. Bruce Russett, H. Alker, K. W. Deutsch and H. Lasswell, *World Handbook of Political and Social Indicators*, Yale University Press, 1964, 374 p.; J. David Singer (ed.), *Quantitative International Politics*; *Insights and Evidence*, New York, 1968, 394 p.; J. D. Singer and Melvin Small, *The Wages of War 1816–1965. A Statistical Handbook*, John Wiley, 1972, 420 p.; Bruce Russett (ed.), *Peace, War and Numbers*, Yale University Press, 1972, 352 p.; V. A. Lefevr, *Konflictuiuscie strukturi*. Moscow, Izd. Vissaia Scola, 1967; I. P. Singh, *Diplommetry*. Bombay, 1970; D. J. Bartholomew and E. E. Bassett, *Let's Look at the Figures*, Penguin Books, 1971; John V. Gillespie and Betty Nesold (eds), *Macro-Quantitative Analysis*, Beverly Hills, Sage, 1971; R. J. Rummel, *The Dimensions of Nations*, Beverly Hills, Sage, 1972.

5. Anatol Rapoport, 'The Uses of Mathematical Isomorphism in General System Theory', in George Klir (ed.), *Trends in General Systems Theory*, London, 1972.

6. Lewis Richardson, *Arms and Insecurity*, Pittsburgh, Pa., 1960; Paul Smoker, *The Arms Race : A Wave Model*, 1966 (Peace Research Society Papers, 4); Urs Luterbacher, *Dimensions Historiques de Modèles Dynamiques de Conflit*, Geneva, 1974, T. L. Saaty, *Mathematical Models of Arms Control, and Disarmament*, New York, Wiley, 1968.

7. Paul Smoker, *International Relations Simulations. A Summary* in *Mathematical Approaches to Politics*, p. 417–64; Lincoln Bloomfield and Barton Whaley, *The Political-Military Exercice*, p. 854-70 (Orbis VIII, 4); Harold Guetzkow, *Some Uses of Mathematics in Simulation of International Relations* in *Mathematical Applications in Political Science*, p. 21–40, Dallas, Arnold Found.

References

ALGER, C. F. 1970a. *Decision-Making in Public Bodies of International Organizations (ILO, WHO, WMO, UN).* (A Preliminary Research Report. Eighth World Congress, International Political Science Association, Munich, September 1970.)

——. 1970b. Methodological Innovation in Research on Intertional Organizations. In : James A. Robinson (ed.), *Political Science Annual*, Vol. 2. Indianapolis, Bobbs-Merrill.

——. 1970c. Research on Research : A Decade of Quantitative and Field Research on International Organizations. *International Organization*, Vol. 24, p. 414–50.

——. 1971. *A Partial Inventory of Data on International Organization.* (Prepared for the meetings of the International Studies Association, San Juan, Puerto Rico, March.)

ALKER, Hayward R., Jr; RUSSETT, Bruce M. 1965. *World Politics in the General Assembly.* New Haven, Conn., Yale University Press.

——. 1969. Supranationalism in the United Nations. In : James N. Rosenau (ed.), *International Politics and Foreign Policy A Reader in Research and Theory.* 2nd ed., rev. New York, Free Press.

AZAR, E.; JOSEPH, D. B.-O., (eds.). 1975. *Theory and Practice of Events Research.* Introduction by Philip M. Burgess. New York, Gordon & Breach. 304 p.

BANKS, S. A.; TEXTOR, R. B. 1963. *A Cross-Polity Survey*, Cambridge, Mass., M.I.T. Press.

BLOOMFIELD, L. 1960. *The United Nations and United States Foreign Policy.* Boston.

BURTON, J. 1974. In: *The Study of World Society: A London Perspective.* Pittsburgh University, International Studies Association, p. 92.

COPLIN, W. D. 1968. The World Court in the International Bargaining Process. In: Robert W. Gregg and Michael Barkun (eds.), *The United Nations System and its Functions: Selected Readings.* Princeton, Van Nostrand.

DAHL, Karl Nandrup. 1968. The Role of ILO Standards in the Global Integration Process. *Journal of Peace Research*, No. 4, p. 309–51.

DEUTSCH, K. W. 1960. Towards an Inventory of Basic Trends and Patterns. In: Comparative and International Politics. *Am. Pol. Sc. Review*, Vol. 54, March, p. 34–57.

FRIEDHEIM, R. L.; KADANE, J. B. 1970. Quantitative Content Analyses of the United Nations Seabed Debate. *International Organizations*, Vol. 24, p. 479–502.

GALTUNG, J. 1970. Diachronic Correlation. Process Analysis and Causal Analysis. *Quality and Quantity*, No. 4, p. 55–94.

——. 1975. Entropy and the General Theory of Peace. *Essays in Peace Research*, Vol. I, p. 47–75. Copenhagen, Chr. Eglers.

HAAS, E. B. 1968. *Collective Security and the Future International System.* Denver, University of Denver. (Monograph No. 1.)

——. 1970. *The Web of Interdependence: The United States and International Organizations.* Englewood Cliffs, N.J., Prentice-Hall.

HOLSTI, O. R.; HOPMANN, P. T.; SULLIVAN, J. D. 1973. *Unity and Disintegration in International Alliances: Comparative Studies.* New York, Wiley-Interscience.

HOVET, T., Jr. 1960. *Bloc Politics in the United Nations.* Cambridge, Mass., Harvard University Press.

LASZLO, E. 1975. A Proposal for Future-Oriented Research at the United Nations. *Planning Review,* Vol. 3, No. 3, May.

MALITZA, M. 1975. Mathematical Approaches in International Relations. *International Social Science Journal,* Vol. XXVII, No. 3, p. 459–67.

MCCLELLAND, C. A. 1972. On the Fourth Wave: Past and Future on the Study of International Systems. In: James Rosenau, Vincent Davis and Maurice East (eds.), *The Analysis of International Politics,* p. 15–40. New York, The Free Press.

NEWCOMBE, H.; ROSS, M.; NEWCOMBE, A. G. 1970. UN Voting Patterns. *International Organization,* Vol. 24, No. 1, Winter, p. 100–21.

RUSSETT, B. M. 1967. *International Regions and the International System: A Study in Political Ecology.* Chicago, Ill., Rand McNally.

RUSSETT, B. M.; ALKER, H.; DEUTSCH, K. W.; LASSWELL, H. 1964. *World Handbook of Political and Social Indicators.* New Haven. Conn., Yale University Press.

TAYLOR, C. L. 1972. *World Handbook of Political and Social Indicators.* New Haven, Conn., Yale University Press, 2nd. ed.

THOMPSON, F. A. 1974. Transnational Political Interests and the Global Environment. *International Organization,* Vol. 28, No. 1, p. 31–60.

VINCENT, J. E. 1971. Predicting Voting Patterns in the General Assembly, *The American Political Science Review,* Vol. 65, No. 2, June, p. 471–98.

VOLGY, T. J.; QUISTGAARD, J. E. 1974a. Correlates of Organizational Rewards in the UN: An Analysis of Environmental and Legislative Variables. *International Organization,* Vol. 28, No. 2, Spring, p. 179–205.

——. 1974b. The Impact of Attributes, Interactions and Legislative Characteristics for United Nations Office-holding: An Interregional Analysis. *International Organization,* Vol. 24, p. 179–250.

6 Functionalism and integration as approaches to international organization

Chadwick F. Alger

Integration and functionalism are labels that cover a great array of research activity in which these terms are defined in a variety of ways. In order to provide an introductory orientation here, they can be defined rather simply. International integration is concerned with the process whereby decisions formerly made by officials of separate nation-States come to be made by officials at a new centre (international organization). International functionalism is concerned with the process whereby specific activities (functions) come to be performed by international organizations rather than by separate nation-State authorities. These areas of inquiry are of critical importance to an increasing number of scholars, practitioners and the general public, as a diversity of issues—such as food, energy, ecology, resources, employment, and inflation—become more obviously trans-national in scope. Their importance is heightened by the fact that concern for these issues, along with projections and predictions into the future, is not matched by concern for the international organizations that are involved and will be required for solutions to problems.

In the last thirty years the number of international organizations has grown at a geometric rate which is now quite familiar, as practitioners have found transnational collaboration an increasing necessity. Scholarship has not generally been very helpful in pointing out the possible consequences of changes in the structure of international systems this activity has

CHADWICK F. ALGER is Professor of Political Science and Public Policy and Director of Programme in Transnational Intellectual Co-operation, Mershon Center, Ohio State University. His research on international organizations has primarily focused on communication, socialization and decision-making processes in the United Nations. He is at present investigating the links between cities and global systems to enable the public to participate more self-consciously and directly in foreign policy-making in national and international organizations.

produced. Indeed, scholarship has not even provided good descriptive accounts of the changing global structures created by this organizational growth. The knowledge gap this has created is striking in the present debates and discussions of relations among the diversity of organizations which comprise the United Nations system. Much of this discussion seems to be guided by a preference for organizational neatness and a preference for hierarchical organization. Is neatness preferred because it produces better results or because we cannot understand complex organizational systems? Is hierarchy preferred because it produces better results, or because we feel more comfortable with it—perhaps by analogy with the presumed organization of nation-States? Research on integration and functionalism should offer enlightenment on the actual and potential impacts of growth in organizations which transcend national boundaries and on the consequences of patterns of linkage between these organizations.

An overview assessment

In my judgement those working under the functionalism and integration labels have made more significant contributions than any others over the past thirty years. This judgement arises out of a perspective through which I view both the nation-State system and the relationship of international-relations scholarship to that system. This perspective views the nation-State system as we know it as *one* historic form of organization for *some* of the activities of humankind. A diversity of enterprises linked people across great distances before the emergence of the nation-State system—in science, religion, ethnic ties, commerce, etc. These processes continued after the creation of the nation-State system and they will continue after it is replaced. Nation-States have had profound impacts on these processes, often nationalizing subsystems or using them for their own ends. But nation-States have also been profoundly affected by transnational processes they have been unable or unwilling to control. Thus the ever-changing organization of humankind can be viewed as a dialogue between territorial and functional forms of organization.

A great shortcoming of international-relations scholarship in the past thirty years has been its overemphasis on nation-States and its neglect of evolving functional activity which overlaps nation-States. Why? An answer would require systematic inquiry, but I can offer several plausible hunches. First, this scholarly field has been dominated by people who have personally experienced wars between nation-States, living in societies in which they have had cataclysmic effects. The capacity of nation-States to produce and employ weapons of mass destruction has much to do with the widespread assumption—never to my knowledge empirically tested—that nation-States (i.e. national governments) are the most important actors with respect to relations among large human aggregates. Second, national boundaries are easily represented on maps that have been prominently displayed on schoolroom walls, and these maps are impregnated in the mind's eye of all of us. We have not had available vivid pictures of the functional overlaps. Third, as a result of these kinds of factors it became customary to aggregate a great deal of information in terms of nation-State units in an ever-spiralling self-fulfilling prophecy. Particularly with the advent of data banks, these sometimes became 'watertight compartments'. A great variety of data was classified in terms of nation-State units, with little concern for the appropriateness of the boxes into which the data were deposited. For example, it no longer mattered which individuals or groups in Columbus, Ohio, were linked to which individuals or groups in Oslo. This datum was categorized and manipulated by the computer as a transaction between the United States and Norway, and probably became part of a per capita figure on transactions between the United States and Norway. This spiralling, self-fulfilling prophecy was also encouraged by the resources wealthy national governments have been able to put into research, which has naturally focused prominently on nation-States (i.e. national governments).

Factors such as these have for the most part imprisoned international-relations scholars, both conceptually and perceptually, in the nation-State system as they believe it to exist at present. Nevertheless, since this system replaced earlier ways of organizing large human aggregates, it must be presumed that it will, in turn, be replaced. A critical concern is to ensure that the presently evolving new system will provide a milieu more hospitable for human life than what we now call the nation-State system. Thus a critical task for scholars studying relations among large human aggregates is to understand dynamics of change and to provide images of alternative forms toward which the nation-State system is moving, or could be moved. Change is increasingly evident, largely as a result of the impact of new technology on travel and communication. A prominent example is geometric increase in the number of both governmental and non-governmental international organizations.

Generally, those engaged in the study of international relations have not coped with the evolving replacement for the nation-State system nor with specification of where this evolution is leading or could lead. Practitioners are far ahead of scholars as they cross increasingly irrelevant nation-State boundaries in efforts to solve a diversity of problems, and seek out profit and pleasure. Scholars have been slow to perceive and interpret new dynamics in international systems. While they are not inattentive to new issues, they are slow to perceive new actors and often meaninglessly aggregate their activity into nation-State units—as when multinational corporations and participation in non-governmental international organizations are treated as attributes of nation-States.

Scholars working on functionalism and integration have made significant contributions because they have freed themselves from the traditional nation-State paradigm sufficiently to inquire into the dynamics of change and, although with less insight, to perceive alternative futures. Succinctly, relations between large human aggregates can be viewed both in terms of territorial and functional organization, and as an interplay, and even struggle, between the two. By viewing these relations in this way, functionalism and integration are able to obtain analytic leverage on the dynamics of system change.

Functionalism and integration have significantly enriched the study of international organizations along several dimensions. First, they have drawn attention to the national and transnational social contexts out of which international organizations arise, and the relationships between these contexts and specific organizational forms. This is an antidote to tendencies to study charters, constituent bodies and problems of international organizations without probing concern for their social contexts. Second, they have directed attention to processes of organizational growth across time. This overcomes tendencies to neglect the pre-charter development of international organizations and the post-charter processes of growth never adequately reflected in charters. Third, they have placed earlier preoccupations with military forces, both as causes of war and instrumentalities for ensuring peace, in more balanced perspective. This overcomes tendencies in many works on international organizations to give secondary attention to the economic and social causes of war and to overemphasize the possibilities for military (collective security and peace-keeping) solutions to the problems of war. Fourth, they have used regions as laboratories for inquiry. This has made research more manageable and has permitted anticipatory study of organizational phenomena not yet relevant to the globe as a whole. Fifth, they have extended the perspective of inquiry in ways that make it possible to draw on a variety of bodies of social science knowledge that were earlier divorced from international-organization research—socialization, learning, attitudes, organizational behaviour, etc. This has overcome tendencies to treat international organizations as a unique domain, rather than as simply one kind of institution in which human behaviour, with many similarities to that in other types of institutions, is equally found.

Emergence of functionalism and integration

Functionalism and integration developed out of earlier thought, debate and experience with balance of power, collective security and world government as approaches to international peace. The perceived failure of balance of power—based on alliances among national military forces to counter potential aggresssors—led to the development of collective security. In this approach a number of nation-States (i.e. national governments) agree in advance to resist any member of the group who commits aggression. In collective security the form of organization is radically different from balance of power, but the means to be used remain the same—military force. Collective security has had limited success partly because big powers have opted out, largely because of their ability to fend for themselves through unilateral use of the same military power that might have been utilized for the collective security of the entire community. Some have proposed world government as a solution to this problem. But proponents of world government have failed to offer plausible prescriptions on how to reach this goal. Indeed, it would seem that a group of nations which cannot make a collective security system work could not directly advance toward world government either.

Inquiry focused on functionalism and integration has usefully confronted the limitations of these approaches and significantly enriched understanding of processes related to the development of international organizations. David Mitrany provided a major impetus to functional thinking in his *A Working Peace System*, first published in 1943—largely basing his work on insight derived from practical experience. Karl Deutsch spurred a complementary line of effort in his work on integration, with the publication of *Political Community at the International Level* in 1954 and *Political Community in the North Atlantic Area* in 1957. It is very important that Mitrany was able to apply insight bridging the barriers which had developed between research and thinking about national organizations and similar effort focused on international organizations. While Deutsch acquired the raw material for his work from case studies, his efforts exemplify growing efforts to bridge the gulf that had come to separate research and thinking on international organizations from the mainstream of social science.

MITRANY'S APPROACH

As set forth by Mitrany,[1] functionalism is based on assumptions about the causes of war and peace:
1. Social and economic maladjustments are the basic causes of war.
2. Social and economic welfare is the precondition of peace.
It is further assumed that:
3. The nation-State system cannot deal with basic social and economic problems because global society is arbitrarily divided into units based on territory rather than units based on problems to be solved.
This leads to the proposal that:
4. Institutions based on function, not territory, would be appropriate for solving basic social and economic problems.
These assumptions of functionalism represent a radical departure from balance of power, collective security and most world-government thinking, which assumes that military force is required to prevent war. First, they point a way out of the dilemma posed by the possibility that military forces of individual nations available for collective security could also be used for war, and the fear that military forces under the control of a world government could be used for world domination. Second, they question the utility of nation-States and suggest the development of complementary units.

Functionalism also presumes to offer means for overcoming suspicion and distrust which have often prevented the building of peace systems.
5. Functional co-operation can begin with non-political, more technical problems.
6. Co-operative experience gained in one functional area can be transferred to another.
These two assumptions of functionalism have unavoidably stimulated extensive debate and inquiry. The fifth has often provoked a rather fruitless debate on whether there are non-political functions and is perhaps more usefully interpreted as an advocacy for initiating co-operation on least controversial problems. This may seem obvious, but it is an assumption profoundly ignored by collective security which advocates initial collaboration on one of the most controversial functions—use of military force.

The sixth assumption is often referred to as 'spillover' which consists of a complex of social and psychological processes. First, there is the assumption that patterns of co-operation in one function will provide examples that can be duplicated in other sectors. Second, there is the assumption that social and economic functions are not independent (e.g. trade and banking) and that functional co-operation in one will generate a need for co-operation in another. Third, there is the notion that participants in functional co-operation will have experiences to dissipate suspicion and distrust on the part of their conterparts in other nation-States and even develop new loyalties to the new institutions in which they work. It is also expected that this eroding of distrust and new loyalties will spread to people at large who derive benefits from functional institutions.

In contrast to world-government schemes, functionalism rejects grand schemes for world order and their implementation through constitutions and charters. Instead, it is assumed that:

7. Co-operation will extend to more and more functions to the point that a 'web of international activities and agencies' will 'overlay political divisions'. (Mitrany, 1966, p. 10–11).
8. Ultimately these agencies will require co-ordinating bodies, which will eventually require planning agencies, which will eventually evolve into a general authority for overall co-ordination.

Mitrany drew insight from the experience of public international bodies dealing with health, transport and communication, which emerged in the nineteenth century, as well as from functional activity within nation-States where he observed that fascination with constitutions and central authority often obscured more basic processes of national integration. By doing so he provided conceptual linkage that made it possible to apply a wide range of social science knowledge to problems in international organ-ization—with respect to attitudes, loyalties, socialization, learning, com-munication, overlapping membership groups, etc. But it remained for scholars working largely under the rubric of regional integration explicitly to identify and explore these linkages.

DEUTSCH'S APPROACH

Karl Deutsch has been a trail-blazer in bridging social science and peren-nial questions of world order, although he has largely ignored Mitrany. After searching social science for concepts and methods of investigation that could build bridges to an understanding of nationalism (1953), Deutsch broadened his perspective to international political communities. His inquiry focused on the conditions that account for 'the absence or presence of significant organized preparations for war or large-scale violence . . .' (1954, p. 34). Deutsch defines a security community as one where such conditions are absent. In his terms, integration is the creation of 'those practices and machinery—those habits and institutions which actually result in the establishment of a security community' (1954, p. 34).

Working jointly with a team of historians, Deutsch (1957) deepened his analysis by drawing on eight cases of attempted integration in North America and Europe between 1707 and 1921. He discovered twelve essential conditions for an amalgamated security community (i.e. one with a central government). These conditions are distinctive with respect to elements drawn from the social sciences (particularly communication) and the fact that they address not only (a) kinds of linkages between nation units, but also (b) their internal characteristics, and (c) similarities and differences between these units.

Linkage between units is concerned with mobility of persons as well as messages, the range of subjects of communications, balance in two-way flows and mutual predictability produced through these communication links. Similarity of units is concerned with compatibility of main values and sharing of a distinctive way of life. Internal characteristics include factors such as economic growth, increasing political and administrative capability, broadening political élites, and expectation of economic gain from integration. This array of variables provides a rich context for inquiry into the development of international organizations. Like Mitrany, Deutsch was an antidote to preoccupation with the concrete structures of international organizations, but he offered greater conceptual richness, particularly through conceptual linkage to a storehouse of social science literature.

Deutsch also made an important distinction between pluralistic and amalgamated security communities: his case studies highlight instances in which a security community had been achieved without amalgamation. The essential conditions of pluralistic security communities seemed to be only three: compatibility of major values, capacity for response to each other's needs, messages and actions and mutual predictability. This represents a profound challenge to those who assert that world peace can only be achieved through world government.

Synthesis of functionalism and integration

Functionalism is generally considered to be one kind of integration, or one aspect of integration, although those studying integration have consumed much printer's ink discussing problems created by the lack of a commonly agreed definition thereof. All definitions derive more or less from the dictionary definition of integration as 'forming parts into a whole'. There is common agreement, however, that joining nations together by force is not integration. As has already been indicated, Deutsch emphasizes the attainment of a ' "sense of community" and of institutions and practices strong and widespread enough to assure, for a "long" time, dependable expectations of "peaceful change" ' (1957, p. 5). While Deutsch recognizes that the achievement of this condition requires 'some kind of organization, even though it may be very loose' (1957, p. 6), his emphasis is on the attainment of a specific condition: no resort to physical force. The mainstream of integration research has followed another path, focusing on a process leading to the creation of a new decision-making unit. Ernst Haas led the way in 1958 in his seminal volume, *The Uniting of Europe*, when he defined integration as 'the process whereby political actors in several distinct national settings are persuaded to shift their loyalties, expectations, and political activities toward a new and larger center, whose institutions possess or demand jurisdiction over the preexisting national states' (p. 16).

In 1964, Haas joined with Philippe Schmitter in an effort to distil what had been learned in the study of economic unions in the European laboratory and apply it to Latin America. Notable in this effort is the time dimension as the authors divide their nine variables into background conditions, conditions at the time of economic union, and process conditions:

1. Background conditions: (a) similarity in power of units joining economic union; (b) rate of transactions (e.g. trade, labour mobility, capital movements, exchange of persons); (c) pluralism in each country (within important groups and in country as a whole); (d) élite complementary (similarity of values of corresponding élites, e.g. military and labour).
2. Conditions at time of economic union: (a) governmental purposes (similarity of views on ultimate political union and eventual character of economic union); (b) powers of union.
3. Process conditions: (a) decision-making style; (b) rate of transaction; (c) adaptability of governments.

Similar to Deutsch's 1957 effort, this list includes variables concerning (a) kinds of linkages between national units, (b) their internal characteristics, and (c) similarities and differences between these units. Haas and Schmitter differ from Deutsch in placing their variables in a time frame. Deutsch (1957) concluded that his twelve 'background conditions' for integration 'may be assembled in almost any sequence, so long only as all of them come into being and take effect' (1957, p. 71). In addition, the Haas and Schmitter framework extends into 'process conditions' within international organizations.

On the other hand, Haas and Schmitter have a slightly different purpose than Deutsch who was endeavouring to discern the conditions for a 'security community'. Haas and Schmitter (1964, p. 707) wished to evaluate the 'chances of automatic politicization'. By this they mean:

Politicization implies that the actors, in response to miscalculations or disappointments with respect to the initial purposes, agree to widen the spectrum of means considered appropriate to attain them. Politicization implies that the actors seek to resolve their problems so as to upgrade common interests and, in the process, delegate more authority to the center. It constitutes one of the properties of integration—the intervening variable between economic and political union—along with the development of new expectations and loyalties on the part of organized interests in the member nations.

Whereas Deutsch was interested primarily in the conditions for a 'no-war' community (as was Mitrany), Haas and Schmitter, and most of those working in the European laboratory, became primarily concerned with the conditions for creating new political unions. While 'politicization' built on insights closely related to Mitrany's notion of 'spillover', it was applied toward different ends—or, as some might say, toward a different dependent variable. This approach came to be labelled 'neo-functionalism'.

Joseph Nye (1971, p. 24) made an effort at 'dissecting the confusing concept of integration' as it had been used in a torrent of books and articles. He advocated breaking apart the concept of integration into a number of variables, development of measurements for each and leaving the relationship between these variables open to empirical verification. He proposed separate measurement of (a) economic integration, (b) social integration and (c) political integration, and provided illustrative variables for each. As summarized in Table 1, economic variables would consist both of regional transactions as a percentage of all economic transactions (trade is the example used in the table), and expenditures for joint services as a percentage of GNP. Social integration would be measured both by mass transactions (such as trade and mail) and élite transactions such as air travel and student exchange. Political integration encompasses four paths followed by integration research: first, institutional integration (PI_1) (proportion of national budgets and staffs involved in an international institution) and the extent of supranationality in decisions; second, interdependence in policy formation (PI_2), particularly with respect to its scope across ministries; third, mutual identity and obligation (PI_3) as reflected in élite and mass polls and by bargaining behaviour; and fourth, the degree of security community (PI_4), i.e. 'reliable expectations of nonviolent relations'. Nye applied this analytic framework in differentiating three major strategies of European integrationists:

Federalism, which begins by emphasizing institutional integration (PI_1) in the belief that this is a prerequisite for achieving policy integration (PI_2), attitudinal integration (PI_3), and a security community (PI_4). Nye cites Clarence Streit's (1961) graphic advocacy of this approach: 'The worst way to cross a chasm is by little steps.'

TABLE I. Regional integration dissected

Type of integration	Subcategories	Type of evidence and measurement operations
Economic (EI)	Trade (EI_t)	Regional exports as percentage of total exports
	Services (EI_s)	Expenditure on joint services as percentage of GNP
Social (SI)	Mass (SI_m)	Transactions (trade, mail, etc.)
	Élites (SI_e)	Intra-regional air passengers; Students in neighbouring countries as percentage of total students, etc.
Political (PI)	Institutional (PI_1) Bureaucratic	Budgets and staff as percentage of budgets and administrative staffs of all member countries
	Jurisdictional	Supranationality of decisions; legal scope; expansion of jurisdiction
	Policy (PI_2)	Scope (percentage of ministries or equivalents affected) Salience (ranking of fields by experts and by expenditure by fields) Extent (Lindberg scale of locus of decision)
	Attitudinal (PI_3)	Élite and mass polls probing identity, intensity, urgency Bargaining behaviour, flexibility in length of time and number of fields
	Security community (PI_4)	Case-studies

Source: Nye, 1971, p. 49.

Functionalism, stressing collaborative effort on specific policy issues of common interest (PI_2) which will spill over into other policy areas. As elaborated by Mitrany, this makes concern for more grandiose institutional integration (PI_1) unnecessary.

Neo-functionalism, which places high emphasis on PI_2 and also intermediate emphasis on PI_1. Nye describes neo-functionalists as 'federalists in functionalist clothing, pursuing federal ends through what appeared to be functionalist means' (1971, p. 51). Even more poetic is his description of neo-functionalism as 'a strategy for attacking the castle of national sovereignty by stealth, with interest groups as mercenaries and technocrats as agents within the walls to open the gates quietly' (1971, p. 54). In other words, Jean Monnet and his followers and collaborators did not have confidence in the 'spillover' assumption of Mitrany, and advocated a deliberate strategy for using economic integration as a base from which supranational political institutions could ultimately be developed. Thus functionalism came to be employed to fill the void in federalist and world government thinking, i.e. by specifying the means to be employed in moving a group of independent nations to the acceptance of some degree of common central government. This synthesis of functionalism and federalism was largely the achievement of practitioners in European integration. Scholars observed their efforts, endeavoured to develop analytic schemes that would help them to understand what they observed and, with varying degrees of rigour, attempted to test and improve functional theory.

Synthesis of research results
for cross-regional comparison

Nye wrote as efforts at regional integration were spreading to other continents and scholars became concerned that their body of knowledge had application only in the laboratory in which it was developed—Europe. He endeavoured to get comparative leverage through comparison of the performance of common markets and regional political organizations in Africa and Latin America. In order to do this he made four modifications in the 'neo-functional approach', with explicit reference to the Haas-Schmitter framework. First, he found 'automatic politicization' as a dependent variable to be Eurocentric, reflecting the interest of 'European neo-functionalists more than the interests of élites in the less developed countries' (p. 58). Instead, Nye chose 'collective decision-making in the policies involved in achieving an economic union' (p. 59). Second, he extended the actors examined to those opposed to integration—beyond 'integrationist technocrats and those interest groups which, for a variety of convergent aims, persuaded governments to create a regional economic organization' (p. 59). Third, enumerated conditions for integration were reformulated in the light of comparative work done on integration processes in 'less developed areas' (specifically adding involvement of actors external to the region, regional ideology, regional identity and élite socialization) (p. 56). Fourth, 'The idea of a single path from quasi-technical tasks to political union by means of spillover is dropped and other potential process forces and paths are included' (p. 56). Nye's effort to adapt to the challenge of cross-region comparison dramatized the degree to which researchers on European integration had initially accepted the paradigm of neo-functionalist actors in Europe—with respect to dependent variable, actors examined, neo-functional variables and disregard for extra-regional factors.

Nye's 'revised version of the neo-functionalist model' (1971, p. 94–5), reproduced as Figure 1, provides a graphic synthesis of the work of many scholars.[2] Simply put, the model states that: integrative potential at the outset (I) may produce activity on the part of governments and groups (II), which produces regional organizations (III) with process mechanisms (IV) that have certain outcomes that feed back (V), and the process continues for a new cycle. Integrative potential at the outset (I) includes four structural conditions not elaborated in the diagrams:

1. Symmetry or economic equality of units.
2. Élite value complementarity.
3. Existence of pluralism (modern associational groups).
4. Capacity of member State to adapt and respond.

Integrative potential includes three perceptual conditions:

1. Perceived equity of distribution of benefits.
2. Perceived external cogency (e.g. external dependence or domination).
3. Low (or exportable) visible costs.

In the context of the appropriate conditions (I), governments (II) create regional organizations (III) and determine the degree of increase or decrease in their activities. As the organization grows (liberalization) or administers its activities, an array of process mechanisms (IV) are set in motion: (a) impact on external actors; (b) rising transactions; (c) functional linkage; (d) deliberate linkage that extends beyond the initial functional linkage, formation of non-governmental regional groups, socialization of participating élites and identitive appeal stimulated by the new centre of activity.

These process mechanisms in turn produce four possible kinds of outcomes (V): politicization, redistribution, externalization and reduction of alternatives. Politicization implies controversy and is a result of divergent interpretations that accompany involvement of more groups and increasing visibility of central institutions. Redistribution results from the differential impact of the organization on groups within nations and across nations. Externalization comes as integration proceeds and member governments are 'increasingly forced to hammer out a collective external position *vis-à-vis* non-participant third parties, because the further integration proceeds, the more likely third parties will be to react to it, either in support or with hostility' (Nye, 1971, p. 93). Reduction of alternatives refers to the reduction in independent alternatives open to political decision-makers as integration moves forward. These outcomes feed back on integration potential and the process continues.

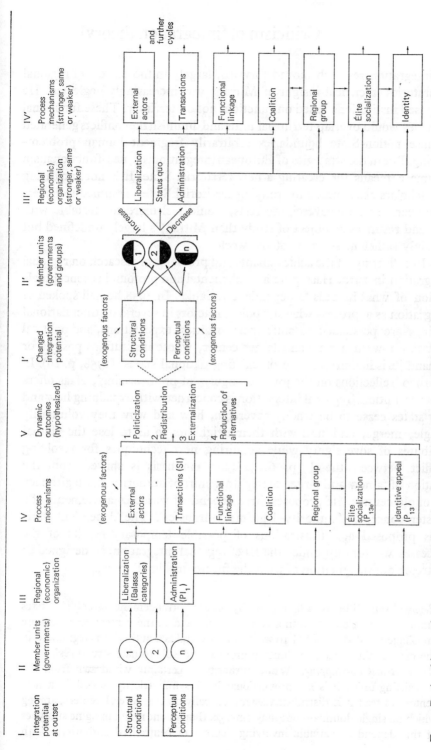

FIG. 1. Regional integration process over time. Arrows indicate a strong relationship, broken arrows a weak relationship, shaded areas of circles indicate groups opposed, and open areas of circles indicate groups in favour (after Nye, 1970, p. 827).

Criticism of 'integration theory'

As integration research moved forward, largely in the context of regional laboratories, a critical insight of Mitrany was increasingly neglected. He proposed institutions based on function, not on territory. These functional activities would overlap territorial units and diminish the conflicts generated because nation-State boundaries arbitrarily fragment human problem-solving. But in the strategies of European integrationists, neo-functionalism became a means for creating a new territorial State. It is not surprising that scholars accustomed to studying territorial States, assumed to have a single centre where sovereignty rests, would feel more comfortable with this end result as an object of study than Mitrany's largely undefined but certainly rather messy view of the world.

In reflecting on the achievements and problems of research on regional integration in 1970, Haas gave a fundamental and profound reconceptualization of what he calls 'a dependent variable'. In 1958 he had spoken of integration as a 'process whereby political actors in several distinct national settings are persuaded to shift their loyalties, expectations, and political activities toward a new and larger center, whose institutions possess or demand jurisdiction over the preexisting national states' (1958, p. 16). In his 1970 'reflections on the joy and anguish of pretheorizing', Haas offers a new definition: 'regional integration is concerned with explaining how and why states cease to be wholly sovereign, how and why they voluntarily mingle, merge, and mix with their neighbors so as to lose the factual attributes of sovereignty while acquiring new techniques for resolving conflict between them' (p. 610). Thus emphasis is shifted from the creation of 'a new and larger center' to a shift of authority and legitimacy out of old centres. He proposes three dependent variables as elements of a 'master concept'—'authority–legitimacy–transfer'. The dependent variables proposed are 'illustrations of possible temporary results of the processes we sum up under the label regional integration, so designed as to stretch our imagination of what the future may hold' (p. 634).

1. *Regional state.* This is 'a hierarchically ordered arrangement resembling states familiar to us. Political authority is concentrated at the center; resources are marshalled and distributed from it. The centralized authority is legitimate in the eyes of the citizens, voluntary groups, and subordinate structures'.
2. *Asymmetrical overlapping.* 'While authority is certainly withdrawn from the preexisting units, it is not proportionately or symmetrically vested in a new center; instead it is distributed asymmetrically among several centers, among which no single dominant one may emerge, though one might imagine subtypes of this dependent variable involving degrees of centralized authority.' With

respect to 'legitimacy in the eyes of citizens . . . the image of infinitely tiered multiple loyalties might be the appropriate one'.

3. *Regional commune*. 'It assumes the kind of interdependence among the participating units which does not permit the identification of a single center of authority or perhaps of any clear center. It is an anarchoid image of a myriad of units which are so highly differentiated in function as to be forced into interdependence. Authority is involved primarily in the sense of having been taken away from previous centers without having found a new single locus. Legitimacy, however it can be imagined, would not take the form of a loyalty akin to nationalism' [p. 635].

In Haas's view, the existing Western European pattern approaches the asymmetrical overlapping image. This starkly underlines the degree to which the regional State image had fostered selective perception by researchers working on European integration.

The greatest limitation of this effort is the vagueness of the description of 'regional commune'. It tends to be a residual category that would include all possibilities outside the other two. It is symptomatic of the hold that the nation-State model has on our thinking when Haas describes it as 'the opposite of a regional state' (p. 635). In this respect he has failed in the difficult task he assigned himself—'to stretch our imagination of what the future may hold' (p. 634). The only clear options described are two provided by European practitioners—the regional State preferred by some and the asymmetrical overlapping system they have created. In this respect scholars absorbed in regional integration are no different from their colleagues working on other aspects of international relations: they have rarely freed themselves from the outlooks of those whose actions they study. Rather, the hallmark of their craft has been legitimization of the operating theories of these officials by translating them into scholarly language. In the process they have also legitimized these practitioners in the eyes of the public at large by accepting their self-proclaimed roles in world affairs—an important part of their operating theories.

Five years later, in 1975, Haas raised even more stringent criticism of regional integration theory, calling it 'obsolete in Western Europe and obsolescent—though still useful—in the rest of the world' (1975, p. 1). Integration has not progressed in Europe as expected because of the inability of the European Community alone to cope with 'matters that transcend the space and the jurisdiction of the community's institutions because they are functions of economic interdependence with trading partners outside of Europe'. These matters include energy, the brain drain, the American research and development challenge, and Europe's inability to produce its own sophisticated weapons, to build nuclear reactors unaided, to launch its own satellites, to stem inflation, to reduce unemployment, to modernize agriculture without huge subsidies and jointly to manage the currencies of member States while maintaining the customs union. Because of benefits which Community members accrue from transactions with non-members, collective action on these issues is channelled into other international organizations and forums as well as into bilateral arrangements.

According to Haas, the Community also encountered unexpected difficulties from within. The 'backwash effects' of the customs union led to demands by less industrialized localities for redistributive policies within the Community. Demand for an 'improved quality of life' also challenged economic growth policies from within at the very time when new challenges were being faced from without. This growing complexity, according to Haas, led member governments to prevent the Commission from acting

because they were undecided whether to seek relief from the pressures of high industrialism through Community action, national action, or joint action with third countries, such as the United States and Japan. Community action was not the obvious choice for Germany, France, and Britain, because each thought it possessed an adequate national capability for action. . . . A clear choice among national, European, and global forms of action was never made. . . . The transnational network of specialists and interests concerned with the post-industrial syndrome developed by leaps and bounds as elaborate industrial consortiums, joint ventures, licensing agreements, and planning groups came into being—all aided by the prior creation of a continental free market for goods, labor, and knowledge [p. 23].

Not only national bureaucracies, but interest groups as well, carefully pick and choose as to whether they demand subnational, national, regional, extra-regional, or globally focused policies; few opt for one of these focuses exclusively [p. 71].

Haas concludes that 'integration theories are becoming obsolete because they are not designed to address the most pressing and important problems on the global agenda of policy and research' (p. 17). Instead of steady movement toward an integrated European Community through the impact of incremental decisions, he discerns a Europe of 'fragmented issue linkage' that includes both regional and extra-regional forums. 'It is foolhardy to predict that the regional focus will triumph in the long run' (p. 62–3). Nevertheless, 'the authority of the Community is quite strong and holding its own in issue areas which continue to be part of the original consensus among governments. . . . The Community continues to make decisions maintaining and even extending the customs union' (p. 65).

Haas discerns that the Communty is at present a 'half-way' house 'which pleases very few', since 'most theorists and practitioners would have the state be either obstinate or obsolete. The fact, however, seems to be that the nation-state is both, and that the present Community system faithfully mirrors this. Which raises the question: Half-way toward where?' (p. 71). As in 1970, Haas describes the Community as an 'asymmetrical overlap', not resembling federal government because of lack of clear-cut division of competences between the centre and the member units with no single centre of authority, no single intelligence centre from which the co-ordination and planning flow, no clear hierarchical lines, and lacking the permanency of a formal constitution' (p. 84–5). Following the same reasoning, Haas discerns that global developments will 'closely resemble the pattern we have imagined for the European Community' (p. 91).

Is 'integration theory' obsolescent?

In what sense is 'integration theory' obsolescent for future inquiry and practice? It is useful to consider this question in the light of the initial purposes for studying regional integration as stated by Haas (1970, p. 608):

The main reason for studying regional integration is thus normative. The units and actions studied provide a living laboratory for observing the peaceful creation of possible new types of human communities at a very high level of organization and of the processes which may lead to such conditions. The study of regional integration is concerned with tasks, transactions, perceptions, and learning, not with sovereignty, military capability, and balances of power. It refuses to dichotomize the behavior of actors between 'high' political and 'low' functional concerns; it is preoccupied with all concerns of actors insofar as they can be used for sketching processes of adaptation and learning free from coercion.

Thus, it was assumed that regions (Europe in particular) were sufficiently isolated from other regions to be used as laboratories for generating knowledge that could be applied to other regions as well as to processes that overlap regions. It is now Haas's judgement that the chosen 'laboratory' is not sufficiently detached from interaction with the world beyond to permit observation of integration processes and the testing of integration theories free from intrusive external factors. Yet, in an unexpected sense, as described in Haas's perceptive efforts to provide an overview of work in the 'laboratory', it is serving as a remarkably useful laboratory for learning about the interplay between simultaneous efforts to solve problems in the context of a variety of territorial units—from subnational to national, to regional units with a variety of boundaries, to global. Haas assumes that regional laboratories are not serving in the fashion intended because the post-industrial era intensifies inter-regional interdependencies. This is why he concludes that regional theory is obsolete in Europe but only obsolescent in Africa, Asia and Latin America. Under this assumption, the laboratory has failed to serve its intended purpose because of the unanticipated impact of technological change on inter-regional relations. Thus, the theory may not necessarily be obsolete, but perhaps the experiment was carried out in the wrong laboratory.

A more serious shortcoming of studies of regional integration has been with respect to the intention of 'observing the peaceful creation of possible new types of human communities at a very high level of organization' (Haas, 1970, p. 608). The nation-State model so permeates thought and perception that it became the yard-stick for measuring regional activity—a model that assumes that nation-States have single centres of authority, single intelligence centres from which co-ordination and planning flow, and clear hierarchical lines. Instead of maximizing opportunity for observing 'new types of human communities', regional integration research has tended to look for the emergence of new territorial units with the characteristics of nation-States. The analytic tools of scholars studying regional integration are so permeated by the nation-State unit of analysis that they cannot anticipate, and are inhibited from perceiving, the emergence of new types of human communities. In this respect they are no different from most international-relations scholars. But this has detracted from the potential value of research on regional integration.

It is symptomatic of the inability of international-relations scholars to specify future States not yet invented by practitioners that, in his 1975 critique, Haas neglects to develop further, or even mention, the regional commune option he vaguely described in 1970. This leaves only two potential future States (in whatever domain we might apply learning from the laboratory): the regional State which was the initial goal of European integrationists and asymmetrical overlapping, the existing condition in Europe. It is also symptomatic of the hold of the nation-State unit on thought that internal fragmentation in European nation-States is not an integral part of these views of the future, despite the fact that Haas acknowledges the 'backwash effects' of the customs union on less-industrialized areas and the ensuing demands for redistributive policies within the Community. Often these 'backwash effects' strike ethnic and nationality groups within nation-States, such as Scotland, Brittany, Sardinia and Sicily. Thus, simultaneous with the 'authority–legitimacy–transfer' from national government to international regional organizations there is a pressure toward 'authority–legitimacy–transfer' to subnational regions. In Europe (within the Community and beyond) periphery regions are striving to develop their own transnational interest group. 'At a moment when the European Parliament is to be elected by universal suffrage', they ask for 'an institutionalized collective representation of all the regions of Europe, representation which can take the form of a second Assembly—a European Assembly of Regions' (Council of Europe, 1975, p. 5). This vision explodes the tyrannical hold of the nation-State as a constituent unit in visions of the future. It is responsive to feelings expressed in debates in the European Council of Local Authorities in the Council of Europe.

Conclusion

The most significant contribution of the literature on functionalism and integration has been the development of conceptual schemes that locate international organizations in the context of national and transnational processes and extensive empirical investigation of these linkages. This has deepened our understanding of the dynamics linking international organizations with their environment. This research has also extended knowledge about decision-making in international organizations. In retrospect, the greatest shortcoming has been the use of these intellectual tools primarily as devices for investigating the emergence of new federal unions. The use of regions as laboratories did not require focus on the emergence of a single centre in the region. Nor did it require that research, and model building, be confined to international organizations with boundaries co-terminous with the defined region. This definition of a laboratory diminished potential for gaining insight on the most challenging part of functional thought—the dynamic interplay between territorial organizations and functional activity that flows across these boundaries. The region could be used as a laboratory for examination of the integrative dynamics of a diversity of functional organizations—subnational, national, regional and global. This would enable research on functionalism and integration to deepen our understanding of what Haas terms 'asymmetrical overlapping' and to discern other models for functional-territorial overlap more clearly.

This shortcoming detracts from the usefulness of work in grappling with an overwhelming challenge faced by practitioners, scholars and the public today—the development of global models that suggest how a variety of functional organizations (governmental and non-governmental), with a variety of territorial boundaries, can develop collaborative linkages with a large number of territorial units towards solving an increasing agenda of problems of global scope. Our ability to respond to this challenge—obviously requiring complex functional and territorial overlaps—is not aided by our tendency to prefer simplistic models in which nation-State boundaries are clearly defined and in which systems of international organizations are arranged in neat hierarchies.

These models must simultaneously contend with a number of difficult issues.

First, and usually neglected in the evaluation of the performance of international organizations, functional overlaps of territorial units perform conflict-management functions as well as serving explicit functional goals. The functionalism and integration literature offers analyses on this issue, in the context of a region with a single boundary, but is not very helpful in the context of a number of overlapping regions.

Second, functional organizations generated by practitioners out of a specific need often perform functions interdependent with organizations generated out of a different need. Relevant models must contend with this interdependence. Work on functionalism and integration, largely as a result of concern with 'spillover', offers very useful insight on these linkages.[3]

Third, most global problems transcend both richer and poorer countries. A greater equalization of wealth, or at least significant movement in that direction, will in all likelihood be required as a basis for fruitful functional collaboration across the rich–poor gap. The literature on functionalism and integration is not very helpful on this issue.

Fourth, existing nation-States are not inevitable territorial components of future global systems. They impose common boundaries on a diversity of functional activities and endeavour to impose hierarchical control on the external linkages of these functional activities. This inhibits external functional collaboration by national functional units (often based on boundaries irrelevant to functional problems) and inhibits the external linkage of subnational functional units. This is particularly a problem with respect to large nation-States (e.g. China, India, the U.S.S.R. and the United States) that range across a diversity of topological, climatic, sociological and ethnic regions. Efforts in Europe to build yet another continental nation-State, and evidence that proposed boundaries are not appropriate for all issue areas, suggests that such nation-States are ana-chronisms in an age of complex functional interdependence. Yet, the very existence of even one or more of them encourages the creation of others (e.g. the existence of the United States and U.S.S.R. stimulated efforts to create a Western European nation-State). Research on functionalism and integration has shed important light on this issue but has not explicitly investigated it because the analytic tools developed were largely applied in the examination of the emergence of new regional nation-States.

Notes

1. Mitrany's thought is scattered in a number of publications. This brief distillation is based on Peter Bock's (1968) overview. For more extensive discussion of Mitrany's thought and its origins, see Haas (1964) and Sewell (1966). For application in a diversity of settings, see Groom and Taylor (1975).

2. For alternative efforts see Leon Linberg's analytic paradigm derived from systems analysis and decision theory (1970), Philippe C. Schmitter's 'A Revised Theory of Regional Integration' (1970), a revision of Haas and Schmitter (1964); and Hayward Alker's application of mathematical formalization to integration logics (1970). The version of Figure 1 used here is taken from Nye (1970) because comprehension is easier than the Nye (1971) version.

3. For a discussion of the shortcomings of 'functional electicism', see Seyom Brown and Larry Fabian's (1975) proposal that would aggregate functional activity into umbrella institutes with respect to specific 'natural systems' such as the oceans, outer space and the atmosphere; and John Ruggie's (1975) alternative formulation of 'policy bundles', such as food–energy–population, energy–money–trade, redistribution–pollution abatement–food, etc.

References

Alker, Hayward R. Jr. 1970. Integration Logics: A Review, Extension, and Critique. *International Organization*, Vol. XXIV, No. 4, Autumn, p. 869–914.

Bock, Peter. 1968. Functionalism and Functional Integration. *International Encyclopedia of Social Sciences*. Vol. 7, p. 534–41. New York, Macmillan Co.

Brown, Seyom; Fabian, Larry L. 1975. Toward Mutual Accountability in the Non-territorial Realms. *International Organization*, Vol. XXIX, No. 3, Summer, p. 877–92.

Caporaso, James A. 1970. Encapsulated Integrative Patterns vs. Spillover: The Cases of Agriculture and Transport Integration in the European Economic Community. *International Studies Quarterly*, Vol. 14, No. 4, December, p. 361–94.

Council of Europe. 1975. Galway Declaration unanimously adopted on 16 October 1975. *First Convention of the Authorities of European Peripheral Regions, Galway, Ireland, 14–16 October 1975*. Strasbourg, Council of Europe.

DEUTSCH, Karl. 1953. *Nationalism and Social Communication: an Inquiry into the Foundations of Nationalism*. New York, John Wiley G.

——. 1954. *Political Community at the International Level*. Garden City, N. Y. Doubleday.

DEUTSCH, Karl et al. 1957. *Political Community and the North Atlantic Area*. Princeton, N.J., Princeton University Press.

GROOM, A. J. R.; TAYLOR, Paul (eds.). 1975. *Functionalism: Theory and Practice in International Relations*. London, University of London Press.

HAAS, Ernst B. 1958. *The Uniting of Europe: Political, Social and Economic Forces, 1950–57*. Stanford, Stanford University Press.

——. 1964. *Beyond the Nation-State*. Stanford, Calif., Stanford University Press.

——. 1970. The Study of Regional Integration : Reflections on the Joy and Anguish of Pretheorizing. *International Organization*, Vol. XXIV, No. 4, Autumn, p. 607–46.

——. 1975. *The Obsolescence of Regional Integration Theory*. Berkeley, Calif., Institute of International Studies.

HAAS, Ernst B.; SCHMITTER, Philippe C. 1964. Economics and Differential Patterns of Political Integration: Projections about Unity in Latin America. *International Organization*, Vol. XVIII. No. 4, Autumn, p. 705–37.

HALLSTEIN, Walter. 1962. *United Europe: Challenge and Opportunity*. Cambridge, Mass., Harvard University Press.

LINDBERG, Leon L. 1970. Political Integration as a Multidimensional Phenomenon Requiring Multivariate Measurement. *International Organization*, Vol. XXIV, No. 4, Autumn, p. 649–731. (Also published as Leon N. Lindberg and Stuart A. Scheingold, *Europe's Would-Be Polity: Patterns of Change in the European Community*, Englewood Cliffs, N.J., Prentice-Hall, 1970.)

MITRANY, David. 1966. *A Working Peace System*. Chicago, Ill., Quadrangle Books.

MONNET, Jean. 1955. *Les États-Unis d'Europe ont Commencé*. Paris, Robert Laffont.

NYE, Joseph S. 1968. Comparative Regional Integration: Concept and Measurement. *International Organization*, Vol. XXII, No. 4, Autumn, p. 855–80.

——. 1970. Comparing Common Markets : a Revised Neofunctionalist Model. *International Organization*, Vol. XXIV, No. 4, Autumn, p. 796-835.

——. 1971. *Peace in Parts*. Boston, Mass., Little, Brown & Company.

RUGGIE, John. 1975. International Responses to Technology: Concepts and Trends. *International Organization*, Vol. XXIX, No. 3, Summer, p. 557–83.

SCHMITTER, Philippe C. 1970. A Revised Theory of Regional Integration. *International Organization*, Vol. XXIV, No. 4, Autumn, p. 836–68.

SEWELL, Patrick. 1966. *Functionalism and World Politics: a Study Based on United Nations Programs Financing Economic Development*. Princeton, N.J., Princeton University Press.

STREIT, Clarence. 1961. *Freedom's Frontier—Atlantic Union Now*. Washington, D.C., Freedom & Union Press.

7 Power and conflict in the study of international organization

Silviu Brucan

Ever since the ideology of liberalism permeated the eighteenth century with its lofty message of unlimited evolutionary progress, idealist thinkers and visionaries, starting with the French philosopher Condorcet, have held forth the promise of a world without war, free of power politics, conflicts and violence. Gradually, that hopeful promise turned into the concept of an international organization that would eliminate war and establish the rule of law in the world.

Woodrow Wilson, a most eloquent spokesman for that school of thought, hailed the League of Nations emerging in the aftermath of the First World War as the new instrument of world peace. Two decades only elapsed and the League worked its way right into the Second World War. Rising from the ruins and genocide of that calamitous conflict, the United Nations was described by its founders as the international organization that would bring an era of peace and harmony. Idealist writers gave momentum to a theory on the depreciation of power in international politics.

To all those who have survived this flurry of excitement of the early days of the United Nations both the promise and the theory now look exceedingly premature. Many an instance of international war has kept breaking out over the last thirty years or so, in which devoted members of the United Nations have played a rather prominent role; although the

SILVIU BRUCAN had been Romania's Ambassador to Washington and its representative to the United Nations before becoming the head of his country's television. He resigned the last post in 1966 and has since been Professor of Social Science at the University of Bucharest. He has taught widely abroad, particularly in the United States and published a book in English: *The Dissolution of Power* (1971), translated into many languages. In 1976, he participated in the third Club of Rome project on reshaping the international order and is currently preparing a book on the Marxist theory of international affairs.

thunder and tumult of the cold war are bygones, the clashes between contending groups of nations, the harsh polemics and rivalries among the great powers, and—looming over everything—the insane nuclear race, all testify to the fact that we are still far away from a warless and harmonious world.

It therefore seems logical to assume that international organizations are not and cannot be insulated from the world they are supposed to regulate, and that consequently power relations and conflicts existing in the world at large are necessarily reflected in the structure and workings of international organizations.

This study proposes to focus on the concepts, approaches and methods which are used in the analysis of power and conflict in international organizations, eventually testing their explanatory power against the background of real events and processes going on in the international arena.

The general approach will be sociological, starting from the conviction that the schools of thought seeking to explain the most complex phenomena of international relations and politics through some unifying concept or single factor have failed to provide a satisfactory theoretical framework for this field. I have in mind theories based on concepts like power, conflict, behaviour, culture or technology, including the traditional schools of geopolitics and racialism. As for class and the class struggle, which remain basic tools of analysis for human society, they are not sufficient to cover the whole *problématique* of world politics, since here the analysis must necessarily operate at both the societal and the global levels, where interactions between nations acquire an impetus of their own, as we shall elaborate later. Economic determinism as the major single factor to be used in explaining world developments is equally inefficient and errorprone, as has been evident in so many cases. Marx and Engels[1] were particularly articulate on this score:

According to the materialist conception of history, the ultimately determining element in history is the production and reproduction of real life. More than this, neither Marx nor I have ever asserted. Hence, if somebody twists this into saying that the economic element is the only determining one, he transforms that proposition into a meaningless, abstract, senseless phrase. The economic situation is the basis, but various elements of the superstructure—political, juridical, philosophical theories, religious views and their future development into systems of dogmas, also exercise their influence upon the course of the historical struggles and in many cases preponderate in determining their form.

This is essentially what I mean by the sociological approach.

Power and international organizations

Our starting premise is that, throughout history, international organizations have always mirrored the world power structure of the given period. Some authors go even further and suggest that international organizations are actually initiated by the predominant powers in order to consolidate their position and to perpetuate long-standing patterns of dependence and domination.

Let us examine these premises with the conceptual tools of analysis and methods available at the present level of knowledge. First, what is power in international relations?

One school of thought views power as the major single core of international politics. Hans Morgenthau, its foremost theoretician, maintains that international politics, like all politics, is a struggle for power; whatever the ultimate aims in international politics, power is always the immediate aim; whenever statesmen strive to realize their goals by means of international politics, they do so by striving for power.[2]

The case seems to be overstated. As K. J. Holsti rightly points out, while Morgenthau implies that power is a major goal of policy or even a determining motive of any political action, he also suggests that power is a relationship and a means to an end. Because of this ambiguity, notes Holsti, 'we do not know what the concept explains or fails to explain in international politics'.[3] Holsti defines power in terms of acts of influence capability and response to the acts. Other authors emphasize the capacity to change the probability of outcomes or to make things happen that would not have happened otherwise.[4]

Whilst all these definitions may help to clarify the meaning of power as an abstract concept, when we deal with international politics, power makes sense if related first and foremost to the nation-State, as the chief actor in the international system. Even if there are forms or manifestations of power that tend to transgress the State (e.g. multinational corporations or transnational organizations), the basic frame of reference remains the nation-State, for, in the last analysis, the latter forms of power need to influence governments in order to achieve their ends. And since international organizations are now built on the principle of State sovereignty, it is essential to grasp the actual relationship between power and nation-State in the workings of the United Nations as well as in defining the limitations of United Nations resolutions in settling disputes between sovereign States.

As for its origin, Morgenthau maintains that power is the result of forces inherent in human nature, and as such a permanent and necessary element in all social relations.[5]

The Marxist theory rejects biological reductionism in explaining social phenomena and, as in the past, when Marxists criticized the transplant of Darwin's evolutionary theory to society and of Spencer's organicism identifying the laws of society with those of biology, they consider it erroneous to pin-point the cause of political power in human nature. Their main argument holds that, while it is certainly true that society comprises biological processes without which it could not exist, society represents a more complex type of material unity, qualitatively different from the biological aggregate. In society, biological laws are integrated within the economic and social relations established among people as well as within the political and ideological conceptions generated by that ambiance, eventually forming a whole that functions in accordance with social laws distinct in many ways from the biological ones. Men who are biologically strong and perfectly fit may well become socially underprivileged and economically poor because of specific conditions in society.

Consequently, power should be explained in social terms rather than in biological ones; in society power is an effect rather than a cause, a means rather than an end. Far from being the primary cause of international politics, power is rather the effect of a historical state of affairs defined both by the material conditions of society and by social and national inequalities. Power politics would not and could not exist if nations were equal in size and might.

There is scientific ground to Morgenthau's proposition that, in both domestic and international politics, the struggle for power is a major factor. However, his generalization that the struggle for power is a permanent element in all social relations is highly debatable.

Hypothetically, if one eliminated the main basis for power, namely social and national inequality, there would be no reason left for domination and struggle against domination, and no reason to exercise power. Nor could industrially advanced nations exploit the poor ones if all nations were at the same level of economic and technological development. In the real world, nevertheless, nations are great and small, mighty and weak, developed and underdeveloped, rich and poor, and so long as such differences and gaps exist, power will remain an important factor in international politics.

Let us now turn to the question of the components of power. What is power made up of and how can one measure power in international organizations?

As a rule, students of comparative politics speak of the following components: natural, economic and technological bases, culture including personnel in science and technology, military force and weaponry, national morale and political cohesion, international prestige and diplomatic ability. Some authors list seven contributing elements: geography, natural resources, technology, population, ideology, morale and leadership.[6] That these are probably the sources of national power seems a quasi-unanimous assumption. There are various criteria used in comparative studies of national power, ranking nations according to geographic area, gross national product, natural resources and, last but not least, military strength. There are also combinations of power assets (e.g. energy production, steel output and population), which researchers extrapolate over decades in future predictions. In present-day international politics, the emphasis in establishing big-power status is on two main elements: economico-technological potential and nuclear weapons. One power theorist holds that every age has its own scale, and concludes that today only a cohesive society with a population of about 200 million people, a national income of at least $300,000 million, a highly advanced technology and weaponry that includes sophisticated and effective nuclear armament can constitute a global power.[7]

Actually, the components of power and national power as a whole have a relative value. Although most of them are measurable quantities and, consequently, nations can be ranked according to more or less objective criteria, what actually counts in international politics is not only such an objective assessment, but also the evaluation of national power by decision-makers and the efficiency of its use in the pursuit of a certain goal. In other words, national power is a potential whose actual value depends on the political capacity to use it and on the degree to which it is related to a definite purpose. As an extreme illustration, Hitler demonstrated political capacity to raise the German potential, but he failed because his goal, world domination, exceeded that potential by far. Therefore, writers distinguish between the operational environment, by which we mean the external objective factors involved in an international situation from the psychological environment, namely the image of external reality shaped under the influence of internal conditions, i.e. the way external reality is perceived and evaluated by nations and their leaders. History provides ample evidence that the images statesmen have of the power of their nation and of its adversaries do not always tally with reality. Marx spoke of 'ideological illusion' and the worst years of the cold war were marked by false images in both the West and the East with respect to the economic viability and political stability in the opposite camp.[8]

Power is sometimes confused with force. In fact, power is primarily and predominantly political, while force in the physical sense of violence is used only when the other means of influence and coercion have failed in determining the particular solution or course of action envisaged by the State wielding power. Surely, in 1956, France and the United Kingdom would have preferred Egypt to renounce the nationalization of the Suez Canal as the result of pressures put on Nasser rather than having to dispatch troops to that end. Force, therefore, should be viewed as the *ultima ratio* of conflict.

How does power fare in international organizations? Is it different from its general condition in the world? From a strictly juridical standpoint, power simply does not exist in the United Nations, for Article 2, paragraph 1 of the Charter solemnly proclaims: 'The Organization is based on the principle of the sovereign equality of all its members.' The same principle is implicit in Article 18 which gives each member of the General Assembly one vote (one nation, one vote). Nevertheless, power relations existing in the world at large are reflected in the United Nations, and to the extent that there is a difference between the voting pattern in the United Nations and the distribution of power in the world, it is due to the contrast between the juridical principle of sovereign equality and the discrepancies of power in the real world. Hence, the idea of the weighted vote to be adopted in the United Nations is essentially an attempt to introduce to the United Nations the actual power relations prevailing on the international scene. At present, these are filtered in the United Nations through the principle of sovereign equality, which may well be one of the underlying reasons why the tendency has grown, over recent years, to remove issues involving relations between the great powers outside the framework of the United Nations. The major protagonists feel they are in a better position to promote their interests outside a system which is too egalitarian and democratic for power politics.

The whole issue may be understood more clearly if considered in the context of the management of power in international society, which is actually the most relevant facet of power for international organizations. Here, one must proceed from the fact that, because in international society there is no centre of authority and power, like the State in domestic society, this vacuum has been filled over the ages by various formulas of centralization of power designed to perform in the international sphere the order-maintaining and integration functions of the State in domestic society—if possible through international organization.

Throughout history, that vacuum produced hegemonic models (e.g. Pax Romana, Pax Britannica) or balance-of-power schemes (e.g. Concert of Europe). Both models theoretically represent the tendency to centralize a system that remains basically decentralized.

Hegemony presupposes a single predominant power, whereas balance of power suggests a scheme within which a number of separate centres of power (sufficiently strong to balance each other in the world arena) function more or less as co-ordinate managers of power in the sense that each is supposed to control its own zone of influence. In his classical essay *On the Balance of Power*, David Hume revealed that, in ancient Greece, all the politics of cities was based on the balance-of-power principle; the rules of the game were set when the Peloponnesian war between Athens and Sparta broke out because one of the protagonists tried to enlarge his league in order to tip the balance in his favour and, thus, acquire a hegemonic status. [9]

Historically, international organizations, albeit in embryo, could be traced back to the experiment of the leagues set up by the Greek cities. Ever since and all the way through the Concert of Europe, the League of Nations, and the United Nations, international organizations have been permeated by the dynamics of power relations. Some historians make an exception of the Concert of Europe (1812–1914), which they hail as the 'golden age of diplomacy' stretching over almost a century of 'international order and stability'. [10] The Concert of Europe is the classical model of balance of power with four or five major powers able to regulate international affairs without having recourse to war against each other. Yet, if one looks more carefully into the matter, one discovers that the 'golden age' was the period of the vast imperialist advance in Africa, Asia and the American continent, when the conquest of colonies became the symbol of great-power status. The 'international order' which prevailed in Europe was chiefly due to the fact that the European powers had got busy with their overseas expansion into other continents and it is perhaps not altogether incidental that the 'golden age' ended at the time when the southern continents were completely divided among the metropoles, and there was nothing left to conquer overseas.

As an international organization endowed with a covenant, an assembly, a council and a permanent secretariat, the League of Nations constituted a radical departure from previous experiments—a real organization with a legal personality, a structure and organs of its own. Thus, the League of Nations was a step forward in international society; for one thing its membership extended to over fifty nations, providing small nations with an opportunity for assertion they had never enjoyed in the past. Yet, the League displayed a conspicuous disparity of power with the great powers holding a controlling influence on the organization. By virtue of their special status in the council, as permanent members, in conjunction with the rule of unanimity, the great powers could always—and actually did—frustrate any action of the League in cases where their vital interests were at stake. This made the League totally ineffective in dealing with the overt acts of aggression initiated by European powers. Actually, the covenant of the League did not even outlaw war specifically, which was a basic constitutional weakness reflecting the mentality of an epoch in which the use of force was the final arbiter of international conflicts.

The United Nations is in many ways a superior type of international organization—much more universal in membership and much more advanced in its guiding legal principles, marking the changes for the better in world politics and in the conscience of nations. However, while the principles and purposes of the United Nations Charter were drafted with a view to the future, the mechanism provided in the Charter bears the imprint of the power realities prevailing at the time. The 'Big Five' of the victorious coalition were given a privileged position in the governmental functions of the Organization, as permanent members of the Security Council. The claim of the drafters of the Charter was that the unanimity principle of the permanent members would limit the freedom of action of the great powers. Yet, the practical consequence has been that the United Nations could not take effective action whenever one of the great powers was directly or indirectly involved. Thus very few military outbreaks indeed qualify for effective United Nations action, for we live in a small and shrinking world in which power is ubiquitous. As Stanley Hoffman puts it: 'In relations among the Great Powers, decisive for the maintenance of world peace, international organizations stand exposed to perpetual defeat.'[11]

Since power relations are never dormant, the whole post-war evolution of the United Nations has followed the shifts in the distribution of power in world politics. For the first fifteen years, the United States, as the leader of both Western and Latin American groups, controlled more than two-thirds of the votes and could easily get its way. This coincided with the cold-war period when most analysts used the model of a bipolar world with the United States and the U.S.S.R. as the protagonists of the two hostile camps, capitalism and socialism, each one tightly lined up behind its leading power. By the end of the 1950s a new political factor—the Third World—began to assert its presence in the United Nations; the Afro-Asian group became the largest group, and gradually, with most Latin American nations joining the Third World, the shift in the composition of the membership and in the power relations within the United Nations became decisive.

In the study of present power realities, most theorists have switched from the bipolar model (United States and U.S.S.R.) to the triangular model (including China in the game), and more recently to the pentagonal model (adding Western Europe and Japan) as versions of the balance-of-power functioning principle. Opponents of the power theory argue that neither of these models is applicable to our present world, as there are now too many autonomous political units acting ever more independently, and therefore it is no longer possible for a small number of major powers to divide the world among themselves and to act thus as co-ordinate managers of power. At the time of the Concert of Europe, the four or five powers were able to do this because there were actually very few sovereign States on the other continents: the colonial empires of the European powers practically covered the whole planet. The situation has since radically changed. Europe itself now has thirty-two independent States. From 1810 onward eighteen republics replaced the Spanish Empire in Latin America; since the Second World War almost twenty Arab States emerged, and in recent decades, in Africa and Asia, scores of new States have arisen over the ruins of the French, British, Dutch and lastly Portuguese empires. Indeed, the number of sovereign States around the world has multiplied to well above 150, and so has the membership of the United Nations.

And it is not only the map that looks different. The real change goes much deeper. Though most of the new States have started with a backward economy and culture, the political activation of the broad masses stimulated by independence and by touches of economic modernization, industrialism and mass communication coupled with increasing education have all resulted in a powerful thrust of national self-assertion that has swept world politics. While it is true that this resurgent movement does not involve power in the traditional sense of the term, it has clearly produced a new international setting in which it is no longer possible for the major powers to run the world, or even to exercise effective control over their allies, partners or clients. This has been conspicuous both in the Viet Nam war and in the Middle East conflict, as well as in voting at the United Nations. Who would have thought twenty years ago that Latin American republics would dare to undertake massive nationalization of American property; that Iceland would defy British trawlers fishing in its extended territorial waters, that tiny Albania would vote systematically in the United Nations against Soviet policy? This is not to say that pressures, threats or arm-twisting from the mighty and rich have been abolished. They are, however, less effective than in the past.

To sum up the point regarding the management of power, let us conclude that the present international system is the most decentralized in modern history. In international organizations, this situation is reflected in the gradual deterioration of the political and military blocs that were set up during the cold war. It is not the voting patterns (which are too often deceptive with their erratic course), but the decentralization process that provides a better and more consistent explanation of trends in the United Nations system.

Parallel to the decentralization process, another significant change has occurred in recent years regarding the dynamics of power itself in the sense that the emphasis and relative weight of the military component of power has been reduced in favour of the economic, technological and politico-diplomatic components which have been enhanced accordingly. This is the profound underlying reason behind the transition to the phase 'from confrontation to negotiation' in the relationship between the major actors; the same reason has led most international observers to switch to the five-centres-of-power scheme, including in the big game Western Europe, as the biggest trader on the world market, and Japan, as a global economic power, though neither possesses a significant and independent military force commensurate with that role. Analysts feel that the pentagonal scheme provides a better tool for explaining actual events on the world scene. And, of course, it is only on the basis of that shift in power that one can explain the success of OPEC in dealing with such powerful interlocutors.

Indeed, the globalization trend powered by modern technology and the tremendous growth of world trade has produced an international environment in which interdependence is the rule. Apparently, the use of force has become counter-productive not only because of the destructive potential of nuclear-missile weapons, but also because modern trade, communication and transportation have tied nations so closely that a decision to opt out of this network in favour of military action looks like an act of madness. The concept of 'limited war' should probably be amended likewise: they occur only in places where military hostilities do not gravely affect international trade.

Do all these things mean that from now on force will be eliminated from the attributes of power? The way we read present history, we see no evidence for such a happy conclusion either now or in the foreseeable future. Despite its setbacks and the severe limitations imposed on force, military strength and its manifestation, the use of force, are here to stay. Apparently, nations which exert power in their foreign policy do feel that they can use the other available means (economic, technological, etc.) as substitutes for force only if they possess the real thing. This is why the nuclear race and the increase in military expenditure have not been seriously affected by the latest developments.

Nevertheless, the actual shift in the dynamics of power, which has brought the economic and technological potential to the forefront, has severely reduced the impact of military strength. Military powers not in a position to use their economic and technological potential as important components of power will continue to maximize the impact of their specific strength in order to improve their relative postures in the 'economic war'.

It is only within that general context that one can explain the impact of the Arab oil embargo, the effectiveness of the new oil prices set by OPEC and the tremendous financial potential acquired by the oil-exporting countries. Whatever the geometry of power, bipolar or pentagonal, analysts must now take a step further and recognize that in world politics there are significant forces at work outside the geometric model.

If one accepts the simplest definition of power in international politics as the capability to influence other nations against their inclination, then surely the oil-exporting countries have successfully passed the test. Many an industrial nation modified its position *vis-à-vis* the Middle East conflict and the new oil prices became effective on 1 January 1974 in spite of protests and threats. As for the financial potential of the oil-exporting countries, the least that can be said is that, since 1974, monetary reforms are no longer the exclusive concern of the 'group of ten' (richest OECD countries).

What kind of power is held by nations which are individually in a developing stage and highly vulnerable? Unlike the traditional type of power embodied in a nation-State, and backed up by impressive military might or by a modern economic potential, the new type of power can be defined properly only in relational terms within a certain system, that is the so-called North–South system; its effectiveness in modifying the behaviour of the system stems from the capability to cause disturbances in its functioning. We call it *systemic power* to underline that it does not exert itself over every international issue or framework, but only within the limits of a given system; its influence is felt to the extent to which decisions affect elements interacting with that system, which explains why the policies of industrial nations which are heavily dependent on oil imports have been more seriously affected than those of nations which import less oil. The energy crisis has revealed that dependence is no longer a one-way street. And global interdependence requires order more than anything else in the international system. The latest developments make it abundantly clear that the world market and the international monetary system cannot be stabilized within the present order with its glaring inequalities and abysmal gaps. Hence we are witnessing the opening stage of a struggle for a new international order reflecting the changes in power relations on the world stage. As Barraclough puts it: 'In the wider perspective of history, it may well turn out that the long term significance of the "oil crisis" is the way it has served as a catalyst for the wider and more fundamental confrontation between the poor nations and the rich, which threatens to engulf the world.'[12]

The weapons in that confrontation are new and so are the rules of the game. Not only energy, but all the new problems that derive from the scientific-technological revolution combined with the social and national revolutions, namely development, world resources, food, pollution, the oceans, etc., are of such nature and dimension that force is both ineffective and dangerous in dealing with them. The discussion stirred up in 1974 by the threats to use force against OPEC countries was highly illuminating in this respect. Obviously, this is the kind of scenario that would cause an upheaval in world production and supply and make the Arab embargo look like a fair bargain. What is more, how can one wage a war against nations scattered over three continents? And what would happen in the meantime to oil exports which have proved to be so vital to the industrialized world? Nor can such problems be solved by one group of nations or another, however strong and numerous; they require global solutions at the world level. Herein lies the new historical tasks of international organizations.

The question thus arises whether the United Nations is equipped to deal with such problems. In the matter of power relations, the United Nations has gone a long way—from George Ball's 'blunt truth that far more clearly than the League, the U.N. was essentially conceived as a club of great powers',[13] to the present state of affairs when great powers complain about the 'tyranny of the majority'. Apparently, the nuclear stalemate outside the United Nations has been compounded by a political stalemate within the Organization. On the one hand, to be effective major decisions require the agreement of the great powers; on the other hand, neither of the major powers or any combination of them can any longer force the United Nations to do something which negatively affects the interests of developing nations.

A sober evaluation of all pertinent factors reveals that the United Nations is going through a transitional stage, the essence of which is adaptation to the new power relations emerging in the world. The process of adaptation is pushed forward by the new historical actors, most of whom did not have a say in Dumbarton Oaks in 1945 when the Charter was drafted and the mechanism set up. However, as any student of history would expect, the beneficiaries of the old order oppose change.

Many authors maintain that the changes required by the establishment of a new international economic order, which has become a major goal of the United Nations ever since the Sixth Special Session held in April and May 1974, entails fundamental changes in the world power structure and its institutional embodiments.

They realize, however, that a complete overhaul of the United Nations Charter, and the existing machinery, desirable as it may be, does not seem a realistic proposition. Historical experience shows how difficult, if not impossible, it is to codify rules and procedures in international law at a time when the new power relations are still in an emerging stage.

An increasing number of Third World authors however emphasize the need to 'democratize' the United Nations, to acquire more control and participation in its decisions, arguing that far-reaching changes are possible even under the present Charter. This approach prevails in the proposals advanced in 1975 by the Group of Experts on the Structure of the United Nations system.[14]

Change must eventually include the question of the power to make decisions and enforce them. Up to now, international organizations have never had power of their own for the very simple reason that, in a State system based on sovereignty, the ability to make decisions is exclusively vested with the individual nations. In order to be able to make decisions and enforce them, an international organization must be empowered by its members to do so. This essentially means that a transfer of power must take place from the nation to the international organization. Whether and when such an evolution, or rather revolution, will occur is a question for futurologists to tackle, and the only reason for mentioning it here is that the study of power in international organizations cannot neglect that important aspect.

The theory of conflict and international organizations

The theory of conflict and conflict-resolution has grown out of the cold war and has long been dominated by the psychological school in international relations. Kenneth Boulding has formulated a theory of conflict as a general social process of which war was a special case, starting from the assumption that in all conflict situations, whether interpersonal, industrial relations (a euphemism for the class struggle), international politics, and even animal life, patterns of behaviour display essential similarities, a common element. He then applied the general models of conflict to various special conflict situations to reveal their divergencies from the basic pattern.[15] On such theoretical bases, Thomas Schelling studied the functions, mechanisms, and strategies for non-verbal communications between parties to violent conflict, and formulated certain rules for bargaining at the negotiating table and for mixing conflict and co-operative behaviour in hostile relationships.[16] Other strategists studied refinements for waging the cold war and armed, with the mathematical theory of games, suggested various ways of exerting pressure on the enemy. A striking illustration of the practice suggested by these strategists was the famous 'balancing on the brink of war' policy adopted in the 1950s by John Foster Dulles, as United States Secretary of State.

Boulding, Rapoport and other theoreticians belong to the psycho-sociological pacifist trend. At the time, they were concerned that the potential of conflict in the international system was such as to lead eventually to catastrophic war, and felt, therefore, that changes were required to divert conflict from violence to debate, to abandon cold-war strategic statecraft and steer away from the dangerous path of the nuclear holocaust. Ultimately, the psycho-sociological approach to international conflict became the theoretical core of the American school of peace research.

In general, the psycho-sociological school, which has been so fertile and creative in microsocial research, has failed to provide a conceptual framework for the analysis of the major phenomena and processes in world politics. Indeed, although one can find some psychic reaction in all conflict situations, even in the most subtle ideological debate, the simplifying analogy between phenomena that are qualitatively different may not take us very far: individual behaviour in a street brawl incited by excessive drinking or jealousy is one thing, social reactions in an industrial strike, a revolution or a war are something else. In the first case, it is the individual psychological motivation that is the determining factor, whereas in a strike, a revolution or a war, important economic, political and military considerations override the psychological ones. What is more, to the extent that collective psychological reactions manifest themselves, these arise in an environment of political and ideological struggle that belongs to the sphere of relations between classes and nations. Even outstanding psychologists now criticize the 'gross oversimplification' implied in the assumption that, because war involves aggressive behaviour on the part of nations, its causes can be explained by examining the determinants of aggressive behaviour in individuals; leaders may engage in a war for strategic reasons and the population at large for reasons of social conformity.[17]

Apparently, the overemphasis on psychological reactions tends to blur the profound social and economic sources of conflict, particularly class antagonisms and economic inequalities in society, as well as disparities in power or in levels of development among nations. As a Marxist, I suggest the following points for consideration: (a) social psychology and even individual psychology (when decision-makers are involved) play an active role in the outbreaks of strikes, revolutions and wars; (b) psychological aspects cannot be dissociated from the social environment in which they originate, nor can they be extracted from the basic conflictual situations existing in society; (c) the pattern of international conflict is not determined by psychological reactions, which are temporary anyway, but rather by deepseated contradictions ingrained in structures of power.

The Soviet sociologist, D. Yermolenko, feels that the methodology for the study of conflict should start with the analysis of economic, technological, geographical, demographic, social, political, military, ideological, psychological and other factors, and on the basis of such analysis should establish the nature and character of the conflict in question, its sources, the stages and levels according to which the danger of aggravation mounts, and the means of resolving or regulating the conflict, and in some cases, of averting it.[18]

Quite interestingly, peace research in Europe has diverged to a considerable degree from its counterpart in the United States. Far from sticking to the narrow behavioural framework of conflict-resolution with its clinical anti-theoretical bias, European researchers have adopted a global perspective and have accepted the starting assumption that the problem of peace is rooted in the very structure of international society, and accordingly that dominance and dependence between nations and between groups of nations produce international conflicts. A tentative inventory of such studies shows that they usually focus on the following types of international conflict:

1. Conflicts generated by the big-power game, major strategic rivalries, phases in the arms race, etc.
2. Conflicts arising from marked differences in size, military strength, population, etc., among nations.
3. Conflicts arising from long-standing patterns of dependence and domination resulting from gaps in economic and technological levels of development.
4. Conflicts between antagonistic socio-economic systems and ideologies.
5. Conflicts caused by social change or civil war with involvement of foreign powers.
6. International conflicts growing out of a bilateral issue in a certain contingency: instant conflicts.

As such studies advance, it becomes increasingly clear that these types of conflict cannot be considered in isolation, since they intersect and interact so that, in most cases, any real conflict is a combination of two or three types.

In digging deeper, one discovers certain relationships between the various types of conflict, their intensity and frequency. For example, some authors maintain that conflicts of the third type break out more frequently if conflicts of the fourth type have been kept under control. As one author puts it: 'Our world is witnessing the coexistence of peaceful coexistence and local wars';[19] other writers go even further and claim that peaceful coexistence is merely the alternative to warfare between the nuclear powers, while conventional local wars in Africa, Asia and Latin America may happily continue.

Istvan Kende has found that out of ninety-seven wars waged in the twenty-five years since 1945, ninety-three were fought in Asia, Africa and Latin America, whilst Europe looks like an almost warless zone of the world. Drawing a neat distinction between international wars (across national frontiers) and intranational wars (civil or class wars), the study provides an interesting comparative approach to the findings of Quincy Wright with regard to the wars waged in a previous period (1900–41) and reaches the conclusion that the situation was nearly reversed in the sense that, whereas in the past 79 per cent were international wars fought across frontiers, in our time the bulk of wars are fought on the territory of a single country. Of these internal wars, those involving foreign participation stand out as most numerous. They are in fact a combination of class wars (fifth type) with wars of independence (third type) according to Kende.[20]

In the early post-war years, it was the ideological conflict that was viewed as the predominant cause of war. The theoretical explanation then was that foreign policy is exclusively or primarily dictated by class interests. The habit of presenting world politics as a clash of opposite ideological poles was in great favour on both sides of what was then called the Iron Curtain.

In recent years, however, Marxist scholars have become increasingly aware that viewing international politics exclusively in class-ideological terms does not prove exceedingly helpful in explaining major political developments—from President De Gaulle's criticism of American hegemony and the harsh Sino-Soviet polemics to the two Soviet-American nuclear treaties and the official statement that the People's Republic of China belongs to the Third World. Nations too, not only classes, play a major role in international politics. Indeed, while nations are made up of classes and other social groups with clashing interests, once nations are consolidated and largely integrated—owing to their common language, territory, economic and cultural traits—they acquire a drive of their own in international politics that cannot be identified with any of their component parts. Thus, the dynamics of relations between nations differ from those of the class struggle, for nations are great and small, rich and poor, developed and underdeveloped, and such disparities and gaps generate types of conflict and co-operation utterly different from those between classes.

S. Sanakoyev, the editor of *International Affairs* (Moscow), writes: 'The foreign policies of States are formed under the impact of hordes of factors, external and internal. They include the struggle between classes and political groups, the level of economic and socio-political development of States, their geographical location, historical traditions, and so on.'[21] It is the complexity of inputs which go into foreign policy-making that explains the diversity of views and positions displayed these days by nations sharing the same ideology and class structure.

The conclusion we draw is that social and national motivations inter-twine, and that their often contradictory interplay is of such nature that, in modern history, periods when the class conflict predominates in world affairs alternate with those when national competition takes precedence. I call this phenomenon the seesaw of class and national motive force in world affairs, for as one gets to the top the other goes down, diminishing its impact on foreign policy. At no time does one or the other wither away; it just recedes into the background, awaiting its turn.[22]

During the First World War the clash between the two groups of powers, the Entente and the Austro-German Alliance, was so sharp and absorbing that Lenin could mention it as one of the conditions that made the Russian Revolution possible. The national motivation was then pre-dominant. When, however, Western chancelleries became aware of what the Revolution was all about, the result was the intervention of fourteen States and the massive support given to the White generals. Class interests prevailed on that occasion.

The Second World War is a classic example of vital national-strategic interests overriding ideological differences between the United States, the United Kingdom and the U.S.S.R., and forging a historical alliance. After the war, as the revolutionary process extended into Eastern Europe, the United States, the United Kingdom and others countered with the 'contain-ment policy', pushing the class conflict and the ideology that goes with it to the top. That was the essence of the cold war.

With the halting of the revolutionary wave in Europe, the centre of social change shifted toward the underdeveloped continents. In the West economic boom and expansion reinforced the conviction that monopoly capitalism had succeeded in controlling its explosive social problems. It was this basic appraisal that produced the switch from the cold war to the Development Decades, from confrontation to negotiation in East–West relations, from the doctrine of massive retaliation to that of 'limited war' made to order for Third World conditions.

Against that background, the nuclear stalemate between the major powers, the French rebellion within NATO and the Sino-Soviet rift, the national resurgence in the developing continents are all manifestations of the new stage in which the predominant motive force in world politics is national-strategic.

As the new nations began to raise their heads, many authors in the West expounded the thesis that civil wars, *coups d'état*, guerrilla and underground movements may well represent the means through which the power structure in the developing nations would be determined in the foreseeable future. In the United Nations the formula was 'indirect aggression'. The real problems of those nations—economic and cultural backwardness, illiteracy, single-crop agriculture, unequal trade relations, etc.—were played down, while the techniques of the power struggle became an obsession.

It was not until the 1960s that the problem of underdevelopment acquired its real dimension in the United Nations. In response, scholarly research work rose to the occasion and began to dig deeper into the multiple sources of conflict in international society.

Here, one should recall the three main contradictions built into imperialism, as formulated by Lenin in 1916, between capital and work, between the metropoles and the colonies, and between the imperialist powers themselves.[23] Certainly, over half a century has elapsed since, and radical changes have occurred in the meantime on the international arena, including the appearance of a new type of contradiction, that between capitalism and socialism. Even Lenin's classical thesis that war is inevitable so long as imperialism exists has been declared irrelevant under present conditions.[24] The reference, of course, is to world war.

Hence, peace researchers have focused on the historical and structural formation of conflicts in contemporary international society. Dieter Senghaas starts from the premise that the development of capitalism and anti-capitalist movements has led to the globalization of international politics and to the emergence of an international society. This society is conceived as an antagonistic totality made up particularly of the following conflict formations: inter-capitalist, West–East, North–South, inter-socialist, inter-Third World, and formations of structural violence where international and national conflict formations intersect. The author views the North–South conflict as originating in the relationship between the capitalist metropoles and their peripheries based on unequal exchange, exploitation and division of labour; the ruling groups in the metropoles find support in the privileged strata of the peripheries, acting as their political agents, and helping the North–South system to function.[25]

With the theoretical and methodological tools of analysis that are thus available, it is now possible to study in a more scientific way the problem of conflict and war as related to international organizations.

Eventually, research should focus on ways and means of resolving conflict or averting its violent manifestations. The starting premise here is that methodologically, conflict is controlled not by constant attempts to suppress or limit it, but by its integration into a strategy of reconciliation, with the goals of the parties that are initially incompatible being absorbed into a higher synthesis where they become compatible.

The main theoretical question in this respect is that in international politics conflict and co-operation are not mutually exclusive notions. In brief, no politics in the international arena is purely co-operative or exclusively conflictual. The very existence of highly conflicting purposes or interests between States implies, and indeed requires, some degree of co-operation among them. One need simply mention, as an illustration, the co-operation between the United States and the U.S.S.R. in drafting the two nuclear treaties on tests and proliferation. On the contrary, even in the closest forms of co-operation between nations there is always an element of conflict, as any student of military blocs or economic groupings, more or less integrated, can easily substantiate. It is the peculiar dialectical relationship between conflict and co-operation in international politics that explains better than anything else the vacillations occurring in East–West or North–South relations.

Another matter to keep in mind is that peace and conflict are not opposites. The opposite of peace is war, the violent manifestation of conflict. But, conflicts need not become violent, they need not necessarily degenerate into a war. There are basic conflicts in international politics that simply cannot be solved by force, by war.

Such conceptual clarifications are essential for the understanding of the means recommended by the United Nations Charter to be used in the settlement of disputes between States, or in averting the passage from conflict to war. Article 33 provides that the parties to any dispute likely to endanger international peace should first of all seek a solution by negotiation, inquiry, mediation, conciliation, arbitration, judicial settlement resort to regional agencies, etc.

Now, what differentiates negotiation, as the most favoured practice, from the other peaceful means ? I submit that it is the element of bargaining, of give-and-take, that makes negotiation distinct from judicial, arbitration or mediation processes.

The trouble is that, nations being what they are, and conflict being an organic feature of inter-State relations, bargaining too often turns negotiation into a dangerous exercise. As previously mentioned, the Cold War strategists developed an entire arsenal of mathematical equations and games designed to distort the process of negotiation into a bargaining exercise on the brink of war. The art of applying power to subdue the other party was considered the main thing in the bargaining process; calculated risk, deterrence 'compellent' threats, balance of terror, were the favourite concepts of strategists. Some of them suggested that rationality in the bargaining process could be taken by the opponent as a sign of weakness, and that, therefore, irrational behaviour was the best way of extracting concessions. A theory of escalation from the first rung—ostensible crisis—to the forty-fourth rung—spasm of insensate war—was formulated as a model of dealing with international conflict.[26]

However, the war in Viet Nam eventually turned into a cold shower for the strategists. Thomas Schelling is coming to the conclusion that the use of force may have a greater effect on the power that uses it than on the victim.[27] Boulding adds to this that violence against those who are morally dedicated reinforces the legitimacy and commitment of the victim, while it undermines those of the aggressor.[28]

Having said this about theories of conflict, let us now see what practice tells us about the effectiveness and competence of international organizations in coping with their main task—the elimination of violence.

Studies on United Nations involvement in international disputes show that over the 1945–65 period, of the 55 disputes referred to the United Nations, only 18 (about 33 per cent) were settled wholly or in part on the basis on United Nations resolutions; the rest were settled outside or remained unsettled.[29] Another study which examined 57 international disputes between 1946 and 1967 found that, in 29 cases (51 per cent), no United Nations action whatsoever was taken.[30] As for regional organizations such as OAS, OAU and the Arab League, their capabilities in settling disputes has likewise proved very low.[31]

One can hardly avoid the conclusion that present international organizations do not have a significant impact on either the outbreak of international conflicts or the settlement of disputes while hostilities are in progress. For one thing, the legal prohibition of the use of force, as provided in the United Nations Charter, has a rather limited effect, since in the sphere of international relations there are no tribunals and police to enforce the law. As for the moral commitment implicit in the voluntary adherence to the Charter by Member States, it has not constituted a more dependable barrier against resorting to violence than the legal one.

However, the performance of the United Nations in controlling conflict has been fairly good in cases where none of the great powers is directly involved, or in situations of emergency perceived by the superpowers as heading towards a nuclear confrontation, both providing the Security Council with the opportunity of liberating conflict-resolution from the dead hand of the unanimity rule. The most sucessful device within this purview has thus far been the peace-keeping forces, as illustrated in the former case (no direct great-power involvement) by the Cyprus conflict, and in the latter (potential nuclear confrontation) by the Middle East.

While in the early years of the United Nations, a Military Staff Committee was constituted and met regularly, the actual military arrangements foreseen in Chapter VII of the Charter and designed to make the United Nations a peace organization 'with teeth', never became a reality. In practice various forms of peace-keeping functioned until the whole idea came to a head during the highly controversial Congo affair. Ever since, the progress of peace-keeping has been pragmatic rather than institutional; both the nature of the action and the creation of the respective forces (scope, command, composition, instructions, etc.) have been defined in each individual conflict according to considerations of practical politics, including availability of money.

In the opinion of Oran Young, great-power acquiescence in playing a secondary role in peace-keeping operations will no longer hold in some cases; growing evidence suggests that the superpowers are becoming more and more aware of their overlapping interests in regulating coercive actions.[32] And one should keep in mind that peace-keeping purports to control armed hostilities rather than to find a solution to the underlying conflict.

The tendency has therefore grown in peace research to focus on the causes of conflicts rather than on fire-fighting initiatives whenever there is a fire alarm. This tendency has been reinforced by the realization that some forms of violence originate in the very structure of international society,[33] and consequently that the elimination of violence presupposes an attack upon its sources.

In this context, there are writers who maintain that present international organizations are equipped to deal exclusively with direct violence, though not very effectively; they are not enabled either legally or functionally to deal with structural or indirect violence, which, according to Galtung, is reflected in unequal power and consequently unequal life chances.[34] One such writer argues that, since international organization is conceived as an adaptation of the modern State-system, it tends to reproduce the basic characteristic of the State-system. And since the quasi-feudal structure of the modern State-system is the very essence of structural violence in international society, it does not come as a surprise that only the elimination of direct, but not of structural violence has been explicitly made part of the function of international organization.[35]

As the decolonization process got under way, the United Nations has played an ever-increasing role in the strategies of newly independent States to reduce the structural violence to which they are subjected. Nevertheless, the First Development Decade (1960–69), so pompously launched by the United Nations has led to a further deterioration of the relative position of the developing nations. While the per capita income in the industrial countries increased by over $650, that in the developing nations increased only by about $40; their share of world trade in exports declined from 21.3 per cent in 1960 to 17.6 per cent in 1969; their external debt burden grew at an alarming rate—from $10,000 million in the early 1960s to $60,000 million at the end of 1969.[36] The widening gap continues to be the law of the North–South system.

In fact, international organizations were not conceived to support an attack on the sources of the basic conflict between the rich nations and the poor. While the decolonization struggle waged within the main bodies of the United Nations, particularly the General Assembly, began in the early 1960s to be increasingly successful, turning the United Nations from a status quo institution into an accelerating factor in decolonization, the international economic and financial organizations have not displayed the same capacity of adaptation. The history of SUNFED (Special United Nations Fund for Economic Development) is illustrative in this respect; although the underdeveloped countries have made strenuous efforts to get the United Nations machinery to secure the transfer of capital from the developed nations to them, so that the poor would no longer be left at the mercy of private or public donors from the rich nations, capital transfer has remained under the control of the latter.[37]

Quite a few studies have provided evidence to show that the World Bank and the International Monetary Fund have had as their foremost goal the stimulation of private capital investment in Third World countries. To achieve this goal, the bank and the fund have not refrained from exerting pressures to make governments change their policies or even from encouraging political groups or parties more sympathetic to large-scale private capital investments in their respective countries.[38]

Such preferential policies are not hard to explain. At the time of the Bretton Woods or the Havana Conferences from which IBRD, IMF and indirectly GATT ensued, the initiators and builders were the rich industrialized nations and, as one may well expect, they created those institutions to regulate international exchange, trade and finance according to their interests. The Gold Exchange Standard set the supremacy of the dollar in the financial system, while the Third World, as we understand it today, simply did not exist.

Today, the situation is radically changed. The Third World is no longer prepared to accept a marginal status in world affairs, and is determined to make full use of all the available international machinery. Following the initiative taken by Algeria on behalf of the Group of 77, the Sixth Special Session of the United Nations General Assembly, held in April and May 1974, adopted two important resolutions on the establishment of a new international economic order and the programme of action required to attain that new order.

Whether international organizations can adapt to the new realities, whether they will prove capable of responding to the new historical challenge is one of the key questions of world order today.

Notes

1. K. Marx and F. Engels, *Selected Works*, Vol. I, p. 443-4. Moscow, Foreign Language Publishing House, 1950.

2. H. J. Morgenthau, *Politics among Nations*, 3rd ed., p. 27, New York, A. Knopf, 1965.

3. K. J. Holsti, 'The Concept of Power in the Study of International Relations', in R. L. Platzgraff (ed.), *Politics and the International System*, p. 134-49, Philadelphia, Pa, Lippincot, 1969.

4. Karl Deutsch, *Politics and Government*, p. 24, Boston, Mass., Houghton Mifflin, 1970.

5. Morgenthau, op. cit., p. 35.

6. N. D. Palmer and H. C. Perkins, *International Relations: The World Community in Transition*, 2nd ed., p. 35-91, Boston, Mass., Houghton Mifflin, 1957.

7. George W. Ball, *The Discipline of Power*, p. 17, Boston, Mass., Little Brown, 1968.

8. The distinction between the operational environment and the psychological one has been thoroughly studied by the psycho-sociological school, particularly by behaviourists (H. Kellman, Otto Klineberg, David Singer, etc.). B. Wasserman reveals that the realists fail to make the real distinction between national interests and interpretations of national interest, for the same facts mean different things to different people. The theorists of decision-making in foreign policy (R. Snyder) emphasize that the situation of conflict as perceived by political leaders is an important factor to be considered in the study of decisions.

9. David Hume, *On the Balance of Power*, quoted by Raymond Aron, *Paix et Guerre entre les Nations*, 4th ed., p. 134-5, Paris, Calmann-Lévy, 1962.

10. E. H. Carr, *Nationalism and After*, p. 6, London, Macmillan, 1945.

11. Stanley Hoffman, *Organizations Internationales et Pouvoir Politique des États*, p. 142, Paris, Armand Colin, 1954.

12. G. Barraclough, 'Wealth and Power : the Politics of Food and Oil', *The New York Review of Books*, No. 13, 7 August 1975, p. 23-30.

13. George Ball, 'Slogans and Realities', *Foreign Affairs* (New York), July 1969, p. 625.

14. E/AC.62/9.

15. K. E. Boulding, *Conflict and Defense*, New York, Harper & Brothers, 1962.

16. Thomas Schelling, *The Strategy of Conflict*, Cambridge. Mass., Harvard University Press, 1963.

17. Herbert Kellman, *International Behavior*, p. 6, New York, Holt, Rinehart & Winston, 1965.
18. D. Yermolenko, 'Sociology and Problems of International Conflict', *International Affairs* (Moscow), No. 8, 1968, p. 47.
19. Istvan Kendef, *Twenty Five Years of Local Wars*, Oslo, International Peace Research Institute, 1969.
20. Ibid.
21. S. Sanakoyev, 'Foreign Policy of Socialism: Sources and Theory', *International Affairs* (Moscow), No. 5, 1975, p. 168.
22. For an extensive presentation, see S. Brucan, *The Dissolution of Power*, New York, A. Knopf, 1971.
23. V. I. Lenin, *Imperialism, the Highest Stage of Capitalism*, New York, International Publishers, 1939.
24. *Statement* of the Conference of Representatives of Communist and Workers' Parties, Moscow, November 1960.
25. Dieter Senghaas, 'Conflict Formations in Contemporary International Society', *Journal of Peace Research* (Oslo), No. 3, 1973, p. 163-84.
26. Herman Kahn, *On Escalation. Metaphors and Scenarios*, London, 1965.
27. Thomas Schelling, *Arms and Influence*, New Haven, Conn., Yale University Press, 1966.
28. K. E. Boulding, 'Rebellion and Authority', *Annals of the American Academy of Political and Social Sciences*, p. 18–185, Philadelphia, Pa., November 1970.
29. Ernst B. Haas, *Collective Security and the Future International System*, Denver, Colo., Social Science Foundation and the Gradual School of International Studies, 1968. (Monograph Series in World Affairs, 5.1.)
30. M. W. Zacher, *United Nations Involvement in Crises and Wars: Past Patterns and Future Possibilities*. Paper delivered at the sixty-sixth Annual Meeting of the American Political Science Association, Los Angeles, Calif., 8–12 September 1970.
31. L. H. Miller, 'The Prospects for Order Through Regional Security, in R. A. Falk and C. E. Black (eds.), *The Future of the International Legal Order*, Vol. I, p. 556-94, Princeton University Press, 1969.
32. Oran R. Young, 'Trends in International Peace-keeping', in Linda B. Miller (ed.), *Dynamics of World Politics*, p. 243, Englewood Cliffs, N.J., Prentice Hall, 1968.
33. Johan Galtung, 'Violence, Peace and Peace Research', *Journal of Peace Research* (Oslo), Vol. 6, No. 3, 1969, p. 167–91.
34. Ibid.
35. Volker Rittberger 'International Organization and Violence', *Journal of Peace Research* (Oslo), No. 3, 1973, p. 217–26.
36. *Final Document* of the Second Ministerial Meeting of the Group of 77, Lima, Peru, November 1971.
37. J. G. Hadwen and J. Kaufman, *How United Nations Decisions are Made*, rev. ed., Leiden, A. W. Sijthoff, 1962.
38. Rittberger, op. cit., p. 221-2.

Part III

Group perspectives

8 The socialist conception of international organization

Grigorii Morozov

Introduction

The socialist conception of international organization is based on the Leninist principles that guide foreign policy.[1] Motivated by a desire for peace and international co-operation, the Soviet Union and other socialist countries participate actively in the work of the United Nations and of many other international organizations.

The socialist view holds that, at the present stage which has been reached in the process of relaxation of international tension, international organizations are acquiring a larger role and a greater degree of responsibility. Many international organizations are now in a better position to realize their positive potentialities proclaimed at the time of their establishment but inhibited in the past by the cold war, whose consequences are still quite clearly in evidence.

In the Soviet Union and other socialist countries enormous significance is attached to implementation of the 'Programme for the Continued Struggle for Peace and International Co-operation and for the Freedom and Independence of Nations', which was approved in 1976 at the Twenty-fifth Congress of the Communist Party of the Soviet Union.[2] This explains why students of international organizations in the socialist countries consider the chief criterion for the usefulness of a particular organization to be the contribution it makes to the realization of détente.

Jurists, historians, economists and sociologists collaborate in formulat-

---

GRIGORII MOROZOV heads the Division of International Organizations at the Institute of World Economics and International Relations of the USSR Academy of Sciences, Moscow. He has published several books and many articles on international organizations and relations.

ing the socialist conception of international organizations.[3] A major scientific monograph on the subject, prepared jointly by scholars from a number of socialist countries, was published a few years ago in connection with the twenty-fifth anniversary of the United Nations.[4]

International organizations and international relations

One of the remarkable features of present-day international relations is the growing part played by international organizations. They had no established role before the Second World War and confined themselves to a few specialized spheres (transport, health, etc.). The League of Nations, offshoot of the 'Versailles system', was a failure as far as the maintenance of peace was concerned.

Socialist doctrine denies any idea of succession linking the United Nations to the League of Nations. The United Nations—the first international organization in history with the genuine ability for the maintenance of peace—was created as a result of the victory of the anti-Hitler coalition in the Second World War.

In the post-war period it is not only quantitative growth but to no lesser extent new qualitative features resulting from major shifts in the world scene which have made international organizations an important element of international relations. Whereas, in the past, international organizations were based solely on the capitalist system of States, the position has now radically altered in that there exists a world socialist system. There now exist in the world international intergovernmental organizations which unite States within the framework of the main social systems, and also international organizations which cut across the dividing lines between these systems and comprise States with different, and sometimes opposing, social systems. These latter organizations represent a highly important feature of contemporary international life, marked as it is by the peaceful coexistence of States with different social systems. The United Nations occupies a central place among these organizations.

The collapse of colonialism and the emergence of a large number of young national States have led to the emergence of international organizations among developing countries. The far-reaching progress made by social movements has also led to the creation of many international non-governmental organizations.

One major characteristic of contemporary international organizations is the result of the scientific and technological revolution. There now exists a host of problems of a global nature which call for broad international co-operation: first and foremost the averting of a nuclear-missile world war; followed by protection of the environment; the peaceful conquest of space; food, energy, raw materials and other problems.

International organizations, in the opinion of those who have studied the matter in the socialist countries, offer outstanding possibilities for co-operation between States in specific fields, and organizations such as the United Nations and certain regional organizations offer an excellent means of settling inter-State disputes. A study of international organizations requires consideration of the political and social factors underlying the fundamental principles and trends of development of international relations in our time. These factors are the disposition and correlation of political and class forces in the international arena, as well as other factors which determine inter-State relations within major social systems, and between States belonging to different systems, including their attitude to the fundamental political and economic problems of our day, starting with that of war and peace. Thus, in studying the international organizations of the capitalist countries, the socialist view takes into account new phenomena in the development of capitalism. These phenomena have led to the setting up of military and political blocs and economic groupings. The socialist view of these organizations is critical, considering that the activity of military blocs enhances the threat of war and that the exclusive character of the economic groupings disrupts the process of internationalizing world economic relations and results in discriminatory attitudes in relations between States belonging to different social systems.

It is clear that there is as yet no generally accepted definition of international organization. In the author's opinion, it is possible, in the light of the basic tenets of the socialist conception, to define an international organization in its most general form as a stable, clearly structured instrument of international co-operation, freely established by its members for the joint solution of common problems and the pooling of efforts within the limits laid down in its statutes. International organizations have, as a rule, at least three member countries, which may be represented by governments, official organizations or non-governmental organizations. International organizations have agreed aims, organs with appropriate terms of reference and also specific institutional features such as statutes, rules of procedure, membership, etc. The aims and activity of an international organization must be in keeping with the universally accepted principles of international law embodied in the Charter of the United Nations and must not have a commercial character or pursue profit-making aims.

Multinational corporations, private international cartels, monopolies and other similar international bodies have nothing to do with international organizations in the true sense of the term.

International intergovernmental organizations (IGOs)

The significance of this group of international organizations lies in the fact that States participate officially in them, and in the importance and variety of the tasks which many of them are called upon to undertake. IGOs are not merely instruments for multilateral diplomacy. Their sphere of activity frequently extends beyond that of political relations between States and embraces many other fields.

Underlying the creation of IGOs is the need for governments to seek joint solutions to major world problems in the interests of peace and the genuine desire of nations and States to enter into economic and cultural relations with each other, even if the accomplishment of this desire is impeded by various factors such as the policy of economic discrimination which is practised by a number of countries in the West.

In order to understand the overall question of participation by socialist States in IGOs in which States with opposing social systems are represented, particular attention must be paid to the Leninist principle that, in foreign policy, it is essential to take into account not only the aggressive schemes of capitalist circles but also the attitudes of sane-thinking bourgeois politicians and opportunities for agreement with the capitalist States.[5] The activity of these IGOs is therefore marked not only by co-operation but also by bitter contention, because peaceful coexistence in no way implies compromise in ideological matters.

The socialist conception of international organization attributes great importance to the role of the young States in IGOs, for whom participation in these organizations is part of the process of consolidating their sovereignty and national independence and of solving their pressing economic and other problems.

International organizations play a fairly large part in present-day international relations, especially in view of the détente situation, but the actual influence of the various organizations can vary enormously depending on their nature, composition and the way in which political forces are disposed within them.

The socialist conception holds that IGOs like States, are part of the overall system of international relations, albeit having a specific role. Whereas States, possessing full rights under international law, constitute first-class members of the system, IGOs on the whole are looked upon as second-class members. Within the system of international relations, IGOs can be classified both according to their real importance and according to formal criteria. In regard to the latter, certain IGOs form part of the general system of international relations both as components of that system and of one of its subsystems in view of their relationship with a larger organization constituting such a subsystem (for example, the United Nations maintains relations with the Specialized Agencies within its system—which is in fact the subsystem here envisaged—and with non-governmental organizations on a consultative basis). Organizations such as Unesco or ILO can be regarded both as part of the United Nations subsystem and as autonomous elements of the general system of international relations. But subsystems (or the aggregate of a number of international organizations bound together by formal links) do not constitute new international organizations; for example, the United Nations 'family' as such—the United Nations subsystem—does not constitute an independent element within the general system, though its components do.

In addition to those already mentioned, the place occupied by an international organization in the hierarchy of international relations depends on a number of other factors: the kind of activity it performs, the size and nature of its membership, etc.

The influence exerted by international organizations on the policies of States and on international relations as a whole is a complex phenomenon. In a certain sense this influence is a two-way process since the situation in international organizations is to a large extent determined by the general processes taking place in the international sphere, while their activity in turn constitutes an integral part of international relations as a whole Their activity as it were transforms international problems, either showing how they can be solved or making it apparent that no solution is possible for the time being. Of great value is the use of specific institutional forms which provide members of international organizations with additional opportunities for talks, joint research, efforts to find solutions, etc. Among recognized forms of activity are the drawing up of draft international agreements, conventions and regulations, codification of elements of international law, and attempts (which, unfortunately, have not yet been sufficiently successful) to employ traditional forms of mediation for settling international conflicts.

While attaching great importance to IGOs, socialist doctrine nevertheless rejects, for the foreseeable future, the possibility that they will evolve towards supranational federations such as a 'world government', 'universal parliament' or similar type of institution which, in the opinion of a number of bourgeois thinkers, would be capable of providing a radical solution to all international problems. We take issue with the advocates of the 'world State' idea chiefly over the question of the frontiers of what is possible for international organizations. Underlying the notion of creating 'universal federations' is the idea that they would be all-powerful, capable of bringing about radical changes in the world and solving even the most complex social and political problems.

International organizations nevertheless occupy in the system of international relations an important place, albeit bounded by objective limits, a place which is determined principally by the objective laws of social development and also by the interests, views and sovereignty of individual States. Within these limits, IGOs naturally enjoy a degree of independence, but their freedom of action is by no means unlimited: questions of war and peace and also fundamental social problems can be solved only as a result of action by States and of interaction and co-operation between the major political forces. IGOs are therefore not self-sufficient; they cannot determine the course of world development. Their role is to help to strengthen peace and inter-State co-operation, giving full weight to the interests of their members, rather than pursuing the aim, which would ensue from the notion of a 'world State', of abolishing national sovereignty. Within well-defined limits, they can also help to solve certain social problems.

As the establishment of a durable system of international security progresses, certain IGOs will inevitably undergo major transformations, change their character and in some cases even cease to exist. A realistic socialist view of foreign policy rests on the fact that the Soviet Union has frequently proposed, as an important step towards détente in the world and on the continent of Europe, the simultaneous disbanding of both the North Atlantic Treaty Organization (NATO) bloc and the Warsaw Treaty Organization (Warsaw Pact). As is well known, the Council for Mutual Economic Assistance (COMECON) is prepared under certain conditions to pursue relations with the European Economic Community (EEC).

The socialist conception is also based on the fact that IGOs possess a specific international legal personality, the character of which consists in its limited scope in comparison with that of States which are fully autonomous entities in international law. In this respect the scope of the legal personality vested in the United Nations, a number of its Specialized Agencies[6] and certain other organizations is greater than for the general run of IGOs.

In studying the activity of IGOs, the socialist approach analyses the working of their machinery. It takes the view that the activity of every part of the structure of any IGO must above all reflect the fundamental principle of modern international law—that of the sovereign equality of States as embodied in the Charter of the United Nations and in the statutes of many IGOs. The true guarantee of peace on earth depends directly on observance of this principle.

IGOs are established for the purpose of joint action by States in their common interest. Member States are juridically equal entities in international intercourse, but at the same time their responsibility and individual contribution to solving the problems of a particular IGO depends on the opportunities available to them in real terms.

The juridical equality of the Member States of IGOs as a principle of international law is not nullified by the fact of their actual inequality, which is determined by many different factors: military and economic strength, size of population, possession of natural resources, etc. The IGOs, established in strict accordance with the universally recognized principles of international law, adhere strictly to the principle of 'one country, one vote'. The unanimous vote rule applied to the permanent members of the Security Council of the United Nations is an expression of the particular responsibility borne by those powers for the fate of the world and the principle of equality between two opposing social systems, necessitating agreed solutions to international problems.

Realization of the potential of IGOs depends mainly on the will of their Member States and the efforts they make towards co-operation and peace. The functional efficiency of the machinery of an IGO, i.e. the quality of the international civil service, is naturally also of considerable importance.

The socialist conception regards compromise and mutual concessions (as long as they are outside the ideological sphere) as important elements in international co-operation between States. The activity of IGOs is indeed inconceivable without them.

IGOs must therefore respect the principles of maintenance of peace and sovereign equality and take the interests of all Member States into account to the greatest possible extent. In terms of their activity, these characteristics should find expression in the decisions they take, which influence the policies of their Member States in one direction or another. We cannot accept the point of view which holds that international organizations 'develop a will which is juridically *independent of the will of the Member States* and superior to it'.[7] Such an interpretation can be employed, as it was during the cold-war period, to enable a group of countries, taking advantage of their 'automatic majority' of votes, to make use of IGOs to impose their will on other countries.

Attempts to infer that decisions taken by IGOs are of a legally binding nature because they derive from a 'supreme' will are in irreconcilable contradiction with the universally accepted character of this category of international organization. It is significant that these IGOs comprise States with differing social systems and differing class structures. The wills of States with different social systems which are members of an IGO cannot be fused together and form some kind of single 'general' or 'supreme' will in the classic sense, i.e. a unified and stable will. Clashing class interests cannot produce a synthesis of wills of this kind. At the same time it is essential to give consideration to the interests of States which are opposed in their social attitudes in order that the activity of such IGOs may achieve just results on the basis of respect for sovereignty and for the interests of all Member States.

The decisions of IGOs should be taken in accordance with a set procedure. These decisions will then reflect the interaction (made up of conflict and co-operation) between the various political forces in the organization in question, and it is this which provides a genuine basis for their legal significance. Other factors which exert an influence on the decisions taken by IGOs include the interest taken by individual regions in the questions under discussion, the positions adopted by groups of States and individual States, etc.

The combined will of these IGOs is distinct from the wills of their individual members in its essence and in its nature. It is formed as a result of decisions arrived at by the members of the IGO, usually by way of compromise. This combination of will is a dynamic force because, in finding a solution to various problems, there is a clash between the wills of the different States, and it is as the result of compromise between them that an agreed position is reached and expressed on any given concrete question. The various wills in this case are not aggregated arithmetically; each one exists independently or inside a homogeneous socio-political group, within whose framework they can be combined. Hence the specific will of an IGO is a complex expression of the positions of the Member States of the organization.

The socialist conception rejects the view of certain bourgeois internationalists who, noting 'the ambiguity . . . of the very concept of international organization', since it does not represent community between its members, draw the conclusion that international organizations are powerless.[8] This kind of pessimistic assertion is belied by facts which bear witness to the positive contribution made by many international organizations to international co-operation.

It is clear, of course, that the fullest possible development of such activity on the part of international organizations is possible only when the overall background of international relations is favourable.

The United Nations

The socialist conception attaches great importance to the United Nations and to many of its Specialized Agencies. The United Nations is considered to be an integral part of present-day international relations.[9] However justified criticism of the United Nations may be, it is undeniable that during the post-war period it was definitely instrumental in averting a new world war.

The United Nations is a unique international organization both in its membership and in the breadth of its competence. One of its most important features is its universality and, above all, the fact that it contains States with opposing social systems.

The Charter of the United Nations reaffirmed the main democratic principles of international law on which peaceful coexistence is based. Events have shown that the Charter has withstood the test of time; it embodies the means necessary to ensure peace and international co-operation.

The key principle of the Charter—that requiring resolutions in the Security Council to be voted unanimously by the permanent members—guarantees co-operation between the permanent members of the council and prevents that organ from being used for purposes which run counter to the interests of peace and security. This principle is tremendously important for young States, small countries and peoples who are struggling for freedom and independence. An example was the USSR's veto in 1961 which prevented the Salazar regime from dragging the United Nations into an adventure against India over the liberation of Goa, Demao and Diu.

The United Nations constitutes a highly important international forum for multilateral discussions. It is the place where vital texts are prepared and it can, in certain circumstances, be the centre for action in defence of peace and for carrying out international co-operative projects.

Analysis of the results of United Nations activity, on the other hand, leads to the conclusion that its potential has not been fully realized. The following observation by L. I. Brezhnev throws light on the reasons for this: 'The United Nations is not some sort of self-sufficient power nor some kind of universal supergovernment. Its actions and the positions it takes up merely reflect the existing balance of forces between the States of the world, which is the prevailing trend in international life.'[10] The results of its work and the extent to which those results conform to the Charter of the United Nations therefore vary at different stages of its activity, depending on the actual balance of forces at any particular time.

The cold-war years had an extremely negative effect on the United Nations. Certain countries, relying on the voting majority they enjoyed (the 'voting machine'), sanctioned, in the name of the United Nations, a number of actions which ran counter to the aims of its Charter. This policy inflicted serious damage on the United Nations. In connection with one of these actions—the 'Korean operation' of 1950–51—an American internationalist wrote: '. . . the UN flag flew at the head of the expedition, but the direction of the war was not really controlled by the United Nations . . . and the more momentous decisions taken during the war were made by [the United States]'.[11] It would be possible to find numerous examples of similar testimony concerning a number of other actions by the United Nations, particularly the 'Congo operation'.

During the cold-war years serious damage was inflicted on the principle of the universality of membership of the United Nations: the socialist countries were subjected to open discrimination. Unfortunately, discriminatory acts of this kind have been practised even recently in the Security Council (as regards the admission of the Democratic Republic of Viet Nam and the Republic of South Viet Nam in 1975).

Even during the cold war, however, the socialist countries and other peace-loving powers were able to achieve a number of positive results during discussions on the struggle for national liberation and other questions—modest but none the less important positive steps, among them the resolution adopted on the initiative of the U.S.S.R. condemning war propaganda in any country and in any form (1947), the proposals by Czechoslovakia concerning the principles of peaceful coexistence and others.

Changes in the balance of power in the world led to similar changes in the disposition of forces within the United Nations, which made it possible to take many useful decisions in vital areas, especially decolonization, disarmament and human rights. An important question in regard to many of these decisions is the extent to which they have been implemented. Over 100 resolutions against the South African racists, for example, are still non-effective. Not enough has been done as regards using the United Nations for the settlement of international conflicts and ensuring peace: Security Council resolution 242 on the Near East, for example, is still unimplemented after many years.

On all the major disputed points the line of demarcation between the Soviet Union and other socialist countries and a number of other powers coincides with that relating to the fundamental principles of the United Nations Charter.

This applies, for example, to the question of United Nations peacekeeping operations which has been under discussion in the United Nations for many years. The USSR insists on the necessity of strict observance of the United Nations Charter, especially the clauses dealing with the decisive role of the Security Council in the conduct of such operations. The stand aiming at setting up the Secretary-General of the United Nations, in opposition to the Security Council, to assume 'effective control' of such operations, has brought about a number of extremely negative consequences (the 'Congo operation', for instance). Firm objections to this attitude are called for. The Charter of the United Nations, which confers upon the Secretary-General important and at the same time clearly defined rights, by no means gives him independent and personal powers to conduct peace-keeping operations.

After many years of a stubbornly negative approach, the countries of the West seem recently more inclined to recognize the primary responsibility of the Security Council for the maintenance of international peace and security, including United Nations peace-keeping operations.

The decision taken at the thirtieth session of the General Assembly of the United Nations concerning the necessity of removing the foreign troops stationed in the Republic of Korea under the United Nations flag is tantamount to a disavowal of the Korean action already mentioned. The history of the United Nations demonstrates the rightfulness of the socialist position and bears witness to the fact that the problem of collective action by the United Nations in defence of peace can be solved only on the basis of strict conformity with the United Nations Charter. Much the same can be said in connection with other questions which have given rise to contention in the United Nations.

Recent United Nations activity shows an increasingly marked preponderance of the constructive over the destructive approach. However, this does not mean that everything is now plain sailing. In response to the weakening of their position resulting from the new balance of forces within the United Nations the Western powers took a number of retaliatory measures against the so-called 'tyranny of the majority'—measures which ran counter to the United Nations Charter. Among these may be mentioned the partial withholding of contributions to the United Nations, the declared intention of curtailing the assistance given to countries which take up, at sessions of the General Assembly, positions displeasing to one of the Western powers, the use of the veto in the Security Council for the purpose of blocking proposals which are inconvenient to a certain group of Western countries, etc. The extreme-leftist views which have in recent years been disseminated within the United Nations create obvious difficulties for the objective discussion of important questions and for rational attempts to find positive solutions to them.

It is clear that no little effort is still required before the United Nations can become a reliable instrument for the preservation of peace and fully justify the hopes placed in it by the peoples.

Economic, humanitarian, scientific and technological problems have in recent years occupied an increasingly large place in the affairs of the United Nations.[12]

A matter meriting attention in this connection is that of determining the correct balance between the various aspects of the United Nations' activity. The socialist approach is based on the fact that the United Nations was founded by the peoples of the anti-Hilter coalition, first and foremost in the interests of preserving peace. Its aim is that the United Nations should become stronger, that its authority in international political affairs should be enhanced, that its political machinery should function effectively and that the governments of Member States of the United Nations should undeviatingly adhere to its Charter.

A different approach affirms the need to concentrate the activity of the United Nations and of the organizations making up the system on economic, scientific and technological co-operation, to the detriment of their political functions. Influential circles in the West, defending this conception, are striving to use the United Nations in order to strengthen their own influence in the countries of the Third World. On the strength of their considerable economic, scientific and technological resources, they hope in this way to make up for the losses they have suffered in fundamental political matters through the shift to their detriment of the balance of power in the United Nations.

The interests of international co-operation, however, and the United Nations' role therein, demonstrate the necessity of giving priority in its activity to political work associated with the preservation of international peace. This does not, of course, mean that it is unnecessary for the United Nations to participate in economic, scientific and technological co-operation, since there is a real need for such co-operation. The United Nations can do much towards solving the political problems which must be solved before a solution can be found to economic and other problems, particularly that of the new international economic order. Affirming the priority of the United Nations' political functions, socialist doctrine supports the economic demands of the developing countries for a restructuring of international economic relations. It is undeniable that the demands of the developing countries, that their sovereignty over their natural resources and their right to nationalize foreign property should be respected and that the principle of equal rights in economic co-operation between peoples should be upheld, are fully justified.

The discussion on economic questions which took place at the sixth and seventh special sessions of the General Assembly of the United Nations demonstrated the direct relationship which exists between furthering the process of détente and solving the pressing problems of international economic relations, especially overcoming the onerous legacy of colonialism in the developing countries.

International intergovernmental organizations of the socialist countries

The significance of the international organizations of the States of the socialist system lies in the co-operative role of the socialist countries in the modern world, and in the special features marking these countries' international relations. The basis of these relations is the principle of proletarian internationalism, founded on the brotherly mutual aid, genuine equality of rights and independence of the countries concerned. The international relations of the socialist countries are characterized by disinterested mutual aid, friendship and co-operation, and the voluntary pooling of forces in the struggle for the victory of socialism. Such general democratic principles of international law as the principles of respect for State sovereignty, equal rights and self-determination of peoples, mutual benefit and non-interference, are reflected in the relations of the socialist countries.

The most important of the international organizations of the socialist countries are the Warsaw Treaty Organization[13] and the Council for Mutual Economic Assistance.[14]

The Warsaw Treaty of friendship, co-operation and mutual assistance was signed on 14 May 1955 in Warsaw and laid the basis of the defensive organization of the European socialist States. The establishment of the Warsaw Treaty Organization was a response by the socialist States to a set of moves by the Western countries signifying a real threat to the socialist States. As we know, NATO was founded in 1949, later to include the Federal Republic of Germany, and the blocs of SEATO, the Baghdad Pact (subsequently CENTO) and ANZUS were established, together with a ring of military bases around the U.S.S.R. and other socialist States.

The Warsaw Treaty Organization has a set of organs (Political Consultative Committee, Unified Military Command, Armed Forces Staff, Military Council) effectively fostering the defensive military strength of its members. The organization reliably ensures the security of the socialist countries in the event of armed attack on them in Europe since it provides for immediate assistance by every means, including the use of armed force. The treaty proclaims its conformity with the Charter of the United Nations and the need to establish a system of security in Europe comprising all States of the continent. The treaty embodies the most important principles of the United Nations Charter. It contains a direct reference to Article 51 of the Charter as the legal basis for the activity of its members.

The link to be created between the organization and the United Nations in the event of the treaty machinery entering into operation is based on the provisions of Chapter VIII of the United Nations Charter. Alongside joint defensive activities, the treaty provides for participation in all steps to ensure international security, co-operation in disarmament, and the development of economic and political ties. The treaty is open to accession by other States, regardless of their social and political systems. Its members have repeatedly proposed to NATO members discussion of the possibility of simultaneous disbandment of both organizations or—as a preliminary step—of dissolution of their military organizations. The NATO countries constantly reject such proposals.

COMECON is an international organization of the socialist countries for economic, scientific and technical co-operation. It was founded in January 1949. There is a COMECON charter and a convention on privileges and immunities. The members of COMECON are Bulgaria, Cuba, Czechoslovakia, the German Democratic Republic, Hungary, the Mongolian People's Republic, Poland, Romania and the U.S.S.R. Under a special agreement Yugoslavia takes part in COMECON activities, while the Democratic People's Republic of Korea and, since the thirtieth session of COMECON in July 1976, the Socialist Republic of Viet Nam, enjoy observer status. In addition, the delegations of the People's Republic of Angola and of the Lao People's Democratic Republic attended the above session as observers. Under agreements concluded, Finland, Mexico and Iraq co-operate with COMECON.

There is an abundant literature on COMECON in the socialist countries. The COMECON charter lays down that the organization's activities should be based on socialist relations between States, and this is fully reflected in the actual conduct of its operations. The charter contains a provision to the effect that all-round economic co-operation shall be developed 'on the basis of consistent implementation of the international socialist division of labour in the interests of constructing socialism and communism in member countries and of securing lasting peace throughout the world'. Among the principles of co-operation, the COMECON charter refers to full equality of rights, respect of sovereignty and national interests, mutual benefit and comradely mutual assistance. The principle of mutual benefit operates in COMECON not in the purely commercial sense but as a principle determined by the general aims of consolidating the world system of socialism and at the same time strengthening each country within the socialist community. Any factors making for competition between COMECON member countries are ruled out, and full freedom is guaranteed for all economic (including trade) relations without any discriminatory stipulations.

The organizational structure of COMECON consists of the supreme authority, i.e. the periodically convened sessions of the collegiate organ—the council, a permanent body—the executive committee of the council, the Committee for Co-operation in the Field of Planning and the Committee for Scientific and Technical Co-operation, permanent commissions on the most important branches of the national economy, which numbered twenty in 1976, and the council secretariat.

All COMECON members are equally represented and have equal rights and obligations. Under the COMECON charter the organs of the council may adopt various legal instruments on organizational and procedural matters. Representation in all organs and voting rights do not depend on the size of financial contributions.

COMECON has set up its own scientific research institutions: the International Institute of Economic Problems of the World Socialist System; and the Institute of Standardization.

COMECON deals with complex and important questions regarding co-operation of the socialist countries. Its activities are directed towards the development of broad mutually beneficial economic ties with all countries, regardless of their social and political systems, on the basis of equality, mutual benefit and non-interference in domestic matters.

The socialist countries also co-operate through other international organizations of theirs, including credit and financial organizations (the International Bank for Economic Co-operation and the International Investments Bank), organizations by industry, organizations in the field of scientific and technical co-operation (including the Joint Institute for Nuclear Research, the International Centre for Scientific and Technical Information, etc.), organizations in the field of transport and communications and others, numbering about thirty in all.

COMECON maintains relations with international organizations of the socialist countries and with other international organizations, including the United Nations (the Economic and Social Council (Ecosoc) and its regional economic commissions), with most of the United Nations Specialized Agencies, the International Atomic Energy Agency (IAEA), the United Nations Conference on Trade and Development (UNCTAD), the United Nations Industrial Development Organization (UNIDO), the United Nations Commission on International Trade Law, the International Organization for Standardization (ISO), the International Federation for Documentation (FID), The World Power Conference, and others.

The principles of co-operation between the Member States of COMECON are laid down both in its charter and in a number of bilateral and multilateral treaties and agreements between socialist countries, in the 'basic principles of the international socialist division of labour' and in agreements regarding the organization of co-operation in railway operation, electricity supply and postal communications, unification of the power systems of Bulgaria, Czechoslovakia, the German Democratic Republic, Hungary, Poland, Romania and the U.S.S.R., multilateral settlements in 'transferable roubles', and a number of other fields.

A matter of the utmost significance is the comprehensive programme for integration of the COMECON member countries, adopted at the twenty-fifth COMECON session. Socialist economic integration represents

a conscious process planned and controlled by the communist and workers' parties and governments of the COMECON member countries, fostering the international socialist division of labour, closer harmony of their economies and the establishment of a modern, highly effective economic structure, a gradual harmonization and evening-out of their levels of economic development, the establishment of deep and lasting ties in the basic economic, scientific and technological branches, the extension and strengthening of their international market, and improved trade and monetary relations.

The COMECON countries account for 37.5 per cent of world industrial production(this proportion is constantly on the increase) and they retain superiority over the capitalist system in terms of economic growth rates.

Ever since its establishment COMECON has demonstrated that it has an exceedingly important part to play in organizing the co-operation of socialist countries.

International non-governmental organizations (NGOs)

Non-governmental organizations form the largest group of international organizations.[15] To the socialist way of thinking, their special nature is primarily due to the increased influence of the public at large on foreign policy, the greater impact of public opinion in international relations and the greater importance of the ideological factor in such relations. Account should also be taken of the processes of economic development and the consequences of the scientific and technological revolution, which has also led to a greater number of specialized NGOs. In recent years there has been a sharp increase in the number of international sports organizations and organizations in the field of culture.

The socialist conception is primarily concerned with NGOs from two aspects. The first relates to social factors and the attitude of NGOs to the preservation of peace. A great deal of attention in this connection is given to such large-scale organizations as the World Federation of Trade Unions, the World Federation of Democratic Youth, the Women's International Democratic Federation, the movement of peace partisans with its supreme authority, the World Peace Council, and so forth. These organizations, which include representatives of various sectors of the public, are carrying on a consistent struggle to preserve peace in the world and are co-operating ever more extensively with such authoritative NGOs as the World Federation of United Nations Associations, the International Council of Scientific Unions, the World Federation of Scientific Workers, the Pugwash movement, and others.

A number of traditionally conservative NGOs (e.g. organizations based on religious beliefs, pacifist or federalist preoccupations, etc.) have recently, under the influence of general trends in world development, started establishing contacts and co-operation with large-scale democratic NGOs, chiefly on matters related to the prevention of war.

The activities of many NGOs, helping to establish a particular social climate, have made a tangible contribution to the settlement of a number of major international conflicts, chiefly in Viet Nam.

A most important stage in the development of NGOs was the World Congress of Forces Making for Peace, held in Moscow in October 1973. This congress, the greatest forum in history of the peace-loving community, was attended by 3,500 delegates from 143 countries, representing over 1,100 national and 120 international organizations and movements. One of the fourteen commissions of the congress concerned itself specially with the co-operation of international non-governmental and intergovernmental organizations.

There are many NGOs of a specialized character according to their aims, membership, and so forth. They vary very considerably in importance. Many scientific organizations, such as the International Council of Scientific Unions (ICSU), do useful work. On the other hand, there are a number of organizations backing the one-sided interests of particular groups opposed to the policy of disarmament.

The socialist conception regards the NGOs as an important channel through which public opinion has a certain influence on the international climate and to some extent on government decision-making.

The NGOs have made a considerable contribution to the adoption of many useful resolutions by the United Nations General Assembly, and to the conclusion of the nuclear test ban treaty, the treaty on the non-proliferation of nuclear weapons and a number of other important instruments in the field of arms limitation.

The activities of NGOs contribute to the development of international law. The draft conventions they prepare on various questions may subsequently be examined by States or by IGOs and so influence the elaboration of standards of international law.

NGOs may influence inter-State co-operation in special fields. Thus the International Geophysical Year (IGY) was promoted by the Special Committee for IGY set up by ICSU. The Scientific Committee on Antarctic Research, the Scientific Committee on Oceanic Research and the Committee for the International Years of the Quiet Sun are organizations concerning themselves with protection of the environment, while other NGOs assist not only the development of science but also in the establishment of a favourable climate in relations between States.

A matter of some interest regarding the part played by NGOs in international relations is their consultative status with IGOs, chiefly the United Nations, Unesco, ILO and others. In recent years a number of works specially devoted to these matters have been published in the U.S.S.R. and other socialist countries. The fact that such links exist between NGOs and the United Nations evinces recognition of the fact that the activities of non-governmental organizations, the information they put out, their links with public circles, and so on, are of interest to the United Nations. At the same time, students of international affairs in the socialist countries are critical of many aspects of this system, for the consultative status arrangements still fall short of what the development of modern international relations in fact calls for.

The thirteenth general conference of the Conference of Non-Governmental Organizations in Consultative Status with the United Nations Economic and Social Council turned its attention in 1976 to many short-comings in this field.

This brief survey of the socialist conception shows that it attaches real significance to international organizations as a means of securing peace, peaceful coexistence and international co-operation. A characteristic feature of this conception is the way in which it links the activities of international organizations to practical issues and seeks to ground all the main aspects of this important problem in theory while never losing sight of the actual significance of the particular organization in question.

The socialist conception is the outcome of a multidisciplinary study of international organizations drawing on the science of international law, the science of international political and economic relations, sociology, history and various other branches of learning. It is not a mere amalgam or patchwork of these branches of knowledge, but an organically unified complex which permits comprehensive examination of all the basic problems of international organizations, studying all international organizations, both intergovernmental and non-governmental, on the basis of Marxist-Leninist methodology.

The proponents of the socialist conception attach great importance to scientific co-operation with students of international organizations who represent other trends and schools, since such co-operation is conducive to the development of science for the benefit of peace and progress.

Notes

1. V. I. Lenin, *Leninskiy Sbornik XXXVI* [Lenin's Almanach], p. 451-5. Moscow, 'Politizdat', 1959, 483 p.

2. L. I. Brezhnev, *Report of the CPSU Central Committee and the Immediate Tasks of the Party in Home and Foreign Policy. XXV Congress of the CPSU, Moscow,* 1976, Moscow, Novosti Press Agency, 1976, 112 p.

3. K. Kocot, *Organizacje Miedzinarodowe. Systematyczny Zarus Zagadnién Prawa Miedzynarodowego* [International Organizations. Review of International Law Problems], Wroclaw, Ossolineum, 1971, 332 p. ; W. Morawiecki, *Funkcje Organizacji Miedzynarodowej* [Functions of International Organizations], Warsaw, Ksiazka i Wiedza, 1971, 459 p. ; G. I. Morozov, *Mezhdunarodniye Organizatzii (Nekotoriye Voprosy Teorii)* [International Organizations. (Some Theoretical Problems)], 2nd ed. rev., Moscow, Izdatel'stvo 'Mysl'. 1974, 332 p.; M. Potočny, *Mezinarodni Organizace* [International Organizations], Prague, 'Svoboda', 1971, 369 p.

4. G. I. Morozov (ed.), *OON. Itogy. Tendentzii. Perspektivy* [The UN. Achievements. Trends. Perspectives], Moscow, Izdatel'stvo 'Mezhdunarodniye Otnosheniya', 1970, 544 p.

5. V. I. Lenin, *Polnoye Sobranize Sochinenii* [Complete Works], Vol. 40, p. 289-90 ; Vol. 41, p. 19-22, 51, 53.

6. G. I. Morozov (ed.), *Spetzyalizirovanniye Ouchrezhdeniya OON v Sovremennom Mire* [Specialized Agencies of the UN in the Contemporary World], Moscow, Izdatel'stvo 'Nauka', 1967, 402 p.

7. C. Rousseau, *Droit International Public*, Vol. II : *Les Sujets de Droit*, p. 451, Paris, Sirey, 797 p.

8. Stanley Hoffmann, 'An Evaluation of the United Nations', in R. A. Falk and S. H. Mendlovitz (eds.), *The Strategy of World Order*, Vol. III : *The United Nations*, p. 793-5, New York, World Law Fund, 1966. 848 p.

9. G. I. Morozov, *Organizatziya Ob'edinionnyh Natziy. (Osnovniye Mezhdunarodno-pravoviye Aspekty Struktury i Deyatel' Nosty)* [The United Nations Organization. (Principal International-Legal Aspects of Structure and Activities)], Moscow,

Izdatel'stvo Mezhdunarodnyh Otnosheniy, 1962, 511 p.; M. Potočny, *OSN-Nastroj Miru a Mezinarodni Spoluprace* [The UN—Instrument of Peace and International Co-operation], Prague, 'Svoboda', 1975, 380 p.; V. G. Shkunaev, *OON v Sovremennom Mire* [The UN in the Contemporary World], Moscow, Izdatel'stvo 'Nauka', 1976, 350 p.; V. L. Israelyan (ed.), *Sovietskiy Soyuz i Organizatziya Ob'edinionnyh Natziy (1961-1965)* [The Soviet Union and the United Nations Organization (1961–1965)], Moscow, 'Nauka', 1968, 687 p.; A. L. Narochnitzky (ed.), *Sovietskiy Soyuz i Organizatziya Ob'edinionnyh Natziy (1966-1970)* [The Soviet Union and the United Nations Organization (1966-1970)], Moscow, Izdatel'stvo 'Nauka', 1975, 535 p.; I. G. Oussatchev (ed.), *Sovietskiy Soyuz v Organizatzii Ob'edinionnyh Natziy* [The Soviet Union in the United Nations], Moscow, Izdatel'stvo 'Nauka', 1965, Vol. I, 454 p.; Vol. 2, 668 p.; A. Yankov, *Organizatziya na Ob'edinenite Natzii* [The United Nations Organization], Sofia, 'Nauka i Izkoustvo', 1965, 329 p.

10. L. I. Brezhnev, *Leninskim Koursom* [Following Lenin's Course], Vol. III, p. 148-9, Moscow, 'Politizdat', 1972.

11. R. M. Maciver, *The Nations and the United Nations*, p. 89, New York, Manhattan Publ. Co., 1969, 186 p.

12. M. M. Maksimova (ed.), *OON i Mezhdunarodnoye Economicheskoye Sotrudnichestvo* [The UN and International Economic Co-operation], Moscow, Izdatel'stvo 'Mysl', 1970, 478 p.

13. A Latzo, *Der Warschauer Vertrag—Instrument zur Sicherung des Friedens* [The Warsaw Treaty Organization—Instrument for Securing Peace], Berlin, Straatsverl. der DDR, 1972, 93 p.; A. Semerdziyez (ed.), *Organizatziyata na Varshavskiya Dogovor. 1955-1975* [Warsaw Treaty Organization. 1955-1975], Sofia, Derz. Voenno Izdatel'stvo, 1975, 275 p.

14. H. de Fiumel, *Rada Wzajmnej Pomocy Gospodarszej* [The Council for Mutual Economic Assistance], Warsaw, 1967.

15. I. I. Kovalenko, *Mezhdunarodhie Nepravitel'stvenniye Organizatzii* [International Non-governmental Organizations], Moscow, Izdatel'stvo 'Mezhdunarodniye Otnosheniya', 1976, 167 p.

9 Western interpretations of international organization as reflected in scholarly writings

Rosalyn Higgins

This chapter looks at the main Western scholarly attitudes to international organization over the last thirty years.

The development of international organization in the post-war era necessarily encouraged various particular types of scholarship. Without purporting to trace their history or cover their scope, we can learn from the substantive topics singled out for study by a generation of scholars of international organizations what their intellectual preoccupations have been. The list of topics is vast and seemingly inexhaustible but the themes undeniably fall into certain major groups that reveal the underlying tensions in international organizations since 1945.

Nearly all the major controversies about the United Nations have been concerned with areas where this basic issue—What type of an institution is the United Nations?—has been very evident. Debates have been conducted over the law-making activities of international organizations, the proper role of their secretariats, their capacity to engage in peace-keeping, and other comparable topics. What these topics, and the vigour of the debate that they have occasioned, have in common is that they all represent crucial stepping-stones along the road where international organizations are transformed into bodies with an ethos of their own, and not treated primarily as vehicles for conference between the member nations.

ROSALYN HIGGINS is a member of the Royal Institute for International Affairs and Professor at the London School of Economics and Political Science. She has written numerous books and articles on international law and international organization, among which *The Development of International Law through the Political Organs of the United Nations* (1963).

Law-making activities
of international organizations

The literature reveals a profound division among Western scholars over the extent to which the United Nations and its Agencies possess, or should be endowed with, the capacity to bind recalcitrant members. So far as the United Nations is concerned, there has been general agreement in the West[1] that the Security Council may bind its members when it takes decisions under Article 25 and Chapter VII of the Charter;[2] and that the General Assembly, exceptionally, may lawfully require States to carry out budgetary decisions taken under Article 17 of the Charter.[3] Beyond that, however—and even in respect of these points there have been dissidents—there has been deep disagreement. The conservative school of thought in the West has taken the view that no further 'law-making' powers are to be imputed. They emphasize the sovereignty of the Member States. Limitations upon this sovereignty are only those conceded by adherence to the clear terms of the Charter itself, or by express subsequent agreement.

It will also be seen that this conservative view about the law-making impact of international organizations is closely linked to arguments about the sources of international law. In this body of writing, the argument has run as follows: sovereign States are only bound through their own consent. In some very limited areas they have consented in advance to be bound by the decisions of an international organ—for example, the United Nations Security Council acting under Chapter VII and Article 25. This must further be correct because, although sovereign States are indeed bound by international law, the sources of international law are to be found in Article 38 of the Statute of the International Court of Justice, and they do not include decisions of international organizations.[4]

It followed that these classical writers sharply distinguished between the practice of international institutions and customary international law. It was urged that political bodies could not make law. These views were buttressed by the belief that nations were bound by principles and rules and not by debates and resolutions.[5]

Those writing in this vein were of a classical training and disposition who sought to place the new impact of international bodies in the traditional legal framework. They found support in those writers who sympathized with the position of minority States within the United Nations, for whom the notion of being bound against their express will was uncomfortable.[6] The intellectual debate was obviously of practical importance to countries like South Africa, for whom the legal quality of various United Nations acts in respect of its racial policies was obviously crucial.

In 1963 a book was published which attempted to provide an intellectual framework for the refutation of these traditionalist assumptions.[7] It suggested that the United Nations was an appropriate forum in which to discern State practice, because in the post-war world this practice was increasingly conducted on a multilateral basis. The traditional hunting ground of diplomatic exchange was now supplemented by State practice as evidenced by a variety of collective acts: votes and public statements made in international organs. This fact, it was contended, existed independently from any argument about the limited law-making powers of an organ *qua* organ:

With the development of international organizations, the votes and views of States have come to have legal significance as evidence of customary law. Moreover, the practice of States comprises their collective acts as well as the total of their individual acts; and the number of occasions on which States see fit to act collectively has been greatly increased by the activities of international organizations. Collective acts of States, repeated by and acquiesced in by sufficient numbers with sufficient frequency, eventually attain the status of law. The existence of the United Nations—and especially its accelerated trend universality of membership since 1955—now provides a very clear, very concentrated focal point for State practice.[8]

There remained, of course, many questions to be answered about the nature and quality of State practice within international organizations before it could be viewed as sufficient to indicate developing customary law. The more conservative groups of writers noted that many decisions and votes in international bodies were politically motivated, and showed no sense of legal obligation. Others responded that political motivation was also present in non-institutionalized bilateral and multilateral diplomacy; it did not automatically disqualify an act from relevance as State practice indicating a custom, It has also been pointed out that the evidencing of the existence of *opinio juris*—a belief of legal requirement—is very hard to come by in the practice of international institutions. For example, a State may vote for a resolution simply because it does not wish to be in the political company of those who vote against it; or it may vote affirmatively, not because it believes the law to be correctly stated in the resolution, but because it does not wish to attract the odium of a negative vote; or it may parallel an affirmative vote with a collateral statement indicating misgivings about the legal validity of the resolution in question. For some Western scholars, these problems are so basic that they negate the possibility of a law-developing—still less a law-making—role for international organizations. But for others the problems, while real, are qualitatively no different from those that appear in assessing the value of State practice outside multilateral institutions.

Even for those who have been willing to concede that the resolutions of international organizations often have some legal significance, there have been major intellectual difficulties in identifying the limits to that proposition. Are resolutions—non-binding in strict terms—legally of greater significance when passed by vast majorities? Are the composition of those majorities significant? Does it matter—and if so, in what circumstances—if the major powers are not part of these majorities? Many Western writers have endeavoured to tackle these problems, some by emphasis on changing methods of decision-making in international organizations,[9] others by a close examination of the component elements of a 'relevant majority'. In the latter group, it has been urged, for example, that though on general issues within the normal scope of the purposes and principles of an institution no single power can effectively exercise a veto (save where specifically provided for) on law development through custom, none the less in certain new and specialized areas, the approval of the actively participating States is a necessity.[10] Reference is made, for example, to the need for the United States and the Soviet Union to support the text of resolutions which purport to reflect practice on outer-space activities.

For certain writers in the West, it has been enough to point out the strictly limited legislative competence of contemporary international organizations.[11] For them—and their view echoes observations that have been made by certain judges in the International Court of Justice[12]—that is the end of the matter. But a group of scholars have insisted that this by no means disposes of the issues. In part, as we have indicated, this is because the actions of the members of organizations—acting in their capacity as States rather than as components of international bodies—may under certain conditions provide the source material for customary international law. But there is another aspect to which certain scholars have drawn attention, namely the fact that acts may operate functionally as law without necessarily being formally binding. In other words, these scholars have been intrigued by the evidence that international institutions may, in the conduct of their business, accrue significant power to themselves because they take actions that have all the effects of legally binding decisions, whether or not they are taken by means that are in a formal sense 'binding'.

This aspect of the problem had been signalled by the handling by the International Court of Justice of the *UN Expenses Case*.[13] Here the Court was faced with the interplay between two propositions: first, that the Security Council and General Assembly were only able[14] to make recommendations about United Nations peace-keeping; and second, that

the Assembly could pass binding decisions about the budget and members'
share thereof. But what if the budget contained authorizations for peace-
keeping expenditure for actions which individual members disapproved?[15]
The Court found that, provided the purposes of the actions were *intra
vires* of the Charter, the Assembly budgetary decisions were binding. The
way in which such interrelationships can lead to operational effectiveness
in an institution, notwithstanding limited legal powers 'to bind' was
little noted by the commentators at the time. But by 1966 one eminent
scholar[16] was observing that 'the characterization of a norm as *formally
binding* is not very significantly connected with its *functional operation* as
law'. Some writers began to observe that claims were being advanced, in
international bodies, which relied on non-binding declaratory resolutions,
and that expectations were being created as to the likely content of
subsequent international decisions on the same subject.[17]

Other writers began to go further. There began to appear important
studies on the competence of international organization. Ingrid Detter,
in a scholarly and well-argued study, went beyond reliance on the constitution as a basis of competence, and even beyond the theory of implied
powers and formal revisions of the basic provisions of competence. And
she went beyond observing the impact of the application of administrative
rules. She provided persuasive evidence that the establishment of subsidiary organs, with all their delegated powers, led to members of United
Nations Agencies being 'bound' by a range of decisions to which they
had never in formal terms given their consent. After a searching study of
contracting-out provisions in certain of the agencies, there remained the
fact that a vast array of operative acts undeniably carry legal consequences
over and above the granting to the organization of any formal powers 'to
bind'. The model that she built distinguished, so far as the effects of this
observation were concerned, primary acts from operative matters, with
States seeking to exercise more control over the institution in respect of
the latter.[18] This marked, perhaps, the beginning of a significant literature
based on a functionalist perspective of international organizations.

This functionalist perspective was evident in other contributions on
this topic of organizational powers. Edward Yemin applied it directly to
a study of the legislative powers to be found in the United Nations and
Specialized Agencies. He too rejected the view that obligations *vis-à-vis*
organizations are only undertaken contractually. States cannot always avoid
legal obligation in respect of rules to which they have not consented. In
France,[19] as well as in Sweden and the United States, the argument was
being advanced that it is often impossible in practicable terms for a State
to avoid the impact of such rules, for it has still greater stakes in fully
participating in the body which it has joined. In a survey of a wide range

of Specialized Agencies, Yemin concluded that, no matter how much States prefer to use the term 'regulatory powers', it is legislative powers that have in fact come into effect.

This 'functionalist' literature was paralleled by studies which sought to ascribe, often as a matter of policy preference, very significant powers to the recommendations of the General Assembly. Thus one study identified the varying circumstances in which the Assembly made declarations, and sought to ascribe relative legal weight to these.[20] Certain European writers contributed to the debate a conceptual analysis of the notion of 'recommendation'[21] and Malintoppi elaborated a thesis of social sanction that accompanies the formulation of recommendations. And Jorge Castañeda took perhaps the most radical position, analysing different types of resolutions and contending that many of them had binding force.[22] In this, he appeared to go beyond the observation (which has now been affirmed by the International Court of Justice)[23] that such resolutions can produce legal effects.

The role of secretariats

The proper role of the secretariat of international organizations has also occasioned much scholarly comment; and this theme too is at the heart of the controversy about what it is that people wish international institutions to be able to do. There have, of course, been biographies on each of the Secretaries-General of the United Nations[24] and the systematic publication of their public papers has been under preparation. A fine early study, which carried its own clear implications as to the sort of international institution the author hoped for, was made available with the publication of Stephen Schwebel's *The Secretary-General of the United Nations* (Harvard, 1959). This was complemented by a later study by Jean Siotis *Essai sur le Secrétariat International* (Geneva, Droz, 1963), which was firmly rooted in diplomatic history but also examined, from a functional point of view, the roles that an international secretariat is called on to play. Leon Gordenker, in *The UN Secretary-General and the Maintenance of Peace* (Columbia University Press, 1967) focused on those aspects of the Secretary-General's role that have caused most controversy.

Peace-keeping

We have suggested that the topics that have attracted most scholarly attention are those that reflect the great debate over the operational powers of international organization. This reflection has sometimes been direct, sometimes indirect. The literature on law-making by international bodies was an example of the former. And the prodigious literature that now exists on the topic of peace-keeping is an example of the latter. However, it may be noted that whereas in the former topic the writings of scholars were of interest primarily to other scholars, so far as peace-keeping is concerned scholarly writtings have closely matched political attitudes taken by Member States. Literature here has been very closely related to actual argumentation in the United Nations, providing perhaps the glosses on such argumentation.

Scholars have—as have States—addressed themselves to the problem of what flows from the failure of the Security Council to implement Article 43 of the United Nations Charter. Article 43 states:

1. All members of the United Nations, in order to contribute to the maintenance of international peace and security, undertake to make available to the Security Council, on its call and in accordance with a special agreement or agreements, armed forces, assistance and facilities, including rights of passage, necessary for the purpose of maintaining international peace and security.
2. Such agreements shall govern the members and types of forces, their degree of readiness and general location, and the nature of the facilities and assistance to be provided.
3. The agreement or agreements shall be negotiated as soon as possible on the initiative of the Security Council. They shall be concluded between the Security Council and Members or between the Security Council and groups of Members and shall be subject to ratification by the signatory States in accordance with their respective constitutional processes.

Thus the original intention was that members would undertake, in accordance with special agreements to be made, to make forces and facilities available. Article 43 was to operate in conjunction with Article 47.[25] However, the arrangements envisaged under Article 43 have never been concluded, because of ideological and political divisions between the West and the socialist countries.

The United Nations has none the less had to decide upon the contribution it should make, in paramilitary terms, in the absence of the implementation of Article 43. Although, as I have sought to show, there has been a substantial divergence of opinion by Western scholars writing on the concept of United Nations powers, there has still been a high degree of concurrence about the proper scope of United Nations military activity. The general Western view has been that the provisions of Article 40 and 41 (which allow for interim measures or diplomatic and economic enforcement action by the Security Council) continue unimpaired, notwithstanding the failure to conclude arrangements under Article 43.

Most writers have taken the position that the absence of agreements under Article 43 means, however, that no State may be compelled to participate in military measures under Article 42 of the Charter, though perhaps (and here there are some differences of opinion to be found)[26] the Security Council may still recommend such measures.

These constitutional issues have intrigued Western writers, who have also written widely on a range of related issues. Is the sole authority to mount a United Nations military action to be found in the Security Council acting by virtue of Article 42 after implementation of Article 43?[27] Or can Article 40, with its general reference to 'such provisional measures as it deems necessary or desirable' be a basis for such action? Does the granting to the Security Council, under Article 24 of the Charter, of the primary responsibility for peace mean that there is no residual peace-keeping role for the General Assembly? And if there is such a role, where is its Charter basis to be found? Indeed, does peace-keeping, within the general purposes and principles of the Charter, have to have a specific Charter basis? Only on the answers to some of these questions have Western writers been in agreement. The majority of them have contended that the Security Council may lawfully recommend peace-keeping, but that the consent of the host State is required.[28] They find too that there is a residual role for the Assembly.[29] On the other questions, however, there has been a wide measure of disagreement. Further, the Soviet view that the 'Uniting for Peace' resolution[30] was unlawful has commanded a substantial measure of agreement in the West.[31]

Western scholars have also addressed themselves in some detail to a range of practical issues that have arisen. In particular, the delicate relationship between the Organization and the State on whose soil the force or military observer group operates has been found worthy of examination.[32] There has been an interplay between the sovereignty of the State and the requirements of international concern that has particularly interested scholars, and Western writers have been concerned also with a distinct set of problems that relate to the proper training of United Nations military personnel. National training programmes, instructions on the relationship of their task to dispute settlement, staff regulations, standardization of pay, comparability of discipline, have been some of the questions studied.[33] There has been interest too—especially in the Nordic countries and Canada—in stand-by plans that can be made in national military units for the provision of United Nations personnel as and when needed.[34]

Nor have Western writers hesitated to state their preferences about the composition of United Nations peace-keeping groups, both as to method and as to substance. There has been a desire to retain discretion for the Secretary-General, rather than to have any *a priori* rules about composition (though the normal exclusion of the veto-wielding powers is generally accepted).[35] At the same time, Western writings have in recent years been more sympathetic to the view that it is desirable in principle to include Eastern European contributions where possible, and that the views of the host government should be given serious attention.

The overwhelming majority of books and articles written on United Nations peace-keeping have been traditionally cast. The newer methodological techniques, including systems analysis, quantitative theory and linkage theory, have not been seriously employed in the study of these problems. The literature in this field, while making use of occasional charts and graphs, follows classical patterns at least so far as methodology is concerned. To be sure, some writers in this area have sought to introduce new conceptual headings;[36] but these have not really indicated serious changes of methodological approach.

For a considerable period of time, peace-keeping, along with technical assistance and co-operation, was seen as an important vindication of functionalist theory. This process seems to have lost much of its momentum today.

The financing of international organizations has been the subject of another body of literature. The subject is very technical with important political and administrative implications. Western writers have generally been in favour of the view that lawfully authorized peace-keeping operations should be assessed, in the same manner as the regular budget, upon the membership at large. At the same time, with the passage of years, it has become acknowledged that this preference, is unlikely to prevail for political reasons. There has been considerable divergence of opinion expressed on many other aspects of financing, including problems relating to budgetary control in the economic and aid fields. Among important works in this field—using conventional methodology—is John Stoessinger's *Financing the United Nations System* (Brookings, 1964) and J. David Singer's *Financing International Organization: the UN Budget Process* (Nijhoff, 1961).

Settlement of disputes

Writers have been concerned with the question of dispute settlement by international organizations. This topic, together with that of voting (to which we refer below) has provided most naturally the stepping-stone from the old traditional techniques to more contemporary approaches to international organization. Early works focused on classical methods of dispute settlement, often those methods mentioned in Chapter VI of the

United Nations Charter. Important contributions in this category included A. Salomon, *L'ONU et le Paix* (Paris, 1948); J. P. Cot, *La Conciliation Internationale* (Paris, Pedone, 1968); W. C. Jenks, *Prospects for International Adjudications* (Oceana, 1964); and Milton Katz, *The Relevance of International Adjudication* (Harvard University Press, 1968). But in more recent years scholars have been concerned with a much wider range of possible ways for settling disputes, drawing heavily on recent insights derived from the theory of conflict resolution. Many of these are identified in S. Bailey, *Ideas and Proposals for Research* (UNITAR paper) and the increasing interrelationship between international theory and conflict resolution in an organizational setting is well illustrated by the range of essays in Raman, *The Settlement of Disputes* (UNITAR, 1977).

Underlying all these major controversies is the question of voting which has obviously been of major importance to scholars of international organizations. Several useful books[37] have been written on this, including Koo, *Voting Procedures in International Political Organizations* (Columbia, 1947); T. J. Kahng, *Law, Politics and the Security Council* (Nijhoff, 1964) and S. Bailey, *Voting in the Security Council* (Indiana University Press, 1975). The growing field of quantitative analysis in international relations theory has had a global impact on the study of international organization.

The difficulties which international organizations have faced over the last few years with a world that seems to be increasingly nationalistic have led to a decline in the volume of writings on international organizations as such. Instead, contemporary scholarly focus is very problem-oriented: disarmament, resources, pollution, economic justice—these themes all fight for our attention, and in the study of them the world of international organizations necessarily plays an important part.

Notes

1. There has been considerable disagreement over which Chapter VII resolutions *do* constitute 'decisions', and over whether it is *only* Chapter VII decisions that may bind. The International Court has held that resolutions other than Chapter VII resolutions may be binding: *Legal Consequences for States of the Continued Presence of South Africa in Namibia* [1971] *ICJ Reports*. See Also, R. Higgins, 'The Advisory Opinion on Namibia: Which UN Resolutions are Binding under Article 25 of the Charter?', *ICLQ*, Vol. 21, 1972, p. 270.

2. Chapter VII of the Charter is headed 'Action with Respect to Threats to the Peace, Breaches of the Peace, and Acts of Aggression'. Article 25 states: 'The Members of the United Nations agree to accept and carry out the decisions of the Security Council in accordance with the present Charter.'

3. Article 17 provides '(1) The General Assembly shall consider and approve the budget of the Organization. (2) The expenses of the Organization shall be borne by the Members as apportioned by the General Assembly.'

4. Article 38 of the Statute refers to the application by the Court of international conventions, international custom, general principles of law, judicial decisions and teachings of the most highly qualified publicists.

5. For example, see Alan James, *International Affairs*, April 1964, p. 301 ; Sir Francis Vallat, *ICLQ*, 1964, p. 1501.

6. See the view of C. W. Manning, *International Affairs*, 1967, p. 211.

7. R. Higgins, *The Development of International Law through the Political Organs of the United Nations*, London, Oxford University Press, for the Royal Institute of International Affairs (RIIA).

8. Ibid., p. 2.

9. For example, the important work done on consensus theory by Bailey, *Voting in the Security Council*, 1969, and C. W. Jenks 'Unanimity, the Veto, Weighted Voting, Special and Simple Majorities and Consensus as Modes of Decision in International Organization', in R. Y. Jennings (ed.), *Cambridge Essays in Honour of Lord McNair*, 1965.

10. See R. Higgins, 'The United Nations and Law Making : The Political Organs', *Proc. AJIL*, 1970, p. 37.

11. With the powers of the EEC, through the issuance of regulations and directives, being an obvious and important exception.

12. See the separate opinion of Judge ad hoc Van Wyk in *South West Africa Cases* (Second Phase), *ICJ Reports*, 1966, 64–215 at 164–173.

13. Case concerning certain expenses of the United Nations, *ICJ Reports*, 1962.

14. Because of the non-implementation of Article 43 of the Charter, which envisaged specific arrangements to be made between members and the Security Council for the provision of United Nations forces.

15. France and the Soviet Union had misgivings about the conduct of the United Nations action in the Congo in the early 1960s; and the Soviet Union had also disapproved the establishment by the General Assembly of UNEF in the Middle East in 1956.

16. Richard Falk, *AJIL*, Vol. 60, 1966.

17. For example, R. Higgins, *Proc. ASIL*, 1970, p. 40.

18. Detter, *Law Making by International Organizations*, 1965.

19. See the 'Introduction' by Michel Virally to Yemin *Legislative Powers in the United Nations and Specialized Agencies*, Sijthoff,

1969 ; and also Virally, 'La Valeur Juridique des Recommendations des Organisations Internationales', *Annuaire Français de Droit International*, p. 66–97, 1956.

20. Asamoah, *The Legal Significance of the Declarations of the General Assembly of the United Nations*, 1966.

21. Malintoppi, *Le Raccomandazioni Internazionali*, Milan, 1958. See also A. J. P. Tammes, 'Decisions of International Organs as a Source of International Law' *Recueil des Cours*, Vol. 94, 1958-II, p. 265-364 ; Blaine Sloan, 'The Binding Force of a 'Recommendation' of the General Assembly of the United Nations' *BYIL*, Vol. 25, 1948, p. 1-33 ; Paitrowski, 'Les Resolutions de l'Assemblée Générale et la Portée du Droit Conventionnel. *Revue de droit international*, Vol. 33, 1955, 111-25, p. 221-42; D. H. Johnson,' The Effect of Resolutions of the General Assembly of the United Nations', *BYIL*, Vol. 32, 1955-56, p. 97-123 ; P. Brugi, *Les Pouvoirs de l'Assemblée Générale des Nations Unies en Matière politique et de Sécurité*, Paris, 1955 ; di Qual, *Les Effets des Résolutions des Nations Unies*, Paris, 1969.

22. J. Castañeda, *Legal Effects of United Nations Resolutions*, Columbia, 1969.

23. 'Legal Consequences for States of the Continued Presence of South Africa in Namibia', *ICJ Reports*, 1971.

24. For example, Lash, *Dag Hammarskjöld: Custodian of the Brush Fire Peace*, 1961 ; *Public Papers of the Secretaries-General of the United Nations*, Vols. I-VII, Columbia University Press ; Georges Langrod, *The International Civil Service*, Sihtoff, 1963.

25. Article 47 provided for a Military Staff Committee to advise the Security Council on its military requirements, the employment and command of forces, the regulation of armaments and 'possible disarmament'.

26. See Bowett, *United Nations Forces*, 1964.

27. Article 42 provides for military enforcement measures.

28. Bowett, op. cit. ; Burns and Heathcote, *Peacekeeping by UN Forces from Suez to the Congo*, Praeger, 1963 ; Rosner, *The United Nations Emergency Force*, Columbia 1963 ; Stengenga, *The UN Force in Cyprus*, Ohio, 1968 ; Wainhouse, *International Peace Observation*, Johns Hopkins, 1966 ; Higgins, *United Nations Peacekeeping*, Vols. I and II, London, Oxford University Press, for the Royal Institute of International Affairs, 1969 and 1971.

29. Bowett, op. cit.

30. General Assembly Resolution 377 (V).

31. J. Andrassy, *AJIL* ; Vol. 50, 1956, p. 563-82 ; Petersen, *International Organization*, Vol. 8, 1959, p. 219-32 ; A. Rossignol, *RGDIP*, Vol. 58, 1954, p. 94 ; Piero Ziccardi, *Comunità Internazionale*, Vol. 12, 1957, p. 221-36, 415-47.

32. Bowett, op. cit.

33. See Fabian, *Soldiers without Enemies,* Brookings, 1970 ; and
    the Monograph Series of the Information Centre on Peace-
    keeping Operations (IPKO).
34. For example, Stenguist, 'The Swedish UN Standby Force
    and Experience', *Peacekeeping: International Challenge and
    Canadian Response,* Canadian Institute of International Affairs,
    1968 (IPKO monograph, 4).
35. The British participation in the Cyprus operation is widely
    seen as an anomaly—albeit a useful and entirely acceptable one.
36. For example, Alan James, *The Politics of Peacekeeping,* Praeger,
    1969.
37. See Bailey, 'New light on Abstentions in the UN Security
    Council', *International Affairs,* 1974, p. 554; GROSS, 'Voting
    in the Security Council: Abstention from Voting and Absence
    from Meetings', *YLJ,* Vol. 60, 1951, p. 224; GROSS, 'Abstention
    and Absence of a Permanent Member in Relation to Voting
    Procedures in the Security Council', *AJIL,* Vol. 44, 1950,
    p. 707 ; McDougal and Gardner, 'The Veto and the Charter :
    An Interpretation for Survival', *AJIL,* Vol. 44, 1950, p. 285 ;
    Stavropoulos, 'The Practice of Voluntary Abstentions by
    Permanent Members of the Security Council under Article 27
    para. 3 of the Charter of the UN', *AJIL,* Vol. 61, 1967, p. 752.

10   A Third World view of international organizations. Action towards a new international economic order

Mohammed Bedjaoui

In the opinion of the developing countries, international organizations, and especially the United Nations, provide an ideal context for the transformation of the international economic order and the development of all peoples. This opinion can be explained: first, by the conception these States have of the role of international organizations and especially of the General Assembly of the United Nations. In spite of the privileged position of the great powers within international organizations, in spite of the existence of limited-membership bodies and the practice of weighted voting, these organizations remain places favourable to contestation, to inspiration and to the creation of new guidelines furthering the interests of the international community.

But the question of how to draw up the 'rules of the international game' for the present and the future, with the participation of all States, new and old alike, leads us to one of the major problems of our time. It concerns the 'reversal of the majority' on the international scene in favour of the new States, and hence the problem, formulated in new terms, of 'majority' and 'minority'.

MOHAMMED BEDJAOUI is a former Minister, a member of the United Nations International Law Commission, an associate of the International Law Institute and, from 1970 to 1979, the Algerian Ambassador in Paris. He is now his country's Ambassador to the United Nations. He has written numerous works on international law and international organizations, among which are: *Fonction Publique Internationale et Influences Nationales* (1958), *La Révolution Algérienne et le Droit* (1961), *Problèmes Récents de Succession d'États dans les États Nouveaux* (1970), *'Terra Nullius', Droits Historiques et Autodétermination* (1975) and *Non-alignement et Droit International* (1976).

This chapter has been adapted from his book, *Towards a New International Economic Order*, which was written for Unesco and published in 1979 as the first volume of a new series entitled, 'New Challenges to International Law'.

A Third World view of international   207
organizations. Action towards a new international
economic order

Number versus force

For thirty years, in addition to its veto in the Security Council, the club of the developed countries had an automatic majoiity in the General Assembly of the United Nations, owing as much to the number of Member States, at that time limited, as to the existence of certain clients.

Some fifty States were godparents to the United Nations at its baptism in San Francisco in 1945. Today, over 150 States are members of the Organization. This tripling of the number of Member States poses complex problems which lie at the heart of the new international economic order and the projected new legal order. The vast increase in the number of States which occurred in the post-war world cannot be considered merely in quantitative terms. For the elaboration of the new order, 'membership' must eclipse the 'leadership' of dominant oligarchies and must give pride of place to 'partnership'.

The problem, however, is that power and number have never been in such a paradoxical relationship as at present.

Formerly, Europe projected its law and power upon the world. It had written the history of the world with its soldiers, merchants, missionaries and lawyers. It dominated the globe in the name of its law, and until 1960 the Third World was virtually non-existent. Today, our world calls for conversions and metamorphoses, grafts and substitutions. We are living at a time when it has become necessary to transfer power and wealth within States as well as among them. We are likewise living at a time when nations are allergic to encroaching leadership.

The problem is not so much the 'transfer of the majority' in itself. This majority, held by the Western countries until the 1950s and 1960s, has now passed to the States of the Third World. The problem is that for the first time in human history, international law is not on the side of force or power. The novelty of our time resides in this signal divorce between law and force. The Western world hitherto possessed material force and imposed on the world its own protective law, in the guise of universal international law. Might and right were therefore on the same side, without serious division or excessive tensions.

If by chance the socialist regime, set up in Russia by the October Revolution of 1917, happened to contest an international legal norm, the 'dominant world' of the time quickly reminded it that the regime was not yet recognized; and when recognition of the U.S.S.R. finally occurred, the homeland of the dictatorship of the proletariat was not dissatisfied to be accepted into the international community, a community where such cardinal principles as the sovereignty of the State and equality between States could be co-opted by the U.S.S.R. in a dialectic turnabout to give it a position of actual equality matching the equality legally conferred, and expressing the U.S.S.R.'s vast material power. In short, this State, which had admittedly contested many rules of bourgeois international law, has none the less accepted the bulk of it without any radical upheaval and without questioning its underlying foundations.

At best, when the socialist camp maintained a more unyielding opposition to various standards of traditional international law, it encountered an environment so hostile that it shut itself in a legal ghetto. It thus raised the barriers of refusal that proved to be without peril for the Western world and without noticeable effect on the international law of those times, which still governed relations between Western and Third World countries. It is none the less historically undeniable that the U.S.S.R. greatly helped to purge international relations and the law of nations of the phenomena of imperialism and colonialism which they contained.

Essentially, however, the socialist camp is adapting to contemporary international law, a law of the international relations of détente and of peaceful co-existence between two blocs, with zones of influence and a more or less friendly division of the world between 'associated competitors'.[1]

Within international institutions, the majority is on the side of the Third World. It possesses a decisive and deciding margin of votes within the General Assembly of the United Nations and the General Conferences of ILO and of Unesco. And for the first time, the power of numbers is opposed to material power. Also for the first time, the real political and economic power in the world, still held by the West, no longer finds its juridical expression embodied in the same way as it still was a few years ago, for example, in the resolutions of the United Nations, ILO, UNCTAD or Unesco. Conversely, the Third World possesses for the first time in these institutions a *right to the creation of law* thanks to the strength of its numbers. This is why it is possible to assert that the Third World countries, which possess neither economic power nor military might, today have the historical privilege of helping by their moral force to give some reality to the ideals embodied in the Charter of the United Nations.

But retaliation was not long in coming in this historic stage of the pre-formation of a new law, with all that this implies with regard to old balances disrupted in varying degrees, and new balances precarious and threatened to a greater or lesser extent. Material power is challenging the power of numbers and is contesting the normative, universal character of the work of international institutions. Does the sum of the resolutions that these institutions adopt owing to the Third World majority constitute positive, peremptory law?

However, before looking at the problem of the necessarily normative

A Third World view of international
organizations. Action towards a new international
economic order   209

value that the resolutions of international organizations hold for the future, it would be preferable to say a little more about the 'automatic majority', as it is called, not without some bitterness, by its opponents.

The life of international organizations is at present dominated by the emergence of a new majority, which has moved the theoretical centre of decision-making towards the countries which are the smallest, weakest and poorest. In one sense, this is quite a natural and unsurprising phenomenon seeing that it is the result of the healthiest play of democratic forces, and that the existence of a majority and a minority in international organizations is in itself perfectly normal. The problems reside in the fact that it is no longer the same majority.

The founders of the United Nations were once in favour of majority rule. Majority of the members present and voting, two-thirds majority for 'important questions' as defined by Article 18, paragraph 2 of the Charter, a qualified majority for the Security Council, where the affirmative vote of nine out of fifteen members must include all the permanent members of the Council—the system functioned under the perfect control of the great powers which dominated the majority.

The Western powers overwhelmed the United Nations. This supremacy was tempered only by the socialist bloc, which made use not so much of a 'strike force' of numbers, which it did not possess, as of its considerable specific gravity, expressed notably in the right of veto that the U.S.S.R. had in the Security Council. Furthermore, the West could marshal a Third World clientèle, which had not yet found its identity, or discovered its political importance or yet become that large quantity of independent States that gave it the power of numbers. The Western world, therefore, found it quite natural to have at its disposal numbers, strength, material power and at the same time the corresponding capacity to create a body of law that would protect that situation. For those who benefited from 'might' and 'right', the world could not be the world without this mastery which they found it natural to hold over both the right to might and the might of right.

In the 1960s and 1970s, especially the latter, this comfortable position was seriously disturbed, without those who enjoyed it, the creators and protectors of the old order, being able to admit that it was precisely their privileged situation, which had lasted for years, that was abnormal. They continue to act in international organizations like States unjustly stripped of some 'right' to supremacy over the minority, while at the same time they incur the obvious reproach of fostering contradictions by ostensibly adhering to the principles of democracy and universality in those organizations.

In fact, thanks to the 'majority rule' from which they profit, the developing countries have opened a substantial breach in the legal edifice constructed in the past by the industrialized States in order to provide a firm base for their domination, and they are taking full advantage of this opening to transform the established order, using the momentum of development. But this numerical importance of the Third World countries only represents a balancing factor, still fragile and uncertain, in the face of the real strength of the industrialized countries and the means to apply pressure that they have at their disposal.

The counter-attack of the industrialized States

CRITICISM OF THE 'AUTOMATIC MAJORITY'

The new majority has been called 'mechanical', and its decisions 'arbitrary', as if international organizations have found themselves subject to a new kind of imperialism, whereas in fact, since the establishment of a new international order is at stake, the common front of the proletarian States is simply a counterstroke, or even a legitimate means of defence against the privileged States.

The developing countries are oddly accused of an 'excessive politicization' of problems within international organizations.

Held to be immature, the new majority is readily accused of irresponsibility in the examination of world problems. It has been said that 'the manner in which the new majority within the United Nations, Unesco and other international organizations is wielded at present is far from being a blessing for the most underprivileged peoples of the world. On the contrary, it is clamorous in form and sterile in substance; it is as inauspicious for the South as for the North, for the East as for the West.'[2]

Those who complain thus of excessive politicization of the problems of international organizations and the dangers of world-wide destabilization concealed by such an attitude, should hearken to the clear and courageous words of the Prime Minister of Luxembourg (and former President of the United Nations General Assembly), Gaston Thorn, who said that 'when the West dominated the world . . . there was not much distinction drawn between politics and economics. Our politics were there to serve our social system, and religion was there to serve our political system. . . . Even at that time, everything was interdependent. And are we now going to refuse the participation of the whole world simply

A Third World view of international   211
organizations. Action towards a new international
economic order

because the ideas that might result are not ours or might not please us?'[3]
He went on:

Basically, this new majority is criticized for having realized too quickly where
the faults were in the Organization, and for having tried to direct it, just as we
did after the war! But the first misunderstanding comes from the erroneous idea
that the United Nations was created in order to constitute an organization of all
the nations of the world, with equal rights for all. That is completely false! Otherwise why would the Security Council exist with permanent members having the
power of veto and others who are not permanent members? This was solely a
club made up of the victors of the last world war who meant to 'lay down the law
for the world'. Two years after its foundation there was no longer any dialogue,
but opposition between East and West and the beginning of the cold war. So, the
original idea dissipated and each or the two Great Powers tried to introduce its
clientèle, while keeping out the other's clientèle as long as possible. It was politics. ... We should not complain about the intrusion of politics into the United
Nations—we created the organization for political reasons, in order to apply our
strategy there. What has happened recently is attributed to the accidents and
failures of a former majority. So they should play the game! ... In the United
Nations the problem is every bit as much one of the new minority that has not
accepted its new position. This minority, while retaining its wealth and military
might, no longer has any power and does not know how to dialogue with people
who were, only yesterday, directly under its control.[4]

Perhaps the inexhaustible arsenal of formulas of all kinds which international law has until now generously offered the industrialized countries
has enabled them to conceal the political reality of the problems within
international organizations. The law of nations was a law of jurisdiction
and of procedure much more than a body of fundamental rules. Legal
inventions and artifices undoubtedly prevented these States for some time
from themselves incurring the well deserved reproach of excessive politicization. According to Addeke Boerma, Director-General of FAO, speaking
during the same debate on the France-Culture radio programme, his
organization essentially 'reflected, in the beginning, the philosophy of the
wealthy nations that wished to promote their interests'.[5]

Amadou-Mahtar M'Bow, the Director-General of Unesco, who also
took part in the debate, noted that 'the record of the former majority is
catastrophic in every field. One must not forget that it was the former
majority which prevented the admission of the People's Republic of China
into Unesco for more than twenty years. Was it a technical vote or a
political vote in an international institution whose purpose is to deal with
science and culture? It can hardly be claimed that the 800 million Chinese

had nothing to contribute to the world in the way of education, science and culture! Yet they were kept away. Solely for political reasons!'[6]

For his part, Sean MacBride declared: 'This majority is criticized for having destroyed international stability. What stability? That of the cold war? That of the Second World War? What stability would be credible without the participation of the Third World? The new nations are criticized for thinking only of themselves. That is perhaps true! But do the great powers ever think much about the small nations?'[7]

In reality the problem is infinitely vaster, and the record of the old majority is identified with that of imperialism, which can be summed up as poverty in the international order and an international order of poverty. In conclusion, one cannot help but subscribe to the forceful statement of the Director-General of Unesco: 'Certain expressions such as "automatic majority" lose all their meaning. During its history the United Nations has seen several dominating groups; however, perhaps none of these posed to the community of nations questions so basically linked to the dignity of man, to justice and equity, as the group of the developing countries when it proclaimed the need to establish a new international economic order among the nations.'[8] The accusation of excessive politicization made by the industrialized States against certain international organizations 'seem rather to reflect the feeling of those who possibly regret the time when the community of States still mirrored only very incompletely the community of the peoples in the world, and who close their minds to the profound reasons for which the new members of this community do not share the view of the industrialized States concerning the principles which should guide their action'.[9]

Furthermore, the process of elaborating international legal norms is much more complex than the critics of the supposed 'automatic majority' would have one believe. It reflects complex power balances. When such diverse countries as Algeria, Chile and India vote together, thereby contributing to the creation of that 'automatic majority' in order to try to promote the new international economic order, one loses sight somewhat too conveniently of the fact that the power of decision-making remains the prerogative of a small group of States which are 'more equal than others'.[10] This is what can be seen if one notes the manner in which the industrialized States point an accusing finger at the developing countries and call them to heel.

A Third World view of international
organizations. Action towards a new international
economic order

213

PERSISTENCE OF THE PHENOMENON OF A VOTING 'CLIENTÈLE'

Sean MacBride has stated that before decolonization 'most of the small
countries which were members of international organizations were clients
or vassals of the great powers who used them as tokens to assure themselves
of a majority on certain question'.[11] This is true and emphasizes the fact
that decolonization served not only to liberate colonized countries, but
also to emancipate to a certain extent many small States from their dependence on the great powers. The freedom of action of these small
countries, alienated in a world dominated by imperialism, was accentuated
and stabilized by the rise of new States resulting directly from
decolonization.

The phenomenon of the client State has not, however, disappeared.
Old or new, the small States are still subject to the effects of the policies
of the great powers which have divided the world into spheres of influence.
Moreover, the small States are far from constituting a homogeneous and
monolithic bloc. They take action, they adopt attitudes and they vote in
accordance with two divisions—an East–West ideological division and a
North–South economic division. That means, to refer only to the developing countries—those sacrificial victims of progress who are less and less
satisfied with the paradise they are promised and demand more and more
their share of present wealth—that the political regimes of these countries
are widely diverse. Without ideological homogeneity and total cohesion in
action, these small countries are always liable to become the victims of
the large ones.

This humiliating situation of 'clients', in the Latin sense of the term,
is what pushed these nations for the most part into the 'non-aligned' camp.
This is a broad and varied movement which is bravely endeavouring to
deprive the great powers of their respective client States, but it does not
confine its members in the straitjacket of any dogma. The solidarity among
these countries is not the result of imposed constraints, but of their
progressive acceptance of principles which they all subscribe to in an
increasing degree as they come to realize more clearly their common
dependence on the great powers. This essential factor is their common
denominator and absorbs all their differences. Living with the same
problems, faced with the same objectives, they realize that their interests
dictate a pooling of their efforts in order to defend positions on which
their future depends.

It would nevertheless be wrong to think that their unity of conviction
or of action is automatically apparent in all spheres of international activity.
Analysis of their votes, as undertaken by various authors, generally shows
that their standpoints diverge more than they converge. To give an example,

using computerized data, a group of young researchers, directed by Marco Mozzati, attempted to retrace the three main stages in the formation of a resolution in the General Assembly of the United Nations, i.e. the agenda as a list of items considered as subjects for decision; the bases for decisions, that is to say the precedents upon which the texts of resolutions are based; and the result of the vote on those resolutions. They arrived at the conclusion that 'the privilege of influencing political choices belongs exclusively to a restricted number of countries—those which combine the methods of political science with the direction of a major international policy'.[12] This research analysed perfectly the mechanisms not only of the systems of domination and the reactions which they provoke, but also of the objective of the battle, that is to say supremacy, which is still the prerogative of the great powers.[13]

One cannot help thinking, therefore, that the 'automatic majority' does not leave them either powerless or even voiceless. On the occasion of the Geneva Diplomatic Conference on Humanitarian Law, where Viet Nam's right to participate was contested, one author wrote:

Artificial minorities—which are the result of arm-twisting and recourse to threats related to the discontinuation of food aid—were used very recently to keep out of a diplomatic conference a government that has been recognized by almost fifty States and is a co-signatory of a solemn international agreement with the United States and the Soviet Union. Multilateral diplomacy, and more particularly its institutionalized forms, entail . . . recourse to majority decisions.[14]

Although attenuated, the phenomenon of the client State at the level of international organizations thus persists. It can nevertheless be seen that as clientèles break up in favour of an independent Third World majority, the imperialist powers are becoming exasperated and even go so far as to manipulate, as has just been seen, not only the means of pressure which they derive from their economic, financial, cultural, or military 'aid', but also the 'food weapon', which represents the most detestable blackmail to ensure support in decisive votes.[15]

Threats to countries which receive aid from a great power go beyond the context of secret diplomacy and come out into the open. When asked by a sub-committee of the Finance Committee of the Senate to present a record of American economic policy with regard to foreign countries, Secretary of State Henry Kissinger took advantage of the opportunity to give a rap on the knuckles to those countries which, while still receiving American aid, did not hesitate to break ranks with the United States in international organizations. Mr Kissinger stated that 'every developing country must begin to understand that our bilateral relations with it will take into account its attitude towards us in international meetings, and especially its votes there on problems to which we attach the greatest importance'. The warning was as brutal as it was unequivocal, and was followed by concrete and direct action: 'I have asked each one of our embassies to explain to the government to which it is accredited that one of the factors by which we will judge the value they accord to their relations with us will be the statements they make and the votes they cast in international assemblies on a rather limited number of subjects we consider crucial.'[16]

The stupefying declarations of Mr Moynihan, the fiery American Ambassador to the United Nations, about the 'effrontery' of Third World delegations that dared abstain from casting their votes with the United States, also received the approval of the head of American diplomacy, and shortly afterwards also received the formal assent of President Ford himself, who had made a public statement along the same lines several days before his Secretary of State.

MAINTENANCE AND 'CO-OPTING' OF DIVERGENCES AMONG THIRD WORLD COUNTRIES

The persistence of the phenomenon of client States is both the cause and the result of the maintenance and co-opting of the divergences that arise among developing countries. Those who hold the power try for their own benefit to co-opt these divergences, which they have frequently created themselves. In spite of the existence of the overwhelming majority enjoyed by the States of the Third World, these States remain for the most part in an inferior situation which corresponds neither to their number, nor to their considerable demographic weight, nor to their enormous resources, nor to the huge potential market which they represent.

In fact, even when the developing countries express their position in perfect unity, the great powers never completely forgo certain privileges that are theirs thanks to the structure and functioning of the United Nations system, to say nothing of the essential field of the preservation of world peace.

It is thus hardly surprising that the necessary modifications in the international order sought by the majority of States, and carried out with difficulty, slowly and progressively, should have to contend, regarding their scope and the time needed to bring them about, with the resistance of the great powers, whose prosperity is too self-assured for them to be sensitive to the enormity of the misery surrounding them. Even when they discover how vulnerable they are economically because of the reactions of the developing countries, the great powers take refuge in their own selfishness instead of promoting a constructive dialogue such as will ensure the salvation of all. As the economic and social situation changes, it is very rare for wisdom to make a spontaneous appearance in order to impose recognition or acceptance of inevitable change, or even less to impose preparation for such change. It is in the nature of things that progress in the international order—which means a questioning of yesterday's certainties and of the precarious comforts of an outmoded order—should be the complex result of reformist attacks and conservative resistance; in other words, the 'algebraic' sum of positive and negative parameters which neutralize each other partially or temporarily in an equation that is constantly being renewed.

One of the extreme means which States 'more equal than others' use to try to ward off the effects of the 'automatic majority' is to aggravate economic and political pressures to the point of destabilizing the regimes of the developing countries.

ECONOMIC AGGRESSION AND POLITICAL DESTABILIZATION

Methods of pressure or reprisal vary widely, the extreme limit being the overthrow of existing governments in certain countries of the Third World. The examples of a great number of African, Asian and Latin American States, especially the Chile of Salvador Allende, are unhappily only too well known and of particular significance in this connection. An examination of these cases would concern the strategy and general tactics of imperialism and would therefore go beyond the framework of the present study dealing with insubordination of the 'client State' in its voting within the international organization. In any event, the examples seem too well known to require detailed reminders. It nevertheless shows that the question of the 'automatic majority' is a subsidiary matter and a false problem, the heart of the issue being that foreign imperialism continues to dominate with impunity the domestic political and economic life of numerous small States, continues to interfere, even militarily, in their national affairs and, *a fortiori*, continues to influence their foreign policy and their votes in international organizations.[17]

This lasting economic domination was tolerated by traditional international law, and this was *a fortiori* true for specific arts of reprisal or pressure of a limited duration which were closely related to acts of true economic aggression. In international law, sovereignty was defined by its political elements, to the exclusion of the economic aspects. Theoretically, this resulted in condemnation by the Charter of the United Nations only of acts damaging the political sovereignty of States. The sanctions provided for in the Charter against acts prejudicial to sovereignty were aimed only

A Third World view of international 217
organizations. Action towards a new international
economic order

at violation of political obligations towards a State, with the exception of breach of economic duties. That is why traditional international law, based upon the classical concept of sovereignty defined uniquely in political terms, majestically ignored the extraordinary situations presented by 'banana republics', dominated by foreign economic cartels and subjected to all sorts of economic pressures by foreign States; and all this, without being able to claim violation of their sovereignty.

In fact, the real political sovereignty of States was in this way rendered non-existent by the confiscation of their economic sovereignty, and traditional international law offered no recourse at all since the political sovereignty of the victim State was, apparently, not directly confiscated.[18]

Under traditional international law, there was no remedy against these situations since imperialism was careful to avoid direct and open violation of the political aspects of sovereignty, limiting itself to undermining its economic bases. Thus disembodied and formal political sovereignty, declaimed like a rite taken from traditional canons, has historically protected the interests of foreign States at the expense of the national interests of the underdeveloped countries.

And even when imperialism passes from permanent and subtle economic aggression, manifold and adaptable, to political destabilization and the overthrow of existing regimes, the rules in traditional international law regarding the responsibility of States, especially regarding definition of and indictment for an internationally illicit act, guarantee that aggressive imperialism, working through its secret services or accredited mercenaries, can act with untroubled impunity. Fond of appearances, traditional international law displays a fundamental incapacity to control situations which are none the less clearly prejudicial to the sovereignty and real independence of the State.

The developing countries are perfectly aware of this sort of violent reaction by the imperialists is an effort to counter their demands for a new international economic order, and they have begun to take steps to protect themselves through mutual support. Within the framework of the movement of non-aligned countries especially, they have gradually formulated rules of solidarity and mutual assistance in the event of economic aggression or destabilization directed agaénts any one of them.[19]

International organizations are beginning to echo these concerns by a stronger and stronger assertion of the right of peoples and States to be in control of their natural resources; by prohibiting all forms of interference, not only in the internal affairs of States but also in their economic affairs; by forbidding the use of force and coercion of any kind in international economic relations, and so forth.

The resolutions and declarations of the United Nations General

Assembly have gradually brought about improvements in the classical system which coincide naturally with the emergence of the Third World and reveal the direction in which the Third World is concerned with enlarging international law. The cornerstone of the new structure is Resolution 2131 (XX), which condemned, for the first time, several kinds of foreign interference that impair the economic independence of the State (various sorts of coercion and economic pressures).

Resolution 2625 (XXV) of 24 October 1970, containing a Declaration on Principles of International Law concerning Friendly Relations and Co-operation among States, emphasized for its part the recognized and codified principle of non-intervention in matters within the domestic jurisdiction of States, drawing from this several conclusions regarding the right of every people to choose freely their political and economic system without any foreign pressure or interference. It also denies States the right to 'use or encourage the use of economic, political or any other type of measures to coerce another State in order to obtain from it the subordination of the exercise of its sovereign rights and to secure from it advantages of any kind'.

These new trends were confirmed by the United Nations General Assembly in 1974 in two important documents. First, the Declaration on the Establishment of a New International Economic Order indicates that this new order should be founded on various principles, including: '(d) The right of every country to adopt the economic and social system that it deems the most appropriate for its own development and not to be subjected to discrimination of any kind as a result'.[20] The second document is the Charter of Economic Rights and Duties of States, which declares that 'every State has the sovereign and inalienable right to choose its economic system as well as its political, social and cultural systems in accordance with the will of its people, without outside interference, coercion or threat in any form whatsoever'.[21] The same Charter, in Article 32, recalls that 'No State may use or encourage the use of economic, political or any other type of measures to coerce another State in order to obtain from it the subordination of the exercise of its sovereign rights'.

It is true that two days after adopting this Charter of Economic Rights and Duties of States, the General Assembly passed Resolution 3314 (XXIX) of 14 December 1974, concerned with the definition of aggression, while remaining silent on the economic aggression that it had forbidden in its Charter two days earlier.[22] In fact, the problem of economic aggression was raised many times during the endless debate in the United Nations on the definition of aggression. But the General Assembly was all too happy to be concluding a quarter-century's debate on the definition to agree to delay even longer while a specific definition of

A Third World view of international   219
organizations. Action towards a new international
economic order

economic aggression was formulated. It can be argued that the General Assembly had all the more reason to stop where it did, since it had already dealt with this particular problem in the Charter of Economic Rights and Duties of States, as well as in the Declaration of Principles of International Law concerning Friendly Relations and Co-operation among States. Likewise, it can be confidently predicted that progress in the establishment of a new international economic order will depend on a more substantial development of norms aimed at prohibiting economic aggression.

To return to the problem of the 'automatic majority', it can thus be seen that the industrialized States still possess sufficiently powerful means to secure the votes of the developing countries. But the pressures of all sorts that they can bring to bear on each of the developing countries are not the only weapons at their disposal. In place of the individual sanction potentially applicable to any State whose vote is not appreciated, they can put the principle of a collective sanction, paralysing international organizations by withdrawing from them and depriving them of their financial contribution.

THREATS TO DESTROY THE MEANS OF INTERNATIONAL CO-OPERATION

Applying a collective sanction to all the Member States of an international organization, certain States have discontinued or reduced their contributions to its budget and have even decided to withdraw from it altogether. Thus the American, French and Swiss parliaments at one moment temporarily suspended payment of their countries' financial contributions to Unesco. The United States even withdrew from ILO in November 1976. The threat of destruction of the means of international co-operation is thus assuming dangerous proportions.

But those wealthier countries which try in this way to 'penalize' the organization as a whole, reacting against what they consider its 'excessive politicization' and the dictates of the 'automatic majority', are most likely penalizing themselves. In fact, international co-operation is an essential element of life and of international relations, and will become more and more so. The advantage, indeed the privilege, of being a member of an international organization and profiting from it, is going to prove as important as belonging to a trade union or professional organization within an industrial State.

The developed States consider that it is precisely the existence of this 'automatic majority' which paralyses real international co-operation. But this is tantamount to seeing such co-operation as subordinate to the will, choices and decisions of the minority. In these circumstances, international co-operation seems to suffer less from paralysis due to an 'automatic majority' than from obstruction by a privileged minority. When the developing countries go so far as to renounce the law of numbers by accepting the technique of consensus, as will be seen later in this work, they demonstrate the strength of their desire to invite dialogue rather than confrontation in the establishment of a new international economic order. In fact, the meagre results achieved so far only serve to emphasize still more the importance of a concession of this size made in the process of elaborating international legal norms by those who are in a numerical majority.

If, in spite of all the legal, para-legal or irregular means which they have in their possession, the industrialized States do not manage to dominate the 'automatic majority', and if, in the end, they are proving powerless to prevent countries as different as Chile, India, Algeria and Iran, from concerting their votes in international forums for the establishment of a new international economic order, then this is proof that the old order is irremediably condemned and that morality, right and even, and above all, efficiency, have abandoned it to seek refuge in the new hope offered by the new order.

Now, the credibility of international organizations depends very much on whether it is possible to give their decisions the necessary weight required by the important qualitative changes that have taken place in a world where States are increasingly conscious of their interdependence. Such a possibility is likely to be wanting for some time yet when one reflects that the advanced States, which are so prompt to criticize the 'automatic majority', continue to enjoy a similar majority in certain international institutions, possess the power of veto in others, and belong to 'exclusive clubs' through which they slow the momentum of the establishment of a new international economic order.

'AUTOMATIC MAJORITY' OF THE INDUSTRIALIZED STATES AND THE POLICY OF 'LIMITED-MEMBERSHIP CLUBS'

A 'syndicate of States' limited in number and great in power, continues to make and proclaim the law for all, as in the age of the sailing ship or the oil lamp. The policy of the 'exclusive club' of the great powers has never disappeared. Its reincarnations can be seen in the 'directories' and other 'limited-membership clubs'.

Certain 'directories', like the one comprising the ten wealthiest countries, which meets periodically to discuss world monetary problems, exist to provide for consultations and unified planning. It would be quite natural for them to consult, but because of the importance of the parti-

A Third World view of international   221
organizations. Action towards a new international
economic order

cipants and their global influence, their consultations amount to decisions
imposed on the whole world. World monetary policy continues to be
formulated in the framework of this all-powerful directory.

This power is wielded outside the relevant international institutions,
and to avoid its being called in question within these institutions, the
industrialized States have made sure that they have tight control over
them. This has been the case since the Second World War in certain
institutions like the International Monetary Fund or the International
Bank for Reconstruction and Development. The system of weighted
voting assures these States of a comfortable automatic majority which
they consider normal.[23] And when, as has been the case for several years,
the interests of these States are threatened by a crisis, they call upon the
feelings of interdependence and solidarity of all as reasons for outlawing
every form of challenge to the established system. Should circumstances
oblige them to open their 'club' to several members of the majority contesting that order, it is only so that they may thus assimilate the challenge.
An author who writes clearly about this phenomenon notes that, 'they
are invited to join this exclusive club of privileged powers, thereby giving
them the possibility of increasing their voting power in certain institutions.
Therefore, instead of a new international order being established, the
proposal is made that these developing countries should themselves be
converted in order to consolidate the established order.[24]

In point of fact, even if they broaden their membership tactically
by opening it to a few Third World countries, with the aim of better
'co-opting' the majority of them, the objective of these exclusive clubs
is actually to extricate the world system from crisis without making any
serious contribution to the emergence of a new and fundamentally more
equitable international order.

One example of negotiations by an ad hoc 'exclusive club' is particularly significant. When the energy crisis exploded in 1973 as a powerful
indicator of a world-wide crisis which had already been in existence several
years, the developing countries quite naturally looked to the United
Nations as a democratic framework for dialogue to build a new economic
order in the wake of the sixth and seventh Special Sessions of the General
Assembly, whereas the industrialized States made it clear that they
preferred negotiations in a more limited context. Overlooking no possible
chance of arriving at a solution to the crisis, the Third World countries
ultimately gave in to the demand of the industrialized States, even while
the problem was still before the United Nations. These were the circumstances in which the North–South conference came into being. Twenty-
eight States took part, two-thirds of which, representing the developing
countries, were chosen by the Third World itself, but only after much

hesitation on the part of the industrialized States. Even then, there were some who anticipated that a choice of this sort would in itself be likely to divide or neutralize the Third World. Among the developing countries finally included were the non-petroleum-producing heavyweights of each of the three continents, that is, Brazil, Zaire and India, as well as several particularly impoverished countries of the so-called 'Fourth World', whose fusion with the others, it was hoped, might provoke the dreamed-of split in the Third World between countries that produced petroleum and those that did not. In addition, the 'necessity' of limiting the number of Member States for the sake of the effectiveness and manageability of the conference, prevented such States as Yugoslavia and Egypt from taking part in it even though a short time before they had played such an important role in the creation of the movement of non-aligned countries, in which they continue to be very active.

With the conference thus composed, there was a danger, for these and other reasons, that it would lead to the self-neutralization of the eighteen developing States, or to a situation in which the whole Third World would mistrust these eighteen representatives who might seem to be hand in glove with the club of the wealthy countries. In the end, in spite of all the game playing, the representatives of the Third World maintained their unity complete and asserted the minimal requirements for a new international economic order, but without being able to get the industrialized countries to make as many concessions to them as they had made to the industrialized countries.

RIGHT OF VETO OF THE GREAT POWERS

Criticisms directed against the developing countries for being able to muster a majority of votes within international organizations can be correctly appreciated only if one makes a comprehensive evaluation of all the facts involved. Among these must be mentioned the notorious and unjust veto power which Article 27 confers on each of the five great powers individually in order to prevent the adoption of decisions not in keeping with their interests.

At the ministerial conference of the non-aligned countries, held in Georgetown in 1972, the foreign ministers took exception to 'the tendency [of the great powers] to monopolize or influence important global decisions'. The Algiers 'summit' of the same movement, held in 1973, condemned the 'disregard for United Nations decisions and the tendency of great powers to monopolize the Organization's activities, to render it inactive or to divert it to their own private interests, [and] contradict the

A Third World view of international   223
organizations. Action towards a new international
economic order

universal nature of the Organization . . .'.[25] In addition, the summit meeting declared that the non-aligned countries would continue to work 'with a view to bringing about a change in international relations towards democracy and equality of all States, and to ensure that decisions which could affect big and small countries are not taken without their full participation on an equal basis'.[26]

The same Algiers summit meeting, which complained of conditions that 'do not fully permit [the United Nations] to perform its mission of peace and development'[27] called for 'improvement of the Organization', and added: 'To this end, the Security Council, the organ primarily responsible for the maintenance of international peace and security, should not be prevented from exercising all the responsibilities conferred on it by the Charter.'[28]

The criticism becomes more pointed with the political declaration of the Colombo summit meeting of 1976, which seems to be one of the rare documents to make an explicit condemnation of the abuse of the veto. In fact, the conference, after welcoming 'the progress made towards the principle of universality of membership of the United Nations' noted that 'the responsibilities and obligations that accompany the veto power . . . continue to be disregarded by some permanent Member States'. It deeply regretted that a Member State, through 'abuse of the veto power', had prevented the admission 'of countries . . . which are fully qualified for such a status [as Members]'.[29]

In point of fact, the machinery of international organizations has some difficulty in functioning smoothly. The institutional imbalance among the principal organs of the United Nations, for example, and the excessive powers inherent in the abuse of the veto could only accentuate this anomaly. The new powers which have emerged on the international scene have underlined the inadequacy of this machinery. In particular, the arbitrary use of the veto power weakens the Organization's credibility. It would seem that this power, which derives from a specific philosophy and well-known intentions, ought not to be left to the total discretion of the countries which benefit from it.

At the thirtieth session of the United Nations General Assembly, a permanent Member of the Security Council, which had on other occasions flaunted its attachment to the principle of universal membership, used its veto to oppose both the admission of the Democratic Republic of Viet Nam and the suspension of South Africa. The Member thus acted in conformity with a sorry idea of universal membership, excluding those that comply with the obligations of the Charter and conversely welcomed those who pride themselves on systematically contravening its provisions.

AVAILABILITY OF THE MEANS
AND NON-AVAILABILITY OF THE USER

To evaluate the real significance of the rather exaggerated criticisms of the 'automatic majority' possessed by the developing countries, and to gauge with some accurary the influence of these countries in standard-setting and institutional action for the establishment of a new international economic order, care must be taken not to confuse possession of a right with its exercise. There is a great difference between the theoretical possession of a right, which the Third World countries legitimately have by virtue of their number, and the actual exercise of that right, presuming that the institutional machinery of the Organization permits it. The measure of that difference is precisely their 'underdevelopment'. And when the means, i.e. the Organization, is available for the assertion of that right, it is the user, i.e. the developing country, which proves to be unready for full exercise of that right.

The sociology of international conferences from this point of view is yet to be written. Evaluation of the respective importance, activity and influence of the governmental delegations within the Organization is particularly instructive. In the main, Third World countries suffer cruelly from a qualitative and quantitative poverty of personnel in all fields. This is one aspect of their 'underdevelopment' which is very clearly visible in the motley kaleidoscope of delegations at international conferences.

The decision-making process in these august forums require the creation of committees, subcommittes, bureaux, drafting committees, co-ordinating units, and so forth, which means that every delegation of a developing country should have enough members to be able to participate usefully in the meetings of every one of these organs. This is scarcely possible for a great number of Third World States, which have neither the human resources nor the necessary financial means to be able to participate on equal terms with the other States in the varied and frequent international meetings. Thus, from the very start, a large number of Third World countries are quantitatively under-represented, and are quite simply unable to participate in all the bodies where international norms are worked out. They cannot be in vigilant attendance and, in the final analysis, play their role to the full. Many of them resign themselves to symbolic participation instead of asserting their interests through fruitful and vigorous action.

This theoretical 'numerical power', condemned by the wealthy States because it produces a 'mechanical majority', must therefore be viewed with some circumspection because the frequently small size of Third World delegations, whose votes can at any moment be secured by

A Third World view of international   225
organizations. Action towards a new international
economic order

the industrialized States which still largely dominate the situation, shows how vulnerable they are.

Though unrecognized by theoreticians, this is a very important and practical aspect of inequality in dialogue, or the inequality which exists between the developed States and the rest in their opportunity for putting their respective positions forward.

PROPOSALS AGAINST THE LAW OF NUMBERS [30]

The existence within the United Nations of a large majority of Third World States has provoked a search among divers coteries for a counter-move to check the law of numbers and perpetuate the supremacy of the great powers. It has not taken long to formulate a number of proposals, some of them old friends, others appearing somewhat newer, directed towards these goals.

Old proposals

Two series of measures have been considered to obstruct majority rule, which is disqualified as soon as it can be used to the advantage of the States and peoples of the Third World, and only in these cases. The first series of measures concerns the General Assembly and aims at the establishment of a system of weighted votes within this body. The other measures aim to modulate the use of veto according to the 'good behaviour' which should be displayed by the Third World States in the context of the General Assembly. Finally, a third series of proposals, more technical in appearance, aims to modify procedural rules so as to take into account abstentions when the majority is calculated.

    Weighting of votes in the General Assembly. The goal clearly being sought in putting forward the idea of weighted voting is the frustration of the principle of 'one State, one vote', which best reflects the sovereign equality of States. To achieve this, it is argued that States are in fact unequal, and it is consequently thought desirable to introduce 'a voting system that would attribute to Member States a weight that would better correspond to their population, their economic importance, their military might, or to any combination of the classical criteria of national power'.[31] The inevitable consequence of this, as one commentator has noted, would be 'to seriously reduce the possibilities of influence of the least powerful, already minimal, to the point at which they would become absolutely negligible. Unification of the international system would no longer be more than a vain phrase, for diplomacy would once again become the privilege of a few'.[32]

A number of proposals for weighting votes in the General Assembly have been made with the aim of neutralizing the advantages that the Third World appears to possess because of its numbers and with the aim of eliminating the Third World from the centres of world decision-making. Some of these proposals are general, others specialized.

Generalized weighting of votes.[33] The first method of weighting votes in the General Assembly to have been put forward is expressed in a general weighting formula that would apply indiscriminately to all States. It would be understood, of course, that coefficients would be allocated to the different States in such a way that the total of the votes granted to the Third World could not, in any circumstance, exceed the total that the developed States would allot to themselves.

This formula would offer the advantage of being simple in conception, easy to use, and efficient in scope, so as to perpetuate the ascendancy of the great powers. It would none the less be true that each State would find itself assigned a coefficient that would immediately determine its ranking on the scale of power, and that this time the formula according to which some States are 'more equal than others', would establish a hierarchy among the great powers themselves.

This is the precise point at which difficulties in admitting such a formula arise for each of the States, except the biggest. (But which one is it?) The Lodge Commission concluded its study on the introduction of a system of weighted voting in the United Nations, by saying that 'there was very little chance that a system of weighted voting would be adopted in the General Assembly in the near future'.[34]

Did this mean that all was lost and that all that the great powers could now do was to admit, willy-nilly, the irreducible nature of the 'majority' held by the Third World? This would clearly be to under-rate the great resourcefulness that the developed world can show in order to maintain its advantages. In this situation, it was not long before the formula of specialized weighting was revived.

Specialized weighting of votes. As the formula of generalized weighting seemed unworkable both for the moment and for the foreseeable future, it was not surprising that specialized weighting of votes by subject was advocated. This type of weighting would as it were be induced from the relative importance of the matters under discussion, as opposed to the general formula of weighting based on the relative power of States.

This formula of weighting, specialized according to the subject, is not new, as we know, and has already been applied in the financial institutions of the United Nations system, where the number of votes which each Member can cast depends on its share of the registered capital. All that the great powers would need to do to have nothing more to fear from

A Third World view of international
organizations. Action towards a new international
economic order   227

the numerical majority of the Third World would be to increase the
number of questions or subjects requiring a weighting of the votes.[35]

Quid pro quos offered for acceptance of weighted voting. It is not surprising that the developing countries were suspicious of the different
formulas for the weighting of votes. Therefore it was decided to interest
them a little more by offering, in exchange for their acceptance, to give
more weight to measures adopted as a result of a weighted vote, and to
move towards reducing the field of application of the veto in the Security
Council.

*Increasing the legal significance of resolutions adopted as a result of a
weighted vote.* One of the snares laid for the Third World States is the
attributing of greater legal force to resolutions adopted by a weighted
vote, especially (a consideration added to increase the attractiveness of
the proposition) in the sphere of international economic co-operation, one
of the central problems of the new international economic order.

But what would this 'greater legal force' granted to resolutions
adopted by the General Assembly signify? The proposals are unclear.
Roughly speaking, it amounts to 'considering that subsequent decisions
of the General Assembly have a legal force superior to that of recommendations'.[36] This proposal is based on the assumption that the resolution does not have in itself any compulsory force if its value is not enhanced
in this way, even if it is adopted by an overwhelming majority of the
States of the world.

As a matter of fact, this is not the real problem, and this so-called
'greater legal force' is not of any real interest when we know that the
weighting of votes can have no other objective than to deprive the Third
World of one of the rare trump cards it holds—the weight of its numbers.

Moderation in the use of the veto. This would in no way do away with
the principle of the veto—which would be the only reform worthy of
real attention—but would, at most, mitigate its use. It is thus proposed
to forgo use of this extremely powerful weapon in marginal affairs and,
in any case, those of little importance, such as 'in the case of creation of a
committee of inquiry'.[37]

It has also been suggested that the veto should not be used in questions
relating to the admission of new States to the United Nations.

Taking abstentions into account. We know that the procedural rules on
voting only take into consideration the votes of Members present and voting
no account being taken of abstentions when the majority is calculated.

One of the particularly decisive consequences of this rule is to permit
adoption of a resolution by a small majority, in spite of the negative vote of the
great powers and the abstention of a substantial number of other States.
This practice serves the interests of the Third World, where many resolu-

tions originate, particularly as regards the new international economic order and the struggle against racism, racial discrimination, apartheid and imperialism in its various forms.

Now the report under examination here considers that these resolutions, unacceptable to a significant number of Member States which are major contributors to the budget of the United Nations, are nevertheless of great importance and could endanger the interests of the great powers.[38] Consequently, the report suggests methods and measures to prevent the adoption of such resolutions.

It was then proposed to take account of abstentions so that the sum of abstentions and negative votes could lead to the rejection of resolutions in the General Assembly.

New approaches

A new effort of the imagination is being made to find a solution to an old problem, namely how to perpetuate the exclusive power of decision of the minority of the great powers in the United Nations system, notwithstanding the overwhelming majority held by the Third World States. A whole range of proposals has been put forward, going from barely concealed blackmail aimed at development aid, to the creation of a new category of 'associate members', a real ghetto in which small States would be confined. The establishment of limited membership forums, parallel to the General Assembly, has also been proposed, where viewpoints of the great powers could carry the day without encountering any resistance.

Financing of development programmes in exchange for the weighting of votes. This would amount to a simple bargain, a straightforward bilateral contract between the members which pay the biggest contributions to the budget of the organization, and the States of the Third World. The biggest payers would finance United Nations programmes devoted to the development of Third World States on condition that the latter accepted the weighting of votes.

To illustrate the relevance of this viewpoint, the same report cites the example of the International Fund for Agricultural Development (IFAD), which provides for a three-way distribution of votes among the members of the Committee for Aid to Development (part of the Organization for Economic Co-operation and Development [OECD-CAD], the members of the Organization of Petroleum Exporting Countries (OPEC), and certain other Third World countries.

In fact, the example mentioned, in which weighted voting is practised, would seem essentially to be an attempt to disqualify the United Nations

A Third World view of international
organizations. Action towards a new international
economic order   229

on the grounds that they are ineffective when it comes to the settlement of the fundamental problems of our time and the establishment of a new international economic order. Furthermore, the result of this system is to sow discord in the Third World.

Motives of largely the same sort seem to be behind the proposal to create a new category of Member States of the organization, the category of 'associate members'.

A new category: the Associate States. The formula, as is well known, would consist of offering the small States, sometimes called 'micro-states', limited participation in the activities and costs of the United Nations. These States would in return be deprived of their right to vote in the United Nations.[39]

This proposal claims to draw on the authority of equity. But where does the 'micro-state' start, and what is the criterion for defining one? One then finds that this name could cover a considerable number of States that it was desired to confine in the Associate State ghetto, stripping them of their right to vote and thus appreciably reducing the already meagre influence of the Third World on global and on its own affairs.

The suggestion to introduce the category of Associate State into the United Nations system must therefore be rejected. One commentator has written, with reason, that the 'United Nations has become the organization of the entire international community. The very fact of belonging to the international community therefore confers the right to enter this organization and it would be a genuine abuse of power to refuse exercise of this right.'[40]

Increase in limited-membership forums. Among the various methods that have been thought up to avoid bringing before the General Assembly the important problems that fall within its jurisdiction, is the proposal for an increase in limited-membership committees or forums, which would be, because of their reduced dimensions, more 'efficient'.[41] The choice of participating States would be made in such a way as not to endanger seriously the major interests of the great powers. With the membership arranged in subtle and clever proportions, this would permit the neutralization of the little power held by the Third World thanks to the law of numbers.

To that would be added the fact that decisions would be made in these committees by consensus, which would only increase the influence of the great powers still more and correspondingly annihilate the influence of the Third World through the effect of dispersion.

Thus the majority of these proposals are merely devices aimed at allowing the great powers to maintain their exclusive hold on all the world's affairs.

These seem to be some of the parameters to be used in weighing the respective importance of the protagonists in the development of international law. They are particularly revealing of the complexity of a situation that it would be wrong to simplify by reducing it to the existence of an 'automatic majority' wielded by the countries of the Third World. But it is a truism to recall that the great powers would not be what they are had they capitulated before this very relative numerical power whose dangers they have intentionally exaggerated. In fact, their power can be appreciated precisely by the way in which they have managed, here and there, to give credence to the idea that such a situation is dangerous. There was then no alternative but to substitute, every time the industrialized States demanded it, another procedure for the law of the majority which they went to extreme lengths to discredit with arguments which ought to have been more fairly presented. Thus dispensing with majority rule was in itself a victory for the industrialized States and demonstrated the reality of their power. The search for another procedure became all the more urgent because the laws of evolution give little hope that the rich will suddenly and freely espouse the views of the poor, or in other words that the wealthy nations will abruptly renounce their privileges. The gradual development of legal norms reflecting a new international economic order thus called for a compromise between the two tendencies, each time that it appeared necessary. This was the principle of consensus, suggested and defended by the industrialized States, but whose essential rule is shown scant respect by them.

Precarious truces: the 'discreet charm' of consensus[42]

The developing countries make a major concession of considerable significance each time they agree to allow unanimous consent to take the place of majority rule. This major concession, made in the hope of concerted action and dialogue in order to develop together a new legal and economic framework for our world, has none the less not always earned for those who made it favourable treatment at the hands of the industrialized States.

To be sure, the very nature of the international community, composed of sovereign States and therefore devoid of any notion of supra-nationality, as well as the structure of international organizations, which deprives them of true decision-making power (with exceptions, as in the Security Council), make recourse to the practice of consensus inevitable. Yet not only does the procedure not guarantee that the resolutions made in this way will be complied with but it also confers, as will be seen, a new form

A Third World view of international
organizations. Action towards a new international
economic order   231

of 'veto' on any State whatsoever. This could mean that not only is the resolution not certain to be binding on States, but it might not even have any legal status in the international organization itself. The traditional problem of the legal value of the resolution as it appeared after the resolution was adopted, now has added to it, or, more exactly, is replaced by, the prior question of the very existence of this resolution. This is a most serious danger which is leading to backward steps, all the more detrimental because at this very moment, what is most needed is a step forward to contribute to the establishment of the new international economic order.

THE ATTRACTION OF CONSENSUS

The circumstances in which consensus made its first appearance in the United Nations in 1964 are well known. A serious crisis had developed over the division of the financial burden of the peace-keeping operations in the Suez Canal zone and in the Congo. The United States demanded a budgetary contribution from all Member States and threatened to have France and the U.S.S.R., who were opposed to this, stripped of their right to vote through application of Article 19 of the Charter, which provides for this sanction in cases of non-contribution to the organization's budget. To avoid obstructing the work of the General Assembly, it was decided to deal only with matters that could be settled without opposition. Consultations were therefore organized prior to each decision.

The procedure of consensus therefore has not come into being just recently, with the 'crisis of international law and the world economy'. It is in itself neither particularly abnormal nor unusual. United Nations bodies had successfully practised it before. Resolutions were adopted in this way using methods with different names, but all coming under the concept of consensus, being passed 'without vote', 'by agreement', 'by consultation of the members', 'by tacit consent', 'by acclamation', on the basis of 'non-objection', or, finally, 'without proceeding to a vote'.[43] Considered in the context of the elaboration, negotiation and adoption of a text, consensus can thus be defined, as 'a practice designed to achieve the elaboration of a text by means of negotiation and its adoption without a vote'. At the Helsinki Conference on Security and Co-operation in Europe, where it was applied, it was designated as being 'the absence of any objection expressed or put forward by a representative as constituting an obstacle to adopting the decision in question'.[44]

However, consensus did not become a more and more widely used working method until after the sixth and seventh Special Sessions of the United Nations General Assembly, the world-wide implications of those sessions being too important to impose any other method for the adoption of rules.

Mr M'Bow adds another reason to all those justifying recourse to consensus and connected with the nature of the international community, the structure of international organizations, and the world-wide implications of the establishment of a new international economic order. He considers that 'the increase in the share represented by voluntary contributions towards the resources made available to international organizations, in particular for activities linked with development', has contributed to consensus taking an even stronger hold on the practices of the United Nations. From this point of view, he notes that 'the world being what it is, it has thus become inevitable that the States which make the most substantial contributions towards voluntary funds should seek to be associated in one way or another with decisions as to how these funds should be used'.[45]

However, this argument, although not unrealistic, must be handled with some caution, for otherwise it would serve first of all to legitimize the claim that 'he who pays the piper calls the tune'. Would there be any difference in kind between this argument and the one used by Henry Kissinger, requiring foreign governments helped by his country to fall into line with the votes cast in the United Nations by the United States? By extension, the argument could also be used to strengthen the decisions of certain States which refuse to pay their contributions to the budgets of international organizations where they lack a majority.

Moreover, this kind of argument, which explains things only partially, can be discarded since a large number of resolutions have also been adopted by consensus in fields that are not dependent on the voluntary financial contributions of Member States. Conversely, and subject to correction, it certainly seems that resolutions have been made otherwise than by consensus in areas where voluntary contributions played a role.

CORRUPTION OF CONSENSUS:
THE FRAUDULENT PRACTICE OF THE RESERVATION

Returning to fundamental problems, one should note the annoying tendency of certain States to 'hedge their bets' by expressing reservations at the moment when a resolution is being adopted by consensus. The technique of consensus allows them to obtain compromise texts which water down, soften and occasionally emasculate resolutions relating to the new international economic order. But once they have achieved this result, they still have recourse to the technique of reservations, which allows them to consider themselves as not concerned by those resolutions. Reservations about secondary points, as well as declarations interpreting all or part of the adopted text, which are admissible techniques, have

A Third World view of international
organizations. Action towards a new international
economic order

233

unfortunately given way to fundamental reservations, which destroy the very meaning of consensus.

This attitude is what is preventing the prompt establishment of a new international legal order, reflecting the economic preoccupations of our world. This temporizing combat, still as effective as ever, is hardly surprising seeing that what is at stake is the development of such important social and economic phenomena. Resistance to change something which is part and parcel of the conditions for progress.

It is nevertheless important to realize that, if the system of reservations were to spread, it would ruin the technique of consensus, the application, the spirit, and the aims of which are incompatible with the procedure of reservations. The temptation is therefore strong for the majority States to renounce the consensus system, which represents an enormous concession on their part, and return to the majority rule whatever the consequences. The industrialized countries, which are now demanding consensus procedure in order to get round majority rule, are the very ones that are helping by their attitude to render the procedure ineffectual and to push the majority States to abandon it in the end.

Furthermore, the use of reservations could lead in some way to the very existence of the resolution adopted by consensus being challenged. Reservation and consensus are fundamentally contradictory, so that, strictly speaking, a resolution cannot have been legally adopted 'by consensus' if it has been the subject of reservations. Thus the rule of consensus has two consequences. The first is that a minority, no matter how small, can refuse to accept decisions that have a strong majority backing, a situation that is the opposite of what could be expected from consensus. The second consequence could be even more serious, however. If consensus is chosen, this implies submission in a certain sense, but only in a certain sense, to a principle of acceptance that might be called 'unanimitarian'.[46] Yet any reservation defeats this principle, and it is legitimate to ask if it does not at the same time nullify the existence of the resolution itself. As soon as it is decided to put the procedure of unanimity in place of the majority technique, one falls into the trap set by the use of the reservation, which is equivalent to recognizing a new kind of veto power for any State formulating such a reservation.

That would be a serious and absurd result of the consensus rule. It is to be hoped that such an interpretation, which is far too mechanical, will not seriously be put forward to challenge the very existence of a resolution that has been consented to by an overwhelming majority of Member States. What actually ought to occur and what does indeed sometimes happen, should consensus fail, is that a vote is taken. In other words, in the final and ultimate stage of one procedure, another is substituted. Majority rule reclaims its rights given the failure of consensus. This is the spirit in which the United Nations General Assembly, examining the working methods of the Special Committee on the Principles of International Law, recalled in Resolution 2103 (XX) that the committee should continue 'the effort to achieve general agreement at every stage of the process of elaboration of the seven principles of international law . . . without prejudice to the applicability of the rules of procedure of the Assembly'.[47] In the same way, UNCITRAL formerly recalled in its report that while 'every endeavour should be made on the part of members of the Commission to reach consensus in making decisions . . . if consensus was not attainable, the Commission would need to abide by its rules of procedure which provided for decisions of the Commission being made by vote'.[48] Otherwise, as one representative declared, 'the progressive development of international law would be impeded if the great majority of States were left at the mercy of a recalcitrant minority'.[49]

What is clear is that the developing countries no longer see any point in the consensus procedure. In order to achieve consensus, they water down certain of their propositions without obtaining their acceptance by a minority of States opposed to them. Their effort thus proves to be in vain. On the standard-setting level, especially as regards the new international economic order, an unsatisfactory result is added to a useless effort, as the search for consensus at any price leads to the adoption of formulas that are either too general, over-ambiguous, or just plain inadequate.

An example of this sort of situation is provided by the standard-setting action of the United Nations with respect to the right of States to nationalize without compensation.

OBSTRUCTION: ADOPTION OF CONFLICTING NORMS

The discussions which were held in Geneva, Mexico City and New York to draw up the Charter of Economic Rights and Duties of States, partly expressed the preoccupations of the Third World and the non-aligned States. When the industrialized States agreed to the inclusion of the right of nationalization in the draft Charter, they attached to it a seemingly natural condition: nationalization was to occur 'in conformity with international law'. It was obvious that States do not resort to it arbitrarily. But to oblige them to conform to 'international law' was, as international law then stood, to impose on them an obligation to give 'fair and prompt' compensation, or even to pay prior compensation. It was to confine them once again in the system of traditional norms, instituted by and for the industrialized States, that is, in a body of rules which offers the poor the

A Third World view of international organizations. Action towards a new international economic order

235

derisory and bitter satisfaction of wasting away in conformity with the law, and offers the rich a powerful justification for prospering in conformity with the same law.

The Sixth Special Session of the General Assembly of the United Nations, at the request of the developing countries, rejected the idea of making the right of nationalization conditional on 'conformity with international law'. It emphasized the right of each State to set the amount of a 'possible indemnity' and the form of its payment. It was understood that any litigation that might result would be settled according to the domestic legislation of the nationalizing States and by the competent legal authorities of that States. The Charter of Economic Rights and Duties of States, however, made compensation not a possibility but a definite principle. Desire for consensus in the United Nations led the Third World countries to make this concession. This compensation must be 'appropriate', none the less taking into account, for every nationalizing State, 'its relevant laws and regulations and all circumstances that the State considers pertinent'.[50] Thus, both in the declaration which marked the conclusion of the Sixth Special Session of the General Assembly, and in the Charter of Economic Rights and Duties of States, nationalization does not come under international law but under the municipal law of each State. In the one case, however, compensation is possible, and in the other it is certain, even though these texts were adopted only seven months apart. The second thus represents a step backwards from the first, even though both are essential for the establishment of a new international economic order.

The desire to compromise in order to obtain the general consensus of Member States illuminated the conflicting interests of the parties concerned by the act of nationalization. The developed countries wanted the principle of compensation accepted, while the developing countries tended, if not to refuse it, then at least to make it subject to very strict conditions, and this for many reasons, notably because of the 'excessive profits'[51] that foreign businesses have made in the Third World.

In conclusion, the practice of consensus is the life-boat that the minority States are themselves sinking through the misuse of reservations, and through behaviour which defies realism. Consensus means, above all, compromise and concession on both sides. If both majority rule and the kind of veto power possessed by the minority are to be rejected, given the structure and nature of the international community, then only consensus is left. It guarantees unanimous acceptance, which is preferable to the acceptance permitted by majority rule, and it protects the democratic ideal, which is completely disregarded in the use of the veto. If comprise were seriously sought by all sides, it would guarantee the smooth progress of international society towards more highly developed stages in its history of service to mankind.

But that point has not been reached and at present we are witnessing counter-attacks aiming to frustrate the democratic principle underlying decision-making within international organizations.

Counter-challenge to the power of numbers: non-enforcement of the resolution

Non-enforcement of resolutions expressing new legal standards is the 'ultimate weapon' available to the industrialized States. It could neutralize everything that is being done to create standards for the establishment of a new international economic order.

Controversy still rages over how far resolutions of international organizations are compulsory and to what extent they are enforceable. These debates are indeed the consequence of the effective non-application of these resolutions by States, but they become a cause of this non-enforcement as well, through a natural phenomenon of action and reaction.

Non-application of resolutions severely affects Third World countries, particularly with regard to the decolonization of southern Africa and the establishment of a new international economic order. The confidence placed in the United Nations by the vast majority of States is thus shaken. In fact, generally speaking, the non-enforcement of the resolutions of an international institution does nothing for its credibility, especially when it is an institution of a universal kind which makes it the world's conscience. While both deeply attached to the existence of the United Nations and cruelly disappointed by its inability to ensure that its resolutions are put into effect, Third World countries are perfectly aware that, unsatisfactory as the instrument is, it is the only one that encourages international co-operation and allows the necessary changes to be made in the economic order.

Not only States, but also the secretariats of international organizations, are sometimes unaware of the existence of the resolutions of those organizations, which shows the complexity of the power relationships that grow up around the problem of the establishment of the new international economic order. It has, for example, been pointed out that documents prepared by the Secretariat of the United Nations did not always conform to the courses of action laid down in the fundamental resolutions relating to the new international order. A resolution of the Economic and Social Council urged the Secretariat to 'respond fully to United Nations resolu-

A *Third World view of international*
organizations. Action towards a new international
economic order   237

tions and decisions and to ensure that documentation prepared by the
Secretariat be fully consistent with the directives of the relevant legislative
texts'.[52]

It seems clear that one of the most fertile springs of thrust towards
the new economic order, could run dry if the resolutions of the United
Nations in this field are not carried out. Leaving aside the credibility or the
prestige of the Organization, dangerous obstructions in the world political
and economic situation could well be the result. Although enforcement of
resolutions has always raised problems because of the nature of the international organization and the fact that the world community is composed
of States, today the problem arises in infinitely more acute terms because
what is at stake is of vital importance to the peace and development of the
planet.

Then again, non-enforcement of resolutions is keenly felt by Third
World States to be a regrettable neutralization of their efforts within the
international organization, as well as being a sort of repudiation of, or
persistent challenge to, any of their own resolutions that are partly related
to those of the organization and are adopted by these States in other
contexts, e.g. within the group of non-aligned countries. That is why,
strongly motivated today by the desire for the establishment of a new
international economic order as they were yesterday by political decolonization, they campaign for the implementation of the resolutions of
international organizations. This is a long-standing and continuing demand
of the non-aligned States.[53]

The organs of the United Nations have reacted to their request and
are concerned with making the resolutions adopted more effective. Thus
the General Assembly, in Resolution 3031 (XXVI) of 18 December 1972,
urged the United Nations Council for Namibia to 'undertake a study on
the compliance of Member States with the relevant United Nations
resolutions'. The Secretary-General expressed his conviction that 'it
would be a far more effective Organization . . . if Member States developed
the habit of consistently responding to and respecting the decisions and
findings of the main organs. It would be a more effective Organization
if Member States were always prepared to put their influence behind the
implementation of the decisions of its organs'.[54] Kurt Waldheim recalled
in 1976 that 'the responsibilities of Governments do not cease when a
resolution is adopted; indeed resolutions usually require determined
action by Governments, in addition to the parties directly concerned if
they are to be translated into reality. I speak with strong feelings on this
matter because the Secretary-General is in sense the custodian of the
decisions of the United Nations. All too often he is called upon to implement them only to find himself with the most limited possibilities of

doing so effectively'.[55] And speaking at the ninth 'summit' of the Organization of African Unity, held in Rabat, Mr Waldheim went so far as to recommend revision of the United Nations Charter in order to oblige all States to comply with the resolutions of the Organization.[56]

It is true that the majority of these stands were motivated primarily by the obstinate refusal of South Africa to implement resolutions concerning political decolonization. But whilst the successes registered in this field today, even in southern Africa, mean that resolutions specifically related to decolonization are being implemented on an increased scale, they ought to provide greater weight to the organization's resolutions as such, regardless of their nature, but especially to those resolutions relative to development and the introduction of a new international economic order.

In fact, to come back to Mr Waldheim's last remark, the Charter, as an organic instrument, has, since it was first drafted, already changed a great deal as a result of its 'glosses'. The General Assembly has made it into something living and evolving, keeping pace with the needs of an international community in the process of transformation. The concept of a 'living charter'—living the life of our world—is thus being raised to an honoured position. By putting aside skimping interpretations which stifle the spirit and imprison the 'soul' of the Charter, and by showing remarkable ability to sense, behind each of its provisions, the breath of our world's aspirations, the developing or non-aligned countries are contributing to the active transformation of international law and relations, and to the ripening to conditions favourable to the introduction of the new international economic order. It has been claimed that certain of the General Assembly's resolutions apparently contradict the Charter itself. Today, however, it is fully recognized that the General Assembly is quite competent to interpret the Charter, not only in its letter but also in its spirit. Thus certain resolutions might indeed appear to be a 'development, of the Charter, but they follow the same lines and go in the same direction. In addition, it is acknowledged that the General Assembly has powers and competences which are inherent in its work. This is the framework within which it takes its decisions, and these cannot be without legal force.

But changes in other sectors remain conditional upon the review of the Charter, which is on the agenda thanks to action undertaken inside and outside the United Nations by the non-aligned and developing countries. An Ad Hoc Committee for the Review of the Charter was set up by Resolution 3349(XXIX). The objective is still the democratization of institutions and of international relations by embodying the right of all States to participate as equals in all decisions of general interest, the United Nations being the vital means of achieving this democratization.

A Third World view of international   239
organizations. Action towards a new international
economic order

This being so, the United Nations must become the principal framework for international relations and to this end bring about its own democratization by universal membership and by the equitable representation of States in all its organs. Furthermore, the United Nations must become the principal body for the democratic elaboration of international decisions on peace and development.

Notes

1. Cf. Edward McWhinney, *Conflit Idéologique et Ordre Public Mondial*, Paris, Pedone, 1970, and by the same author, *The International Law of Détente*. See also Mohammed Bedjaoui, 'Non-alignement et Droit International, *Collected Courses of The Hague Acadmy of International Law* (The Hague), Vol. 151, p. 415–20 and *passim*.

2. Statement by Samuel Pisar during a broadcast debate, quoted by Eric Laurent in, *Un Monde à Refaire, Débats de France-Culture. Trois Jours pour la Planète*, p. 109, Paris, Éditions Mengès, 1977.

   Criticism directed at the new world majority has sometimes taken a contemptuous and racist twist. The Third World is treated as primitive and stupid: 'Suddenly certain peoples wake up early one morning, decide that they are nations and dare to condemn Zionism. Why should they feel ashamed, since they have just barely come down out of the trees? . . . Just as it would be shameful to choose the rector of a university from qualified nursery school teachers, it ought to be even more scandalous for nations that have just come down out of the trees to consider themselves world leaders. . . . The African States have shown their stupidity. . . . Their vote in the United Nations could only be the result of pressure from the Moslem oil-producing States, for could primitives have their own ideas? Thus they gave in to the Moslems, the very people who traded slaves all over Africa, treating black people like animals. There is no doubt that if Israel could shower dollars on the African States, these States would all be ready to vote in the United Nations for a condemnation of all Moslems as racist nations. But penniless Israel tried to give the Africans something better than money: help in the acquisition of knowledge in order to draw them closer, if possible, to the civilized world.' (Aharon Shamir, 'They Have Just come Down out of the Trees, and They Condemn Zionism', *Yedioth Aharanot*, 14 November 1975). See also page 215, concerning the official statements of the United States Ambassador to the United Nations, Mr Moynihan.

3. Statement by Gaston Thorn quoted by Laurent, op. cit., p. 122.
4. Laurent, op. cit., p. 120-1.
5. Laurent, op. cit., p. 112.
6. Laurent, op. cit., p. 119. Mr M'Bow states that he does not understand what is meant by automatic majority: 'But automatic in relation to what? It is as though its detractors presented it as an absolutely irresponsible majority, voting anything, simply because it has a majority. Really, one ought to avoid caricatures and grant a little credibility to this majority!' (ibid., p. 129).
7. Ibid., p. 114.
8. Address given by Amadou-Mahtar M'Bow in Paris on 21 March 1978 to the International Diplomatic Academy on 'Consensus in International Organizations'.
9. LAURENT, op. cit., p. 7.
10. Pierre-Marie Martin, 'Le Nouvel Ordre Économique International', *Revue Générale de Droit International Public*, No. 2, 1976, p. 503.
11. Ibid., p. 114.
12. Consiglio Nazionale delle Ricerche, *Manual for the Study of International Organizations and Relations*, covering the period from the first session of the General Assembly (opened 10 January 1946) to the thirtieth session (closed 17 December 1975). Collective work under the direction of Marco Mozzati, published by CESDOC, University of Padua, with the help of Unesco (unpaged volume with continuous numbering of the resolutions in the order of the General Assembly sessions).
13. The study of international relations *stricto sensu* using computerized analysis of votes, reveals the bipolar and not multicentred character of the international political system. But an examination of the votes, notably with regard to the political interpretation of the Charter, which gives rise to incessant controversies and increases the possibilities for countries to group together, disperse or remain isolated, shows that the international organization, created by the Charter as the instrument of institutional society, represents an alternative to power politics.
14. Jean Siotis, paper presented to the International Expert Meeting on the Study of the Role of International Organizations in the Contemporary World, Geneva, 15–19 March 1976, Unesco doc. SHC–76/CONF.623/9 of 8 March 1976.
15. Cf. Bedjaoui, op. cit., p. 32-4, the passages relating to food power and food diplomacy. In 1976, Algeria publicly denounced 'grain aid'—which turned out, on top of it all, to be a purely commercial transaction in the form of a simple contract for the sale of wheat—which the United States consented to grant only in return for the muting of Algeria's criticism of American policy in general and the war against Viet Nam in particular.
16. Cf. the French newspaper *Le Monde*, 1–2 February 1976.

A Third World view of international   241
organizations. Action towards a new international
economic order

17. A statement made on 17 December 1977, by Yvon Bourges, French Minister of National Defence, is noteworthy for its exceptional and meritorious frankness in reviving the notion of 'gunboat diplomacy', for there, too, force is considered to be the prop of diplomacy. 'What a country like France', stated the Minister, 'expects from its armed forces is not dissociable from the part it intends to play in the world. . . . An action may prove to be necessary . . . in order to protect our interests outside our national territory should those interests be seriously threatened. . . . Now that France has become one of the leading industrial and commercial powers, it must look to its sources of supply. This is how our military capacity can be spoken of as being directly tied to the foreign activities of the country and as supporting our foreign policy and strengthening our diplomacy.'

18. Cf. Bedjaoui, op. cit., p. 86-7 et seq. President Salvador Allende stated to the United Nations General Assembly, that 'a group of corporations can with impunity interfere in the most vital workings of the life of a nation, even going so far as to disrupt it completely' (doc. A/PV 2096, 4 December 1972). In condemnation of 'the enslaving and uncontrolled activity of multinational corporations', he added : 'At the third session of UNCTAD, I referred to the phenomenon of the transnational corporations and drew attention to the staggering increase in their economic power, political influence, and corrupting effect. . . . We are witnessing a pitched battle between the great transnational corporations and sovereign States, for the latter's fundamental political, economic and military decisions are being interfered with. . . . In a word, the enrire political structure of the world is being undermined.'

    Since the tragic fall of President Allende, part of the mystery has been cleared up thanks to the inquiries of the American Senate and of journalists about the combined subversive activities of the CIA and certain multinational corporations.

19. Cf. Mohammed Bedjaoui, 'Non-alignement et Droit International', *Collected Courses of The Hague Academy of International Law*, op. cit. Also the final declarations of the Fourth and Fifth Conferences of the Non-aligned Countries (Algiers, September 1973, and Colombo, August 1976) as well as the Lima programme of solidarity and mutual aid adopted by the Conference of Foreign Ministers of the Non-aligned Countries (Lima, 25–30 August 1975). Finally, in addition to non-alignment, the final declaration of the first meeting of the Heads of State of the petroleum-producing countries (First Summit Meeting of OPEC) held in Algiers in March 1975. In particular, at the Fourth Conference of Heads of State and Government of the Non-aligned Countries, held in Algiers in September 1973, the participants roundly condemned 'resort to any kind of aggression in economic relations by

means of pressure, coercion, economic blockades, the freezing
of credits or any other direct or indirect measures aimed at
limiting the sovereignty of States and at obstructing the
country's right to developmental self-determination' (Resolution NAC/ALG/CONF.4/EC./Res.3 of 9 September 1973).

20. Resolution 3201(S.VI) of the Special Session of the General
Assembly of 1 May 1974, containing a Declaration on the
Establishment of a New International Economic Order.

21. Resolution 3281(XXIX) of the General Assembly of 12 December 1974, Chapter II, Article 1.

22. Nevertheless, it may be wondered whether economic aggression
or economic domination is not one of those 'other forms of
alien domination' to which Article 7 of the Resolution on a
Definition of Aggression refers, the Article states: 'Nothing in
this definition, and in particular Article 3, may in any way
prejudice the right to self-determination, freedom and independence . . . of peoples forcibly deprived of that right . . .
particularly peoples under colonialist and racist regimes or
other forms of alien domination; nor the right of such peoples
to struggle to that end and to seek and receive support, in
accordance with the principles of the Charter and in accordance
with the . . . Declaration [on Principles of International Law
concerning Friendly Relations].'

23. Cf. Eric David, 'Quelques Réflexions sur l'Égalité Économique
des États', *Revue Belge de Droit International*, 1974, p. 399.

24. Idriss Jazairi, 'Le Concept de Solidarité International pour
le Développement', *Progrès des Peuples et Solidarité Mondiale*,
p. 21, Geneva, International Institute for Labour Studies,
1977.

25. Political declaration, paragraph 81.

26. Ibid., paragraph 26.

27. Ibid., paragraph 80.

28. Ibid., paragraph 82.

29. Political declaration, XIX, The United Nations, paragraph 151.

30. This section refers to the critical analysis contained in a recent
American document, distributed at the United Nations on
28 February 1978, for the time being in mimeographed form,
and entitled: 'Report of the Secretary of State to the President
on Reform and Restructuring of the United Nations System',
Washington, D. C., 28 February 1978.

31. 'Report of the Secretary of State . . ., op. cit., p. 17.

32. Michel VIRALLY, *L'Organisation Mondiale*, p. 291, Paris,
Librairie Armand Colin, 1972 (Collection 'U', series 'Droit
International Public').

33. This is what the 'Report of the Secretary of State . . .' (op.
cit., p. 18) calls 'generalized introduction of the weighted vote
to the General Assembly'.

34. 'Report of the Secretary of State . . .', op. cit., p. 19.

35. cf., above p. 207 *et seq.*

36. 'Report of the Secretary of State . . .', op. cit., p. 23.

A Third World view of international
organizations. Action towards a new international
economic order   243

37. Ibid., p. 21. The objective is explained in this way: 'To bring about acceptance by the majority of the Members of the United Nations of appreciable modifications in the voting procedures of the General Assembly, without excessive dilution of the veto power.'

38. 'The content and orientation of debates in the General Assembly have a considerable effect on the climate of world intellectual opinion and on the way in which problems of general interest are perceived. Consequently, even if the majority of resolutions of the General Assembly are by their nature only recommendations, they are important and the United States must not overlook tendencies that go against its interests.' (ibid., p. 19).

39. 'Such a formula could, for example, lighten the burden of the small States by exempting them from contributing to the financing of the expenses of the United Nations. In return, they could renounce their right to vote' (ibid., p. 23-4).

40. Virally, op. cit., p. 266.

41. cf., above p. 220 *et seq.*

42. Unesco intends to initiate studies 'to explore the political, sociological, cultural and legal bases of consensus as a method of formulating the position of the international community and as a means of resolving or by-passing conflicts of opinion and interests by tying in consensus with certain traditional practices and institutions'. On the principle of consensus, see: A. D'Amato, 'On Consensus', *Canadian Yearbook of International Law*, p. 104-22, 1970; Suzanne Bastid, 'Observations sur une Étape dans le Développement Progressif et la Codification des Principes du Droit International', *Recueil d'Études de Droit International en Hommage à Paul Guggenheim*, p. 132-45, Geneva, 1968, and 'Observations sur la Pratique du Consensus', *Festschrift für Wengler*, p.11-25, Berlin, 1973; H. Cassan, 'Le Consensus dans la Pratique des Nations Unies', *Annuaire Français du Droit International*, p. 456, 1974; A. Cassese, 'Consensus and Some of its Pitfalls', *Rivista di Diritto Internazionale*, p. 754-61, 1975; Jean Charpentier, 'La Procédure de Non-objection', *Revue Générale de Droit International Public*, p. 862-77, 1966; B. Conforti, 'Le Rôle de l'Accord dans le Système des Nations Unies', *Collected Courses of The Hague Academy of International Law*, Vol. 2, 1974; Wilfrid Jenks, 'Unanimity, the Veto, Weighted Voting, Special and Simple Majorities and Consensus as Modes of Decisions in International Organizations', *Cambridge Essays in International Law, Essays in Honour of Lord McNair*, p. 48-64, London, 1965, Guy de Lacharrière, 'Consensus et Nations Unies', *Annuaire Français de Droit International*, p. 9-14, 1968; Paul Reuter, 'Quelques Réflexions sur le Vocabulaire du Droit International', *Mélanges Trotabas*, p. 423, Paris, 1970; L. G. Sohn, 'Voting Procedures in the United Nations Conferences for the Codification of International Law', *American Journal of International Law*, 1975, p. 310. Arnold Tammes, 'Decisions of International

Organs as a Source of International Law', *Collected Courses of The Hague Academy of International Law*, 1958, II, p. 285–302. Daniel Vignes, 'Will the Third Conference on the Law of the Sea Work According to the Consensus Rule ?', *American Journal of International Law*, 1975, p. 119–29. A. Watt, *The United Nations, Confrontation or Consensus*, Australian Institute of International Affairs, 1970.

43. Cf. *Repertory of Practice of United Nations Organs* (5 vol.) and *Supplements*, 1, 2 and 3 (9 vols.), as well as *Repertoire of the Practice of the Security Council* (7 vols.), especially for Articles 18 (paragraphs 32–8), (paragraphs 54–6), 27 (paragraph 7), 67 (paragraphs 34–5); in Supplement 1, especially Articles 18 (paragraph 4), 27 (paragraph 5) and 67 (paragraph 5); in Supplement 2, Article 67 (paragraph 3); Supplement 3, Articles 18 (paragraphs 9–16) and 67 (paragraph 3). Also see documents A/8426, *Report of the Special Committee on the Rationalization of Procedures and Organization of the General Assembly* (paragraphs 288–9); A/PV 2229–2231 (1974) and A/PV 2349 (debates in the General Assembly); A/AC 121/SR.1, *Special Committee on Peacekeeping Operations; A/6230 Special Committee on Principles of International Law; E/SR 1921, Economic and Social Council*, etc.

44. Amadou-Mahtar M'Bow, 'Consensus in International Organizations', op. cit.

45. Ibid.

46. Consensus is certainly not synonymous with unanimity. It is perfectly compatible with the expression of a reservation, provided that the reservation is not considered by its author to be a formal objection that would then obstruct the whole system of consensus. Where a reservation would not constitute a formal objection, i.e. where it would not signify a 'vote against', consensus and unanimity can be equated, but only from the point of view of result, of course, not from the point of view of nature. Constantin Stavropoulos, former legal counsellor of the United Nations, summarizes the situation well when he says that consensus is 'a practice by which a minority of delegations which do not approve a resolution entirely are satisfied with formulating their reservations for the record without insisting on voting against the resolution. Consensus does not necessarily imply a rule of unanimity requiring the positive support of all participants, which would be the same as giving each one a veto. The practice of consensus is essentially a manner of proceeding which avoids formal objections.' (*UNITAR News*, Vol. 6, No. 1, p. 23).

47. When this committee finished its work, Resolution 2625(XXV), containing a declaration on these seven principles, was adopted by a perfect consensus.

48. Doc. A/7216, General Assembly, 23rd Session, Supplement No. 16, p. 480, paragraph 35.

A Third World view of international 245
organizations. Action towards a new international
economic order

49. Declaration by M. K. Yasseen (Iraq), Sixth Commission, 1083rd meeting, 29 November 1968. The representative of Lebanon on the Special Committee on the Principles of International Law had stated, on behalf of the non-aligned countries, that 'the attempt to secure general agreement does not mean the imposition of the unanimity rule and, ultimately, the imposition of the will sometimes of a small minority on an overwhelming majority . . .' (Report of the Special Committee, doc. A/6230, 21st Session, meeting of 27 June 1966, paragraph 571).

50. Resolution 3281(XXIX) of the United Nations General Assembly of 12 December 1974, Article 2, paragraph 2, subsection (c).

51. Cf. Diaz Albonico, 'La Théorie Chilienne des Bénéfices Excessifs', *Annuaire de l'Association des Auditeurs et Anciens de l'Académie de Droit Intervational* (The Hague) 1972–73, *Auditeurs de l'Académie de Droit International* (The Hague) 1972–73, Vol. 42/43, p. 62–3.

52. Economic and Social Council, sixty-first session, Res. 2042(LXI), 5 August 1976.

53. From the very first Conference of Heads of State or Government of the Non-aligned Countries, held in Belgrade in September 1961, the participants were faced with the problem of the implementation of United Nations resolutions. Their second conference held in Cairo in October 1964, when the question of the liberation of countries that were still dependent was on the agenda, raised the problem of the eradication of colonialism, apartheid and racism. The third and fourth 'summits', respectively held in Lusaka in 1970 and in Algiers in 1973, deeply regretted the persistent tendency to ignore resolutions of the United Nations and to default in their implementation. The fifth 'summit', held in Colombo in August 1976, expressed its serious concern at the 'non-implementation of numerous decisions of the United Nations, especially because of the refusal of certain Member States to submit themselves to these decisions, or because of their obstinate violation of the fundamental principles of the United Nations, as well as of its decisions'.

54. United Nations, official documents, twenty-eighth session, 'Introduction to the Annual Report on the Organization's Activity, 16 June 1972–15 June 1973', supplement 1A, doc. A/9001.

55. 'Introduction to the Annual Report on the Organization's Activity', 1976.

56. Speech of the Secretary-General of the United Nations at Rabat, 12 June 1972.